Fostering Research on the Economic and Social Impacts of Information Technology

REPORT OF A WORKSHOP

Steering Committee on Research Opportunities Relating to Economic and Social Impacts of Computing and Communications

Computer Science and Telecommunications Board

Commission on Physical Sciences, Mathematics, and Applications

National Research Council

NATIONAL ACADEMY PRESS
Washington, D.C. 1998

NATIONAL ACADEMY PRESS • 2101 Constitution Avenue, N.W. • Washington, DC 20418

NOTICE: The project that is the subject of this report was approved by the Governing Board of the National Research Council, whose members are drawn from the councils of the National Academy of Sciences, the National Academy of Engineering, and the Institute of Medicine. The members of the workshop steering committee responsible for the report were chosen for their special competences and with regard for appropriate balance.

This study was supported by Grant No. SRS-95285584 between the National Academy of Sciences and the National Science Foundation. Any opinions, findings, conclusions, or recommendations expressed in this publication are those of the author(s) and do not necessarily reflect the view of the organizations or agencies that provided support for this project.

Library of Congress Catalog Card Number 98-86542
International Standard Book Number 0-309-06032-X

Additional copies of this report are available from:

National Academy Press
2101 Constitution Ave., NW
Box 285
Washington, DC 20055
800-624-6242
202-334-3313 (in the Washington metropolitan area)
http://www.nap.edu

Copyright 1998 by the National Academy of Sciences. All rights reserved.

Printed in the United States of America

STEERING COMMITTEE ON RESEARCH OPPORTUNITIES RELATING TO ECONOMIC AND SOCIAL IMPACTS OF COMPUTING AND COMMUNICATIONS

HAL VARIAN, University of California at Berkeley, *Chair*
FRANCES ALLEN, IBM T.J. Watson Research Center
ERIK BRYNJOLFSSON, Massachusetts Institute of Technology
JORGE SCHEMENT, Pennsylvania State University
SCOTT SHENKER, Xerox Palo Alto Research Center
LEE SPROULL, Boston University
RICHARD SUTCH, University of California at Berkeley

Staff

MARJORY S. BLUMENTHAL, Director
JANE BORTNICK GRIFFITH, Interim Director
PAUL SEMENZA, Program Officer (through July 1997)
JON EISENBERG, Program Officer
JULIE C. LEE, Administrative Assistant (through August 1997)
MICKELLE RODGERS, Project Assistant
RITA GASKINS, Project Assistant

COMPUTER SCIENCE AND TELECOMMUNICATIONS BOARD

DAVID D. CLARK, Massachusetts Institute of Technology, *Chair*
FRANCES E. ALLEN, IBM T.J. Watson Research Center
JAMES CHIDDIX, Time Warner Cable
JEFF DOZIER, University of California at Santa Barbara
A.G. FRASER, AT&T Corporation
SUSAN L. GRAHAM, University of California at Berkeley
JAMES GRAY, Microsoft Corporation
BARBARA J. GROSZ, Harvard University
PATRICK M. HANRAHAN, Stanford University
JUDITH HEMPEL, University of California at San Francisco
DEBORAH A. JOSEPH, University of Wisconsin
BUTLER W. LAMPSON, Microsoft Corporation
EDWARD D. LAZOWSKA, University of Washington
DAVID LIDDLE, Interval Research
BARBARA H. LISKOV, Massachusetts Institute of Technology
JOHN MAJOR, QUALCOMM, Inc.
DAVID G. MESSERSCHMITT, University of California at Berkeley
DONALD NORMAN, Hewlett-Packard Company
RAYMOND OZZIE, Iris Associates, Inc.
DONALD SIMBORG, KnowMed Systems
LESLIE L. VADASZ, Intel Corporation

MARJORY S. BLUMENTHAL, Director
JANE BORTNICK GRIFFITH, Interim Director (1998)
HERBERT S. LIN, Senior Staff Officer
JERRY R. SHEEHAN, Program Officer
ALAN S. INOUYE, Program Officer
JON EISENBERG, Program Officer
JANET BRISCOE, Administrative Associate
LISA L. SHUM, Project Assistant
MICKELLE RODGERS, Project Assistant
NICCI DOWD, Project Assistant
RITA GASKINS, Project Assistant

COMMISSION ON PHYSICAL SCIENCES, MATHEMATICS, AND APPLICATIONS

ROBERT J. HERMANN, United Technologies Corporation, *Co-chair*
W. CARL LINEBERGER, University of Colorado, *Co-chair*
PETER M. BANKS, Environmental Research Institute of Michigan
WILLIAM BROWDER, Princeton University
LAWRENCE D. BROWN, University of Pennsylvania
RONALD G. DOUGLAS, Texas A&M University
JOHN E. ESTES, University of California at Santa Barbara
MARTHA P. HAYNES, Cornell University
L. LOUIS HEGEDUS, Elf Atochem North America, Inc.
JOHN E. HOPCROFT, Cornell University
CAROL M. JANTZEN, Westinghouse Savannah River Company
PAUL G. KAMINSKI, Technovation, Inc.
KENNETH H. KELLER, University of Minnesota
KENNETH I. KELLERMANN, National Radio Astronomy Observatory
MARGARET G. KIVELSON, University of California at Los Angeles
DANIEL KLEPPNER, Massachusetts Institute of Technology
JOHN KREICK, Sanders, a Lockheed Martin Company
MARSHA I. LESTER, University of Pennsylvania
NICHOLAS P. SAMIOS, Brookhaven National Laboratory
CHANG-LIN TIEN, University of California at Berkeley

NORMAN METZGER, Executive Director

The National Academy of Sciences is a private, nonprofit, self-perpetuating society of distinguished scholars engaged in scientific and engineering research, dedicated to the furtherance of science and technology and to their use for the general welfare. Upon the authority of the charter granted to it by the Congress in 1863, the Academy has a mandate that requires it to advise the federal government on scientific and technical matters. Dr. Bruce Alberts is president of the National Academy of Sciences.

The National Academy of Engineering was established in 1964, under the charter of the National Academy of Sciences, as a parallel organization of outstanding engineers. It is autonomous in its administration and in the selection of its members, sharing with the National Academy of Sciences the responsibility for advising the federal government. The National Academy of Engineering also sponsors engineering programs aimed at meeting national needs, encourages education and research, and recognizes the superior achievements of engineers. Dr. William A. Wulf is president of the National Academy of Engineering.

The Institute of Medicine was established in 1970 by the National Academy of Sciences to secure the services of eminent members of appropriate professions in the examination of policy matters pertaining to the health of the public. The Institute acts under the responsibility given to the National Academy of Sciences by its congressional charter to be an adviser to the federal government and, upon its own initiative, to identify issues of medical care, research, and education. Dr. Kenneth I. Shine is president of the Institute of Medicine.

The National Research Council was organized by the National Academy of Sciences in 1916 to associate the broad community of science and technology with the Academy's purposes of furthering knowledge and advising the federal government. Functioning in accordance with general policies determined by the Academy, the Council has become the principal operating agency of both the National Academy of Sciences and the National Academy of Engineering in providing services to the government, the public, and the scientific and engineering communities. The Council is administered jointly by both Academies and the Institute of Medicine. Dr. Bruce Alberts and Dr. William A. Wulf are chairman and vice chairman, respectively, of the National Research Council.

Preface

To aid in identifying fruitful approaches to assessment of both the positive and negative impacts of using information technologies, the National Science Foundation asked the Computer Science and Telecommunications Board (CSTB) of the National Research Council (NRC) to gather perspectives on the problem from experts in several relevant disciplines—in particular, economics, sociology, psychology, and anthropology, as well as computer science and engineering. It was thought that a sharing of ideas among individuals with pertinent experience as well as openness to the benefits of interdisciplinary analysis might suggest new ways of addressing what has proved so far to be a complex and difficult undertaking—assessing the diverse outcomes in a variety of contexts of the growing use of computing and communications technology. The results of this exploration are intended to be useful to the National Science Foundation in its efforts to assess the impacts of computing and communications technology, to provide examples of successful research and pose interesting questions to the research community, and to inform policy makers about the nature and utility of such research.

The context for this project included recent legislation and administration efforts (e.g., enactment of the Government Performance and Results Act, establishment of the Federal Accounting Standards Advisory Board) as well as ongoing oversight activities aimed at assessing the outcomes and impacts of federal programs, including research and development programs. It also included the National Science Board's interest in expanding the body of science and technology indicators to include those relating to impacts on the economy and society of information technology's use.

In addition, as a result of reductions in federal regulation or elimination of federal programs, a number of conventional federal sources of data have disappeared (e.g., data on telecommunications from the Federal Communications Commission, data on early Internet use from the National Science Foundation in connection with its operation of the former NSFNET). One result has been to focus more attention on what can and cannot be measured and on how different disciplines can contribute to better public understanding of the linkages among research and development, computing and communications science and technology, and the larger economy and society.

CSTB formed the multidisciplinary Steering Committee on Research Opportunities Relating to Economic and Social Impacts of Computing and Communications, which met in February 1997 to organize a workshop held on June 30 and July 1, 1997 (Appendix A gives the agenda and lists participants). The steering committee sought to identify topics amenable to research, especially interdisciplinary efforts calling for collaboration involving computer scientists, economists, and others. The workshop featured discussion of specific kinds of impacts along with examination of methodological issues, availability of valid data for research, and approaches relevant to assessing the outcomes of information technology's use.

An objective of the workshop was to identify and stimulate thinking about potential research topics, as well as to obtain perspectives on how to develop a more systematic understanding of outcomes important to public policy making. To this end, workshop participants considered possible gaps in knowledge, open research questions, areas where quantitative and qualitative data as well as new methodology are needed, and areas that appear to experts to be well covered. The workshop was also designed to illuminate how and where new research interest could be stimulated in a range of disciplines. In addition, the steering committee explored how to promote and support such interdisciplinary research.

To broaden the base of common understanding among the multidisciplinary participants in the workshop, the steering committee requested position papers from participants (Appendix B includes a selection of these papers) and also commissioned two background papers (presented in Appendix C). These papers contributed to discussions at the workshop and to the steering committee's efforts to synthesize workshop participants' observations on key impact areas and associated analytical challenges. In addition to meeting physically, the steering committee shared information by electronic mail and through a special World Wide Web site, which it used to develop workshop and report materials.

Given the broad nature of the task addressed by the workshop, and in keeping with the activity's limited budget and time frame, the steering committee adopted the approach of selecting and developing for presentation in its report a set of important and instructive examples compiled from the research topics, issues, and research approaches discussed at the workshop, as well as in submitted position papers. The resulting workshop report thus presents examples of important topics and fruitful approaches within several branches of social science rather than attempting to be comprehensive in considering the full range of possible topics. In the report, the fields of anthropology, demography, education, and

PREFACE   ix

political science are underrepresented, and the text has little to say about library science, bibliometrics, or information science. Omission of a number of interesting or significant topics reflects the exploratory nature of the project rather than a value judgment on the part of the steering committee. The topics of the creation and growth of the computer industry itself, among the most obvious of the economic and social impacts of computing and telecommunications, have been excluded here because they merit a report in their own right.

The bibliography suggests further reading that provides broad coverage of many of the issues touched on in this workshop report. Many of the references, including a number of review articles, are themselves replete with pointers to other work. Where possible the report includes references to significant Web sites addressing the impacts of computing and communications.

The workshop steering committee is grateful to Eileen Collins, who originated the idea of an interdisciplinary exploration of the impacts of computing and communications, and Les Gasser, both of the National Science Foundation (NSF), for their support of the project and for ongoing guidance. Their commitment to the importance of interdisciplinary interaction was fundamental to the design of the workshop. Funding for the report came from both the NSF Division of Science Resources Studies and the NSF Division of Information and Intelligent Systems.

The workshop steering committee acknowledges the contributions of the workshop participants, both through papers written as part of workshop activities and during discussions at the workshop itself. The steering committee also wishes to thank the NRC staff for their assistance with the workshop and the preparation of the final report, including Marjory Blumenthal, Paul Semenza, Jon Eisenberg, Julie C. Lee, Mickelle Rodgers, and Rita Gaskins. Finally, the steering committee is grateful to the reviewers for helping to sharpen and improve the report through their comments. Responsibility for the report remains with the workshop steering committee.

Acknowledgment of Reviewers

This report has been reviewed by individuals chosen for their diverse perspectives and technical expertise, in accordance with procedures approved by the National Research Council's (NRC's) Report Review Committee. The purpose of this independent review is to provide candid and critical comments that will assist the authors and the NRC in making the published report as sound as possible and to ensure that the report meets institutional standards for objectivity, evidence, and responsiveness to the study charge. The contents of the review comments and draft manuscript remain confidential to protect the integrity of the deliberative process. We wish to thank the following individuals for their participation in the review of this report:

Robert McC. Adams, University of California at San Diego,
Michael Arbib, University of Southern California,
Anita Borg, Xerox Palo Alto Research Center,
Yale Braunstein, University of California at Berkeley,
John S. Chipman, University of Minnesota,
David Farber, University of Pennsylvania,
Irene Greif, Lotus Development Corporation,
Donna Hoffman, Vanderbilt University,
Heather Hudson, University of San Francisco,
James Morris, Carnegie Mellon University,
Milton Mueller, Rutgers University,
Jean-Michael Rendu, Newmont Mining Corporation,
Henry W. Riecken, University of Pennsylvania School of Medicine (emeritus),

Peter Temin, Massachusetts Institute of Technology,
Timothy Van Zandt, Princeton University, and
Terry Winograd, Stanford University.

Although the individuals listed above provided many constructive comments and suggestions, responsibility for the final content of this report rests solely with the workshop steering committee and the NRC.

Contents

EXECUTIVE SUMMARY 1

1 INTRODUCTION 7
   1.1 Growth Trends, 9
      1.1.1 Computing Power, 9
      1.1.2 Demographics of Computer Ownership, 10
      1.1.3 Internet Use, 12
      1.1.4 Global Connectivity, 13
   1.2 Some Major Challenges, 14
      1.2.1 Productivity and Organizational Change, 14
      1.2.2 Information Technology and Wage Inequality, 16
      1.2.3 Design of Technology and Standards Setting, 16
   1.3 Role of Social Science, 18

2 ILLUSTRATIVE EXAMPLES AND UNANSWERED QUESTIONS 21
   2.1 Households and Community, 21
      2.1.1 Computer Use in the Home, 22
      2.1.2 Differential Impacts of Technology, 24
      2.1.3 Community, 24
      2.1.4 Education, 26
   2.2 Social Infrastructure: Universal Service, 29
   2.3 Business, Labor, and Organizational Processes, 32
      2.3.1 Location: Internationalization and Telecommuting, 32
      2.3.2 Labor and Information Technology, 35

2.3.3 Organizations and Processes, 39
2.3.4 Social Science and the Workplace, 46
2.4 Information Economy and Society, 48
2.4.1 Protection of Intellectual Property, 48
2.4.2 Free Speech and Content, 52
2.4.3 Privacy, 53
2.4.4 Information Use and Value, 56
2.4.5 Pricing Models and Content, 60
2.4.6 Pricing Information, 61
2.4.7 Network Externalities, 65
2.4.8 Auctions, 66
2.4.9 Electronic Commerce, 67
2.5 Illustrative Broad Topics for Ongoing Research, 72

3 DATA—THE BASIS FOR NEW KNOWLEDGE 78
3.1 Types and Uses of Data, 78
3.1.1 Data from Experiments, 79
3.1.2 Panel Data, 81
3.1.3 Data from Time-Use Studies, 82
3.1.4 Metadata, 83
3.2 Availability of and Access to Data, 84
3.2.1 Data Collected by the Private Sector, 85
3.2.2 The Need for Firm-level Data, 86
3.2.3 Data Collected by Government, 88
3.3 New Types of Data, 89
3.3.1 Documenting the Effects of Technology Deployment, 89
3.3.2 Data on Social Interactions from the Internet, 92
3.3.3 The Internet as a Window into How Commercial Transactions Are Conducted, 93
3.4 Time and Tools for Gathering and Interpreting Data, 93
3.4.1 The Time Required to Do Good Social Science, 93
3.4.2 Appropriate Subject Pools and Instrumentation, 95
3.5 Approaches to Meeting Requirements for Data, 95

4 OPTIONS FOR FOSTERING INTERDISCIPLINARY RESEARCH AND IMPROVING ACCESS TO RESULTS 101
4.1 Encouraging Interdisciplinary Studies and Collaboration, 102
4.2 Funding to Strengthen Interdisciplinary Research, 103
4.3 Making the Results of Interdisciplinary Research More Accessible, 105

BIBLIOGRAPHY 106

APPENDIXES

A WORKSHOP AGENDA AND PARTICIPANTS 127
B POSITION PAPERS SUBMITTED BY WORKSHOP
  PARTICIPANTS 131
  Research on Information Technology Impacts
    Paul Attewell *(Graduate School and University Center,
    City University of New York)*, 133

  What If All Information Were Readily Available to All?
    Joseph Farrell *(Department of Economics, University of California,
    Berkeley)*, 138

  Critical Issues Relating to Impacts of Information Technology: Areas for
  Future Research and Discussion
    Alexander J. Field *(Santa Clara University)*, 139

  Computer-mediated Communications
    Claude S. Fischer *(Department of Sociology, University of
    California, Berkeley)*, 142

  Impacts of Information Technology: Behaviors and Metrics
    Amy Friedlander *(Corporation for National Research
    Initiatives)*, 144

  Five Critical Issues Relating to Impacts of Information Technology
    Michael Froomkin *(School of Law, University of Miami)*, 147

  Cultural Influences on the Process and Impacts of Computerization
    Rob Kling *(Center for Social Informatics, Indiana University)*, 150

  Questions for Research
    Jeffrey K. MacKie-Mason *(Department of Economics,
    and School of Information, University of Michigan)*, 152

  Electronic Interactions
    Paul Resnick *(AT&T Laboratories)*, 156

  Social Impact of Information Technology
    Frank Stafford *(University of Michigan)*, 158

  The Uncalming Effects of Digital Technology
    Mark Weiser *(Xerox Palo Alto Research Center)*, 160

C COMMISSIONED PAPERS

Infrastructure: The Utility of Past As Prologue?
Amy Friedlander *(Corporation for National Research Initiatives, Reston, Virginia)*, 165

Computer And Communication Technologies: Impacts on the Organization of Enterprise and the Establishment and Maintenance of Civil Society
John Leslie King and Kenneth L. Kraemer
(University of California, Irvine), 188

Executive Summary

There has been a revolution in computing and communications in the past few decades, and all indications are that technological progress and use of information technology will continue at a rapid pace. These advances present many significant opportunities but also pose major challenges. Today, innovations in information technology are having wide-ranging effects across numerous domains of society, and policy makers, although currently lacking sufficient understanding and analysis of the consequences of their decisions, are acting on issues involving economic productivity, intellectual property rights, privacy protection, and affordability of and access to information, among other concerns. Choices made now will have long-lasting consequences, and attention must be paid not only to their technological merit, but also to their social and economic impacts.[1]

Despite the significance of these impacts for society, there has been relatively little investment in research to help understand, predict, and shape them. Among the reasons for this underinvestment are the rapid emergence of these phenomena and the difficulties in conducting the interdisciplinary work required to understand them. In the cross-cutting arena of the information economy, research on how information technology affects organizations and economic productivity can lead to better use of the technology for the benefit of society and individuals alike. Improved knowledge of how people interact with computing and communications technology, the circumstances under which people will benefit from it, and the differential impacts that such technology has on different communities can be incorporated as well into decisions affecting technology design and deployment.

To explore possibilities for research on the impacts of information technology and ways to assess these impacts, the Steering Committee on Research

Opportunities Relating to Economic and Social Impacts of Computing and Communications held a 2-day workshop on June 30 and July 1, 1997, involving participants with expertise in economics, social sciences, and computer science and engineering. Since this was an endeavor of limited budget and time frame, centered on discussions and interactions among participants at a single workshop, the workshop steering committee focused on identifying and developing examples of some significant research issues and concerns, rather than aiming to cover the full range of relevant topics. The content of this workshop report thus reflects suggestions made and issues raised in workshop activities and in the position papers submitted by workshop participants.

Chapter 1 outlines some of the trends in the growth of computing and communications discussed at the workshop and highlights several policy areas— including economic productivity, wage inequality, and technology design—in which interdisciplinary research involving both information technologists and social scientists can contribute to a better understanding of the economic and social impacts of information technology. The value of the social science approach, which draws on systematically developed theories of human behavior in combination with sound supporting data, is contrasted with the overreliance on anecdotes, extrapolation, and sloganeering that often characterizes the writing of pundits.

Chapter 2 presents examples of cross-cutting research that has been conducted to understand information technology's influence in personal, community, and business activities and gives suggestions regarding important open research questions. Incorporating examples given at the workshop and in position papers, it indicates some ways in which use of methodology from economics and the social sciences might contribute to important advances, and it describes how interdisciplinary research between social scientists and information technology researchers might help to improve knowledge of outcomes affecting private life and the household, the community, the social infrastructure, and business and the workplace. Chapter 2 concludes with a list of broad research topics offered by the steering committee as examples of promising areas for ongoing research.

Social science research depends on researchers having access to enough reliable data to establish a basis for reaching valid conclusions. Chapter 3 provides a brief overview of the types of data used by social scientists in their investigations and describes some of the problems encountered in data collection, management, and use. According to some workshop participants, researchers working at the intersection of information technology and socioeconomic issues confront a number of challenges related to the availability of data. Chapter 3 concludes with some suggested approaches to meeting these challenges.

Based on discussions at the June 1997 workshop and on material in the position papers submitted by its participants, the steering committee identified several options for fostering interdisciplinary research and making the results of this research more accessible to the public and policy makers. Chapter 4 presents these options.

The appendixes list the workshop agenda and participants and include a selection of the position papers submitted, as well as two additional background papers commissioned for the workshop.

EXAMPLES OF THE APPLICABILITY OF SOCIAL SCIENCE RESEARCH

Presented at the 1997 workshop and in participants' position papers was an array of examples showing applications of the results of social science research to improve understanding of the economic and social impacts of information technology in different domains, including the following:

- Private life and the household—Social experiments can be used to measure the impact of computerization on household members' behavior.
- Community—Sociological studies can illustrate the differential impact of technology on user communities and members of organizations.
- Social infrastructure—Economic analysis and historical studies can be used to illustrate some of the policy trade-offs involved in universal service.[2]
- Business and labor
  —Social science methods can be used to examine decisions about organizational structure.
  —Economic analysis of changes in labor markets can contribute to effective economic policy.
  —Historical studies of technological adoption of the electric motor are relevant to current issues in computer technology.
  —Sociological studies of technical support communities can contribute to better practices within those communities.
- Information economy and society
  —Historical analysis of intellectual property disputes can yield insight into current problems in this area.
  —Economic analysis of networks can lead to greater understanding of market phenomena.
  —Economic analysis of pricing can shed light on how online commerce will be conducted.

ILLUSTRATIVE BROAD TOPICS FOR ONGOING RESEARCH

Workshop discussions and position papers yielded numerous suggestions for research topics. The list below was compiled by the steering committee as an illustrative set of promising areas for research.

- Interdisciplinary study of information indicators—Researchers have recognized and begun to analyze the increasing role that information plays in all aspects of society. Interdisciplinary study could help to identify and define a set of broadly accepted measures of access to, and the use and impact of, information and information technology. Composite information indicators such as an interconnectivity index (characterizing the extent to which individuals, organizations, and businesses are linked to each other) and a marginalization index (characterizing the extent to which the benefits of information and information technology are not available to certain segments of society) could be established.
- Impacts of information technology on labor market structure—To enable informed decision making on critical policy issues such as how to respond to increasing wage inequality (involving, for example, efforts to assess the potential benefits of additional investment in training), it is important to understand to what extent and how the use of computers might affect wage distribution.
- Productivity and its relationship to work practices and organizational structures for the use of information technology—Gains in productivity come not only when new technology is introduced but also when new ways are found to use the technologies. Compilation of work that has already been done in this area is needed. Continued research also could illuminate how better to quantify the economic inputs and outputs associated with use of computers.
- Intellectual property issues—Policy makers considering revisions to intellectual property law or international agreements, as well as firms evaluating possible approaches to protecting intellectual property, would benefit from continued theoretical and empirical research.
- Social issues addressed at the protocol level—Widespread use of the Internet has ramifications in such far-reaching concerns as intellectual property rights, privacy protection, and data filtering. Exploring how these concerns might be addressed at the protocol level—through policies, rules, and conventions for the exchange and use of information—could prove to be a promising approach to addressing complex social issues arising from the use of new computer and communications technology.

APPROACHES TO MEETING REQUIREMENTS FOR DATA

As was noted in workshop discussions and some of the position papers submitted by participants, approaches such as the following could contribute to meeting the requirements for data needed to study the economic and social impacts of information technology:

- Making data related to the social and economic impacts of computing and communications available to the research community through a clearinghouse;
- Exploring ways for researchers to obtain access to private-sector data;
- Increasing data collection efforts by government;

EXECUTIVE SUMMARY

- Exploring the development of new multipurpose data sets by the research community;
- Establishing stronger ties with industry associations to facilitate collaborative research; and
- Exploring in workshop sessions uses of the Internet as a source of data on social interactions that take into account ethical and privacy issues associated with data collection, archiving, and reporting.

OPTIONS FOR FOSTERING INTERDISCIPLINARY RESEARCH AND IMPROVING ACCESS TO THE RESULTS OF RESEARCH

Based on discussions at the June 1997 workshop and material in participants' position papers, the steering committee identified several options for fostering interdisciplinary research and making the results of such research more accessible to the public and policy makers.

- Encouraging interdisciplinary studies and collaboration between researchers in information technology and researchers in the social sciences and economics through use of the following:
    —Interdisciplinary workshops to convene researchers with expertise in a range of fields to explore successful approaches to conducting research on the impacts of information technology, as well as to foster increased collaborative work;
    —Interdisciplinary curricula to help prepare students for collaborative work with researchers in other fields; and
    —Interdisciplinary fellowships to stimulate intellectual cross-fertilization and development of professional contacts.
- Funding to strengthen interdisciplinary research through the use of the following:
    —Evaluation of large technology system research proposals with attention to their inclusion of interdisciplinary research on behavioral, social, legal, and economic implications;
    —Synergistic use of major research programs that build or deploy prototypes of computing and communications systems, so as to improve understanding of impacts and to enhance outcomes; and
    —Collaboration with private foundations and industry so as to leverage resources.
- Making the results of interdisciplinary research more accessible through the use of mechanisms such as the following:
    —A World Wide Web page containing headlines and abstracts of policy-relevant social science research, pointers to the print and/or online published results, and regularly updated reviews of literature summarizing the state of

the art in various fields as well as directories of specialists in particular areas; and

—Supplemental ways of disseminating the results of research, such as by providing testimony at hearings held by policy makers or organizing specialized briefings for policy makers.

NOTES

1. Throughout this report, the term "impacts" is used as a shorthand expression to indicate a complex set of multicausal, multidimensional outcomes of the use of technology. Technology does not typically have a single impact, but rather a range of different outcomes depending on the context or settings. For more discussion, see Box 1.1 in Chapter 1 and Attewell's and Kling's papers in Appendix B of this volume.
2. Universal service is the practice of making telecommunications and information services—such as basic telephone service—available at an affordable price to all people within a specified jurisdictional area.

1

Introduction

It is becoming increasingly clear that the growth of computing and communications technology is exceeding our understanding of its economic and social impacts (Box 1.1).[1] The processing power of microchips is doubling every 18 months. From 1989 to 1995, Internet traffic doubled every 12 months, and it is now doubling every 6 to 9 months. When plots of trends over time require a logarithmic scale on the vertical axis, something interesting must be going on! Accompanying and supporting these dramatic increases in the power and use of new information technologies has been the declining cost of communications as a result of both technological improvements and increased competition in a sector long dominated by monopoly (and in other countries often state-owned) enterprises.

At the same time, there has been comparatively little investment in research to help understand how information technology has affected and will affect our society. The United States, and indeed the world, are facing critical policy issues—involving intellectual property rights, privacy, free speech, education, and other crucial concerns—armed with very little understanding and analysis of the consequences of possible choices.

For several reasons, too little social science research has been done to date in this area. Certainly the phenomena associated with information technology have developed rapidly in comparison with academic calendars and funding cycles. In addition, serious investigation of a number of complex technological, economic, and social issues requires interdisciplinary work to which there are currently many barriers. It is rare, for example, to see economists and sociologists collaborating, much less sociologists and computer scientists. One of the reasons is

BOX 1.1
"Impacts" and Technological Determinism

One of the most common findings in prior studies of information technology's (IT's) impact has been that outcomes are far from uniform across all settings and contexts. In earlier years we looked for *the* impact of IT on, say, organizational centralization, and scholars tended to hew to one end or the other of a bipolar spectrum: centralization versus decentralization, upskilling or deskilling, job destroying versus job creating. What scholars found, in almost every case, was that this was an unproductive way to conceptualize the issue. One almost always found evidence of both extremes of outcomes or impacts as well as many points in between (see Attewell and Rule, 1989). We finally realized that we were asking the wrong question. We should have asked, In what contexts does outcome A typically predominate, and in what contexts does outcome B tend to prevail, and when does one see A and B in equal measure?

We found that a technology does not usually have *an* impact. The context or setting in which the same technology is used often produces strikingly different "impacts." This phenomenon has been discussed in terms of "Web models" (Kling), or "structural contingency theory" (Attewell) or Robey's "Plus Ca Change" model. All imply that we fully appreciate the role of context in technology outcomes and that we therefore expend sufficient research effort to measure the context, and to delineate its interactions with the technology. If we fail to do this, we return to the old "black box" paradigm, that is, attempting to measure only the input (say, a particular software program) and the outcome (say, kids' test scores) without bothering with the context (the classroom, the kids' family backgrounds) or the causal mechanisms.

Black box research on impacts often discovered "inconsistent" outcomes across studies but proved unable to show why there was so much variation, because it neglected to measure the contextual variables that were moderating the effects of the input on the output. For example, the old paradigm would phrase a research question so as to ask whether or not home PCs would improve kids' school performance. In contrast, research within the current contextual paradigm would ask under what conditions having PCs at home affects students' school outcomes. A piece of my own work has indicated, for example, that having a home PC currently has a minimal effect on the school performance scores of poor and minority kids but is associated with substantial positive effects on the school performance of kids with high socioeconomic status (SES), when other factors are controlled for (Attewell and Battle, 1997). Race and class/SES, in this example, prove to be very important contextual features moderating the impact of home PCs on school performance.

It is important to understand that because of the last three decades of research and the importance of context as discussed above, many distinguished scholars of technology avoid the term "technology impact." Using this term in framing the question would be viewed by some of them as indicating an ignorance of the body of scholarship in technology studies. For them, the term "impact" connotes a kind of technological determinism that is very dated and widely discredited. Personally, I am not so averse to the term "impact," but I do agree with their larger point about avoiding models based on simple technological determinism.

—Paul Attewell, "Research on Information Technology Impacts"
(see Appendix B of this volume)

the investment of time and energy required by both technologists and social scientists to understand enough of an unfamiliar discipline area to enable serious progress in joint efforts. Also, research funding agencies and programs are generally not organized to exploit interdisciplinary opportunities.

To aid in identifying fruitful approaches to assessment of both the positive and negative impacts of using information technologies, the National Science Foundation asked the Computer Science and Telecommunications Board (CSTB) of the National Research Council to gather perspectives on the problem from experts in several relevant disciplines, such as economics, sociology, and psychology, as well as computer science and engineering. It was thought that a gathering of a group with pertinent experience as well as openness to the benefits of interdisciplinary analysis might suggest new ways of addressing what has proved so far to be a complex and difficult undertaking—assessing the diverse outcomes in a variety of contexts of the growing use of computing and communications technology. The results of this exploration are intended to be useful to the National Science Foundation in its efforts to assess the impacts of computing and communications technology, to provide examples of successful research and pose interesting questions to the research community, and to inform policy makers about the nature and utility of such research.

The Steering Committee on Research Opportunities Relating to Economic and Social Impacts of Computing and Communications organized a workshop to explore opportunities for research on the impacts of information technology and ways to assess these impacts. Since this was an endeavor of limited budget and time frame, and to be based in large part on input received at a single workshop, the committee adopted the approach of identifying and developing some significant examples and issues, rather than performing a more comprehensive study of the full range of relevant topics. The content of this report reflects areas of interest and issues raised in the workshop and the position papers submitted by workshop participants and subsequent work by the steering committee.

This chapter illustrates the dramatic increases in computing power and the penetration of new communications technology, and it highlights several key areas where impacts of these trends are being felt. It concludes by discussing the role of social science in characterizing these impacts.

1.1 GROWTH TRENDS

1.1.1 Computing Power

Computers have become so affordable and ubiquitous in part because of the remarkable improvements in semiconductors. Since the 1960s, semiconductor chip makers have increased the density of transistor circuits at a rate of about 10 percent a year. Combined with numerous other technological advances, this capability has led to a doubling of microprocessor power every 18 months (Fig-

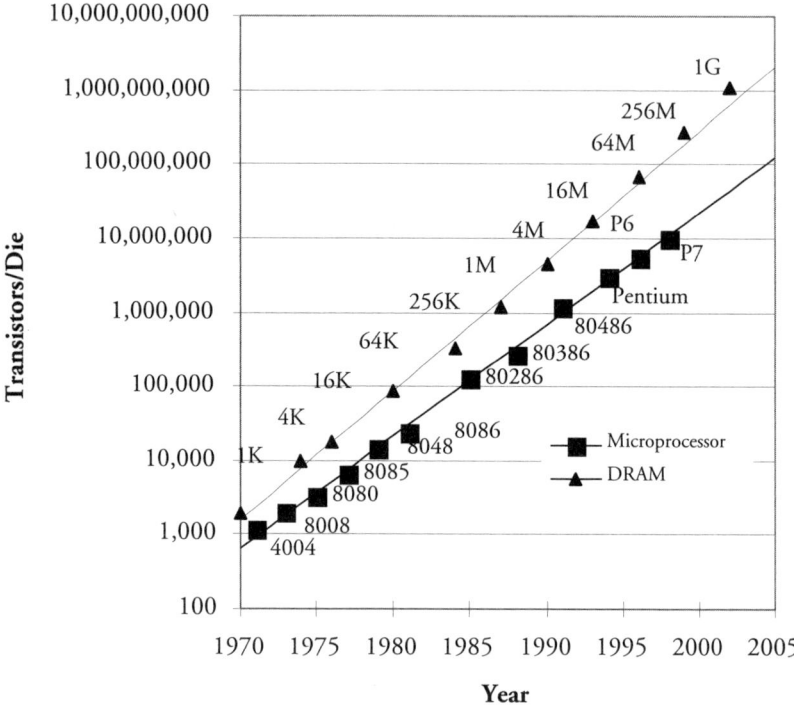

FIGURE 1.1 Moore's Law: The number of transistors per chip has grown exponentially for several decades and is projected to continue to do so for some time to come. SOURCE: Brynjolfsson and Yang (1996), using data from the U.S. Bureau of Economic Analysis and from Intel Corporation.

ure 1.1), a trend known in the computer industry as "Moore's Law" after a 1964 prediction by Gordon Moore, a founder of Intel Corporation. Improvements in semiconductors and other components account for the annual 20 to 30 percent decline in the quality-adjusted price for computers (Berndt and Griliches, 1993; Gordon, 1990), even as the costs of other industrial equipment have been increasing steadily (Figure 1.2). At the same time, businesses and consumers have chosen to increase their spending on computers, suggesting that they find new uses of computers worthwhile. As a result, the real quantity of computer power deployed, which reflects both increased spending and increased computer power per dollar spent, has grown tremendously over the past several decades (Figure 1.3).

1.1.2 Demographics of Computer Ownership

A recent survey of more than 50,000 households found that more than 40 million U.S. households now own PCs [2] (Computer Intelligence, 1997). Owner-

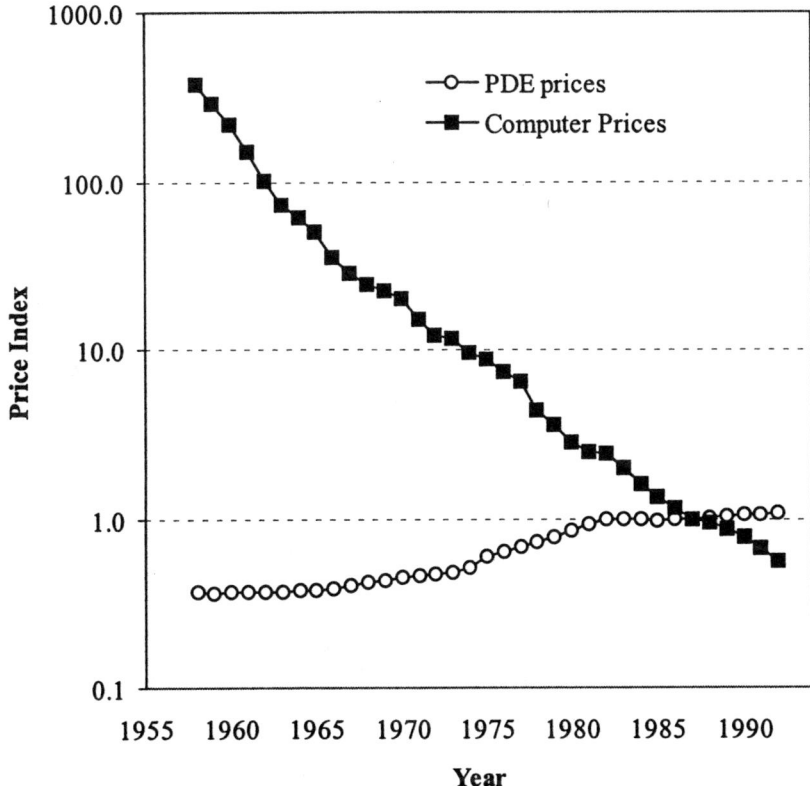

FIGURE 1.2 Real computer prices. The price of computers has declined relative to the costs of other types of producers' durable equipment (PDE). SOURCE: Brynjolfsson and Yang (1997), using data from the U.S. Department of Commerce.

ship patterns correlate strongly with age and income. About 20 percent of households with incomes between $10,000 and $20,000, but more than 60 percent of households with incomes of $60,000 to $75,000, have computers. Some of the largest annual gains in computer ownership were found in middle-income groups. For example, households in the $40,000 to $50,000 income group reached the 50 percent level, and there was a nearly 5 percent increase in penetration in the $20,000 to $30,000 income group. Almost 60 percent of households with children own a computer today.

An earlier RAND analysis by Anderson et al. (1995) examined computer ownership data from the 1993 Current Population Survey conducted by the Bureau of the Census. They categorized computer ownership according to income, education, race/ethnicity, age, sex, and location of residence. This study found that income and educational status were associated with significant differences in

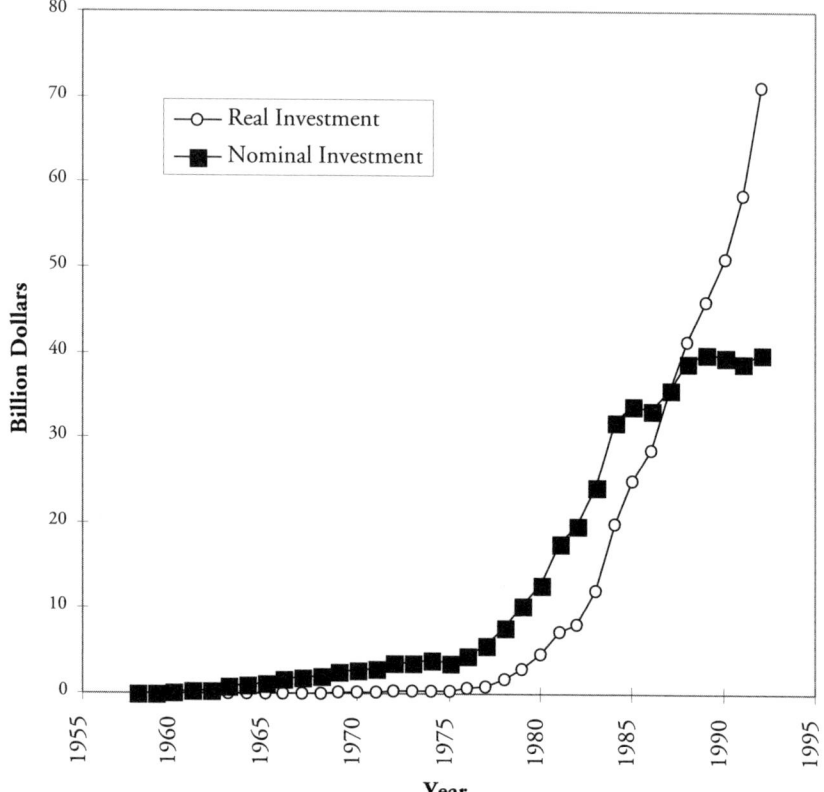

FIGURE 1.3 Nominal and real computer investment. SOURCE: Brynjolfsson and Yang (1997) using data from the U.S. Bureau of Economic Analysis.

computer ownership. For example, about 7 percent of the lowest-income quartile of households had computers at home, whereas nearly 55 percent of the highest-earning quartile had computers at home.[3] In 1993, about 13 percent of individuals over the age of 15 who did not have a high school diploma had a home computer, whereas 49 percent of college graduates had a home computer.

1.1.3 Internet Use

The most reliable figure on Internet use is the number of computer and network domains connected directly to the Internet, all of which must have a public Internet address. According to conservative estimates from a recently conducted Internet domain survey (Network Wizards, 1998), the number of Internet host computers grew from 1.313 million in January 1993 to almost 30 million in January 1998.[4]

The number of individuals who use the Internet is very difficult to measure, in part because the definition of users is somewhat fuzzy. Users might be subscribers to a consumer Internet service or other computer service that includes the Internet as a component, or they might be potential users with access to the Internet at their workplace. Matrix Information and Directory Services (Quarterman, 1997) estimated that as of January 1997 about 71 million people worldwide had access to e-mail. When access to information by file transfer protocol (FTP) or the World Wide Web (WWW) was the criterion used, the figure was about 57 million people worldwide.

Project 2000[5] at Vanderbilt University has conducted several carefully designed surveys of Internet and Web use. One study (Hoffman et al., 1996) examined Internet use by age, education, and sex using a telephone sample of 3,785 respondents. It found significant differences in usage patterns across these demographic groups. For example, only 13.5 percent of those with a high school diploma or less reported using the Web once or more per week, whereas nearly 56 percent of those with a college degree reported weekly use. Hoffman and Novak's most recent estimates, based on Nielson Media Research's Spring 1997 Internet Demographic Study, showed that 45 million people in the United States 16 years of age and older, or about 22 percent of the population, had accessed the Web at least once (Hoffman et al., 1997a).

Another study (CommerceNet/Nielsen Media Research, 1997), in which 9,000 people were interviewed, estimated that 58 million adults in the United States and Canada used the Internet on a regular basis. More than half of the respondents said that they had been online within 24 hours of the interview.

Although e-mail appears to be the most widely used Internet service, the World Wide Web is one of the fastest growing services. A Baruch College-Harris Poll (1997) survey of 1,000 U.S. households conducted in the spring of 1997 indicated that the number of adult Web users had nearly doubled—to 40 million people, or 21 percent of adults—from the previous year. About a quarter of these were people in their forties.

According to Matrix Information and Directory Services (Quarterman, 1997), about 36 million individuals worldwide have the technical capability to distribute or publish information via FTP or WWW. The Netcraft Web Server Survey found 525,915 publicly accessible Web servers in an exhaustive search in November 1996; by December 1997 the number had risen to more than 1.6 million (Netcraft, 1996, 1997).

1.1.4 Global Connectivity

According to a study by the International Data Corporation, the surge in Internet use is a global phenomenon (International Data Corporation, 1997a). The study estimated a worldwide total of 91 million users as of November 1997, with 14 million users in the Asia/Pacific region, 20 million in Europe, and around 1 million in both Africa and South America.

1.2 SOME MAJOR CHALLENGES

The studies cited above are, of course, based on particular samples and research methodologies; it is hard to appraise their accuracy without more detailed investigation. Moreover, among the variables that make measurement difficult and contribute to inconsistent results are disparate definitions of "use" and "access." However, these studies clearly indicate that computer and Internet growth is a significant, widespread, and global phenomenon. Although use of information technology is most prevalent among businesses and highly educated, high-income, North American households, all demographic groups in the developed world show a pattern of significantly increasing use.

A phenomenon this ubiquitous and growing this rapidly is clearly important. As the three examples below illustrate, social science research can help policy makers and others to better understand and shape the interactions between technology and society.

1.2.1 Productivity and Organizational Change

In the long run productivity is the primary determinant of our standard of living and the economic resources available to address societal challenges and problems. Understanding whether and how computers affect economic productivity is a critical issue for policy makers as well as business leaders. In 1987, the economist Robert Solow quipped, "We see the computer age everywhere except in the productivity statistics" (Solow, 1987). Solow's comment reflects the fact that, despite the tremendous advances in computer power and affordability shown in Figures 1.1 to 1.3, the aggregate statistics suggest that economic productivity has grown more slowly since about 1973 than it did in the period from 1950 to 1973.

There are many possible explanations for the apparent slowdown in productivity despite the advances made possible by computerization.[6] Analysis is complicated by the fact that many of the benefits of the computer age are not reflected in the official statistics on output and productivity. Managers typically cite improved quality, variety, timeliness, and customer service as important reasons for their investments in computers, yet these aspects of output go largely unmeasured.[7] Furthermore, the growth of productivity in the service sector is difficult if not impossible to measure. Zvi Griliches, for example, has estimated that the "unmeasurable" sectors of the economy grew from 53 percent of the total in 1948 to about 74 percent in 1994 (Griliches, 1994). Ironically, there is apparently less information in the information age about the value of output than there was in the industrial era. New and better metrics clearly are needed to help in understanding how productivity in the information age should be gauged and evaluated.[8]

Another aspect of the productivity paradox may be unrealistically high expectations about the potential of computers to affect output. Investment in computerization is still a relatively small share of the total economy, and so the possible impact of computerization on the whole may be limited. Based on the quantity of computer power purchased each year, it is possible to calculate the expected contribution computers "should" be making to economic growth under the assumption that capital investment in computers is earning a "normal" rate of return. Various researchers have undertaken such an exercise, and the estimates cluster around 0.3 to 4 percent of additional growth in the economy owing to technological advances in computers each year.[9] Perhaps, then, the measured slowdown in productivity would have been even more pronounced had it not been for the contributions made by computers.

A constant stream of new discoveries and advances is required just to keep productivity growth from falling to zero, and part of the promise of computers is their ability to engender such new discoveries. In earlier decades, growth in productivity was the result of innovations such as electricity, automobiles, the radio, jet engines, plastics, and even corrugated cardboard (Denison, 1985). Today, new products and services, innovative business processes and organizational forms, and even new industries can be traced to advances in information technology. Moreover, like earlier general-purpose technologies such as the steam engine and electricity, computers have changed the nature of work in myriad minor and major ways, thus magnifying their economic and social impact.

David (1989, 1990) found that the electrification of factories had its greatest effect after factories had been radically reorganized (see section 2.3.3 for more details). Similarly, case studies suggest that realizing the full benefit of computer technologies also often requires a significant rethinking of how business works. As a result, the ways in which computers are used may be more important than the quantity of investment. In one instance, a large medical products manufacturer found that effective use of computerization required changes in two dozen work practices and policies, including those related to inventory, incentive systems, worker training, job responsibilities, and hiring criteria. Initially, productivity fell because the new system did not work smoothly. However, by focusing on the interactions among the work practices, the company was able eventually to reap substantial rewards from use of the technology (Brynjolfsson et al., 1997).

Understanding exactly which work policies and practices need to be changed and which changes are most important in various contexts—for example, what frequency and amount of training are required for workers to adapt to new technologies—are critical research issues. Collection of further case studies can help, but there is a particular need for analysis leading to broader insights that can be generalized across numerous companies and situations. Here again, lack of good data on how businesses are changing has hampered progress. Section 2.3.3, "Organizations and Processes," discusses these issues in more detail.

1.2.2 Information Technology and Wage Inequality

For more than 20 years, the gap separating high-wage earners from low-wage earners has continued to increase in the United States. For example, the ratio of the wages earned by males at the 75th percentile of the distribution to those at the 25th percentile has grown from 1.75 to 1 in the 1970s to 2.25 to 1 in the early 1990s, and the wages of those at the more extreme percentiles have moved farther from the median (Murphy and Welch, 1993). By some measures, the poorest members of society are worse off than they were a generation ago. Most economists attribute much of the increase in inequality to an increase in the demand for skilled labor and also link that shift in demand to technical change. For example, Autor et al. (1997) showed that the increase in inequality was largest in those industries that were the heaviest users of information technology. However, it remains unclear *how* use of IT changes labor markets. Thus, it is difficult to predict whether the growth in wage inequality will continue and what policy makers can do about it.

Is the growth of inequality a temporary phenomenon that will correct itself? Should society invest more heavily in education to dampen the negative effects of technological change? What is the role of corporate reorganization in changing the demand for different types of workers? These are some of the important questions that can be addressed only by further research on the economic and social impacts of computing and communications. Section 2.3.2, "Labor and Information Technology," discusses this subject in more detail.

1.2.3 Design of Technology and Standards Setting

Social science has much to contribute to the design of appropriate technology. Today the question facing many technologists is not, How do we do it? but, What should we do? As determinants of technology development, design issues involving human-computer interfaces (see Box 1.2), pricing and "versioning" (the provision of different qualities or versions of a good that sell at different prices), evaluation, and product life cycles have become more important than the traditional engineering concerns. Social scientists can help to design the questionnaires, marketing studies, pricing policies, and interfaces necessary to develop successful information technology.

Standards development is another aspect of technology design in which social science can play a very useful role. Technical standards are the basis for interconnection and communication among information technology systems. However, an important aspect of standards is that once adopted, they can be very difficult to change because of their highly distributed nature and the consequent

> **BOX 1.2**
> **Human-Computer Interface Design**
>
> As a result of technology advances, interface designers can now attempt to make human-computer interfaces more personable by incorporating human-like attributes such as speech or representations of human faces using pictures, simulations, or animation. When technologists introduce human-like attributes into interfaces, they change the user's experience from one of human-machine interaction to one that approximates some features of human social interaction. Even though such interfaces only partially represent human attributes and clearly are not "real," users still respond somewhat as though they were interacting with a person rather than a machine.
>
> Social science research has explored how people react to more human-like interfaces. For example, Clifford Nass and his colleagues demonstrated that when people interacted with computers that had human-like attributes, they applied such rules as "Be polite when delivering evaluations" and "Praise of others is more accurate than praise of self" when they assessed computer software (Nass et al., 1994).
>
> Lee Sproull and her colleagues demonstrated that people made their own behavior more social when they interacted with human-like interface agents. For example, people reported that they were more altruistic when they answered standard personality-test questions asked by a talking face displayed on a screen than when they answered the same questions displayed in a text window (Sproull et al., 1996).
>
> In neither case did the researchers ask the conventional questions about ease of use: Was the audio easy to hear and understand? Were the visual images sharp and clear? Were the instructions easy to understand? Instead the researchers asked, Did users respond to these computer programs in ways reminiscent of ways they would respond to a human being?
>
> Trying to introduce human attributes into interfaces is not necessarily the right approach.[1] However, if technologists do attempt to make computer interfaces more human-like, then social scientists can use theories of social interaction to help technologists understand and predict how people will react to these interfaces, thus increasing the acceptance and utility of the computing technology.
>
> ---
> [1] A recent Computer Science and Telecommunications Board report (CSTB, 1997b) discusses promising research in interface design.

need for broad-range, costly alternations of user behavior and infrastructure. For example, technical standards developed and adopted now for electronic payment—such as the proposed Secure Transactions (SET) standard for credit card transactions over the Internet—may be in use for some time, and careful thought should be given to their implications.

Thus far, information technology standards setting has been successful in not hindering the dramatic growth just described. However, technical standards are playing an increasing role in policy considerations, and some current issues require the development of standards that address social, legal, and policy concerns. See sections 2.4.1, "Protection of Intellectual Property," 2.4.3, "Privacy," and 2.4.9, "Electronic Commerce," for further discussion.

1.3 ROLE OF SOCIAL SCIENCE

There is no shortage of pundits who will forecast the future of the information society. Much of their writing is based on extrapolation or slogans, neither of which is an effective guide to crafting public policy and designing technology. One month everyone is talking about "information 'haves' and 'have-nots'"; the next month it is "agent-based commerce." Rarely do articles in the mass media refer to social science research, such as studies of differential access to computers or economic studies of a variety of mechanisms for automated trading, that would be highly relevant to these issues.

For the purposes of this report, the core social sciences are taken to be anthropology, economics, history,[10] political science, sociology, and social psychology. Closely allied are the fields of demography, information science, law, and organizational studies—areas that have a significant social science component and are also highly relevant to research on the impacts of information technology. These disciplines use dramatically different methods. Economics, for example, is highly quantitative, whereas anthropology and history are typically much more descriptive.

An advantage offered by social science is that it can help technologists and policy makers to understand how people and social institutions behave in response to current technology developments and what the effects of particular changes might be. Changes might be introduced at the microlevel, for example, by technologists who make computer interfaces more personable, or at the macrolevel, for example, by policy makers who put in place new intellectual property protection frameworks. At either end of and along the entire continuum, social science data and theory can help decision makers make better-informed decisions.

The collection of reliable data—such as data on the penetration or use of a particular technology—is an endeavor in which the methodology of social science can make an important contribution. For example, as noted in section 1.1.3, measurement of how many people use the Internet is complicated by the current lack of widely accepted, precise definitions of "use." Defining terms appropriately and precisely is basic to social science methodology, as are assessing the reliability of survey data and increasing the reliability by using particular techniques for sampling, increasing response rates, and assessing the impact of missing data.

The technology-related work that has been done by social scientists is not widely known either to policy makers or to technology designers in part because it is published in academic journals, which are relatively inaccessible, and disseminated only to a relatively small audience. The World Wide Web may allow such studies to become more accessible. However, the typical problem is not in gaining access to scholarly journals and other such sources of pertinent studies, but rather in knowing what to search for. Also, scholarly work is often inaccessible to the lay reader.

Much of the data on the computer and communications industry comes from market research firms whose data complements that generated by social scientists. Both types of data are necessary, and both are worthwhile. One distinction is that the commercial sources make money by selling their data; nobody makes money directly from social science data. But the primary distinction is that social scientists do not simply count things. When they count (to answer how much, how many, how frequently), a theoretical context, involving systematic theories of human behavior, motivates the counts. Thus, for example, a sociologist interested in electronic group dynamics might ask about the relationship between unpleasant events in the group and a decline in group membership. She might count the frequency of "flames" (hostile messages) or "spams" (electronic junk mail) or flames about spams, or how much time people spend deleting flames and spams from their mailboxes, as indicators of unpleasant events. In assessing how those numbers correlate with changes in the size of group membership, the goal is not to count, but rather to understand how the frequency of one kind of behavior affects the dynamics of a social institution. Such understanding enables more reliable forecasts and more trustworthy inferences about causal relationships.

The value of social science research comes not from tracking the frequency of use of the latest technologies but rather from helping to develop common social and economic principles that can be applied to new circumstances. Those designing or relying on technology and those making policy decisions about the use of technology without reference to systematic theories of human behavior or economics will likely find themselves approaching each new issue in ignorance. Given the rapid pace of technological change, this approach has both economic and social costs.

In summary, the ongoing computing and communications revolution requires serious social science investigation. Such work would be valuable for both social policy and technology design. Many choices being made now will be costly or difficult to modify in the future. To help answer the challenges introduced above, new areas of research, improved collection of data, and new collaborations are called for. The chapters that follow examine these issues.

NOTES

1. Throughout this report, the term "impacts" is used as a shorthand expression to indicate a complex set of multicausal, multidimensional technology outcomes. Technology does not typically have a single impact, but rather a range of different outcomes depending on the context or settings. For more discussion, see Box 1.1 as well as Attewell's and Kling's papers in Appendix B of this volume.

2. The Computer Technology Index survey used a sample designed to be representative of all U.S. households and had a 66 percent response rate.
3. Evidence is emerging that the advent of PCs priced below $1,000 is allowing lower-income households to enter the market for personal computers (Hoffman and Novak, 1998).
4. Network Wizards changed the method used to collect data starting with the January 1998 survey and cautioned that care is required in comparing figures derived by using the old and new methods. The extent of growth is unmistakable, however. The last survey conducted with the old method found nearly 20 million hosts in July 1997—which would correspond to roughly 26 million hosts if the new survey method had been used. See Network Wizards (1998) for a discussion of this issue.
5. Project 2000 publications are available online at <http://www2000.ogsm.vandervilt.edu/>.
6. To some, the slowdown in the growth of officially measured productivity seems at odds with the many examples of how computerization has contributed to advances in the past two decades. Automatic teller machines enable banks to handle millions of transactions at all hours of the day and in numerous locations, a capability made possible by computer networking. Volumes of transactions are handled that would be inconceivable without computers. In addition, many modern manufacturers operate with a fraction of the labor previously required while handling far greater product variety. Retailing, medicine, transportation and logistics, communications, and virtually every other industry are in the midst of a computer-enabled transformation.
7. Citing unmeasured improvements in these and other areas, the Boskin Commission recently estimated that the consumer price index overestimates inflation by approximately 1 percent (Advisory Commission to Study the Consumer Price Index, 1996). This implies that growth in productivity has been underestimated by a comparable amount.
8. One tack that several researchers have recently taken is to rely on firm-level data instead of national or industry-level data. For instance, Brynjolfsson and Hitt (1996, 1997) and Lichtenberg (1995) have found that there is, in fact, a strong positive correlation between IT use and productivity at the firm level. See also CSTB (1994a).
9. See, for instance, Brynjolfsson (1996a,b), Oliner and Sichel (1994), Jorgenson and Stiroh (1995), and Lau and Tokutsu (1992).
10. Although history is not usually classified as a social science, historical analysis can play a valuable role closely allied to that of the social sciences in helping to characterize the impacts of computing and communications.

2

Illustrative Examples and Unanswered Questions

This chapter discusses a selection of social science studies that have provided useful insights for understanding the impacts of computing and communications and shaping public policy. The aim is to give a flavor of the results produced by earlier studies and to introduce some areas viewed as especially promising for future research, including points raised and issues discussed at the June 1997 workshop and in position papers submitted by the participants. It is not intended to be comprehensive; the points and issues discussed illustrate the range and value of social science research and provide a basis for framing important research questions. The chapter concludes with an illustrative set of broad topics for ongoing research drawn from the discussion presented below.

Since the range of potential impacts associated with information technology is vast, the examples and issues outlined below are organized according to the domains in which they are extraordinarily important: private life, including households and community; social infrastructure; and business, including labor and organizational process. Cutting across all of these are issues integral to life in an information economy and society—among them protection of intellectual property, pricing of information, and electronic commerce. Another significant impact of computing and communications is the changing boundaries between these domains—between people and organizations, organizations and nations, and the private and public sectors.

2.1 HOUSEHOLDS AND COMMUNITY

Americans are rushing to furnish their homes with a host of devices for sending, receiving, and processing huge quantities of information through di-

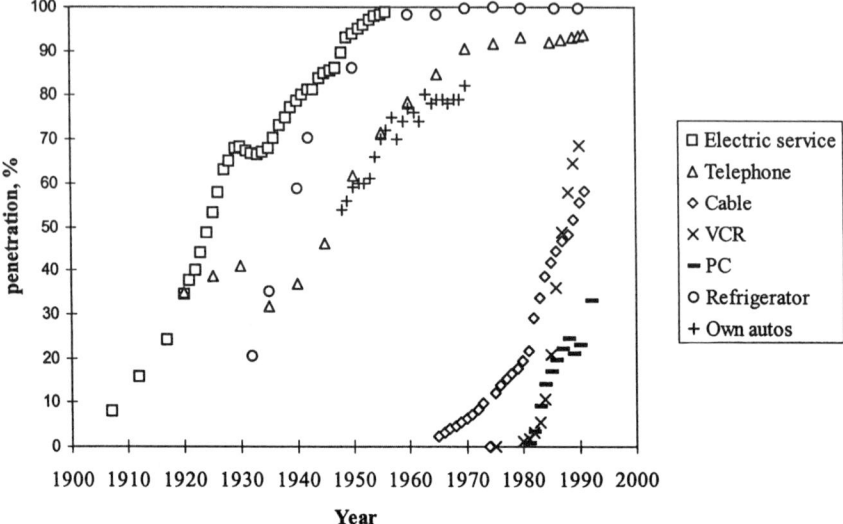

FIGURE 2.1 Penetration of various household devices in the U.S. market over the 20th century. SOURCE: Data from Belinfante (1991), Electronic Industries Association (1984-1990, 1992), Television Bureau of Advertising (1991), and U.S. Bureau of the Census (1986, 1990-1992).

verse media across multitudes of channels. Figure 2.1 shows trends in acquisition of devices such as personal computers compared with ownership of two consumer staples—refrigerators and automobiles. If one could lift the roof from the characteristic U.S. home, one would see that it looks increasingly like a multiplex theater. What once took place in the town square, in the neighborhood tavern, on market day, or in the library can now occur as easily in the study or in the bedroom. Computers and advanced communications are also playing increasingly significant roles in community organizations and in education.

2.1.1 Computer Use in the Home

Computer use in the home is a relatively recent phenomenon, and one that has changed considerably in the past two decades. At first, a majority of use was work-related. Today computers are more accepted as a household technology, with an increasing amount of software and other development targeted to the home. (For further discussion and a model for the interaction of the household and technology, see Venkatesh, 1996.)

Descriptive studies of computer use in the home are relatively rare and almost always very "thin," that is, based on a small number of survey questions.

More intensive and extensive study of computer use in the home is required to understand what people use the computer for; how computer use substitutes for other activities; and how it affects family dynamics, children's educational performance, adults' employment activities, and so forth. But even the best descriptive studies inevitably confound household computer use and its effects with effects stemming from household income and educational status. Households with greater resources are much more likely to have and use computers, and they are likely to use them in different ways. In this situation it is difficult to understand how much of any described effect is due to the technology and how much is due to ancillary resources the household brings to bear on such challenges as understanding how to use software, troubleshoot technical problems, select software for children, and incorporate computers into family activities. A good way to untangle the effects of technology from the effects of other household resources such as income and education is to conduct field experiments in which households are given current technology and well-designed training and support to compensate at least in part for limited income and educational resources.

The Homenet Project (Kraut et al., 1996; Kiesler et al., 1997), organized by social scientists at Carnegie Mellon University, is a field experiment documenting the use and effects of household computers in more than 100 households in Pittsburgh, Pennsylvania. Families were selected for demographic diversity, and a matched sample of eligible but not-selected families was also tracked. Each selected family was given a computer, modem, extra telephone line, full Internet accounts for each family member above age 8 who wanted one, software, training, online support, and access to an evening telephone help desk. In exchange for receiving technology and technical support, families agreed to participate in a variety of data collection efforts, including surveys, home interviews, and automated logging of software use.

Data collection and analysis are still under way, but the researchers have already been able to document important findings:

- Even with hardware and software designed for ease of use, personal training, and personal support, people found the technology hard to understand and use. Significantly, many of those who stopped (or never started) use blamed themselves rather than the technology for their problems. Generational effects persist even when both older and younger generations have the same access to the same technology. People in the household under the age of 19 use the computer more than people older than 19.
- Use of electronic mail is better than use of the Web as a predictor of later e-mail and Web use.
- Household income and educational levels are not valid as predictors of Internet use when all the people compared have adequate technology and support.

2.1.2 Differential Impacts of Technology

It is rhetorically convenient to talk as though technology is used by everyone in the same way and affects everyone similarly, regardless of their life circumstances. Thus, such generalizations as "e-mail flattens organizational hierarchies" or "people who spend time online reduce their face-to-face interaction" are common.

Historians of earlier technologies such as the telephone have noted that people use the same technology differently and that it has different effects, depending on a person's age, gender, income level, geographic location, and other circumstances (see, e.g., Fischer, 1992; Mueller and Schement, 1996).

Numerous researchers have reached the same conclusion about computers. Attewell and Battle (1997) showed that equivalent technological capability in homes is associated with higher school test scores when family income is higher. The Homenet study (Kraut et al., 1996; Kiesler et al., 1997; described above in section 2.1.1) demonstrates that the same technology in the home is used differently by males and females, and also by teenagers and adults. A RAND study of retirees (Bikson et al., 1991) showed that the same technology is used differently by recent retirees and same-age counterparts who have continued to work. Section 2.3.4 gives examples of the differential impact of e-mail use in scientific communities.

An important related question is understanding why some people who made use of the Internet at some time then stopped using it. Demographic studies of the populations of network users and nonusers are required. The developing population of people who experimented with Internet use but did not become long-term users deserves analysis. One study of this topic, using Nielson data from more than 14,000 households, discovered that Internet "drop-outs" were less likely than those who continue using the Internet to have developed social relationships and roles online (Chung, 1998).

Research on differential impacts holds a very important message to those, such as policy makers and others, wishing to understand the interactions between technology and society as a single, uniform impact: they will forever be disappointed or deluded. It is vital to recognize that the "same" technology has different effects in different social and organizational circumstances. Indeed, one of the most important contributions that social science research can make is in exploring how social and organizational conditions—such as income, age, sex, or work status—affect and are affected by how technology is used.

2.1.3 Community

The Internet offers a new locus for communication and participation. According to a *Business Week*/Harris poll released April 28, 1997, of the 89 percent of those surveyed who used e-mail, nearly one-third considered themselves part of an online community. Forty-two percent of those involved in an online community said that it was related to their profession, 35 percent said that their community was a social group, and 18 percent said that it revolved around a hobby.

The shift away from traditional notions of public space may threaten older forms of community. Polls show, for example, that more New Jerseyans know the names of the mayors of New York and Philadelphia than know the names of the mayors in their own towns. Although regions vary, this decline in localism seems to be a characteristic of the U.S. political landscape. Large media networks collect audiences by concentrating on stories that appeal to large blocks of viewers and readers. Thus suburban and rural citizens are quite likely to recognize the name of a city official for whom they cannot in fact vote. Individuals who commute to distant workplaces and whose personal networks are spread geographically are further disconnected. The possibility that localism may become increasingly irrelevant to increasing numbers of Americans signals social and political change of a profound nature. For as long as community has remained intact, for example, libraries and churches and schools have functioned to bring people together, to educate newcomers, and to reinforce the virtues of citizenship.

Today the number of potential secondary anonymous relationships has increased vastly as individuals seek to accomplish tasks by relying on mediated information received from strangers. Home-centered, individualistic, information-heavy approaches to carrying out their personal and professional lives offer people opportunities to bypass both the traditional community and the public sphere.

Hard evidence on the issue of localism and engagement with the community is very mixed. For example, Americans today change homes and communities at about half the rate that they did in the mid-19th century, and even less than they did in the 1950s. It is possible to argue that people are less involved on a daily basis with their neighbors—and more with people elsewhere—than they were a century ago, but the degree of that change is as yet unestimated. Such change may also be a result of other phenomena in the early 20th century—rural to urban migration, the streetcar in cities, and the automobile in rural areas—rather than new communications.

In a sense, the questions first raised by the University of Chicago school of sociology (e.g., Park, 1916, 1955) in the early part of this century persist in their relevance: How does community form out of the ferment of diverse cultural experiences? How does democracy emerge from the diverse cultural experiences of immigrants? At the end of the 20th century such questions are still being asked; but whereas the Chicago school focused on the role of the newspaper as an agent for assimilation and teaching democracy, the question today is under what conditions new information technology and media will bring Americans together or pull them apart. Box 2.1 illustrates some interesting areas meriting further exploration.

> **BOX 2.1**
> **Community in the Information Age**
>
> **Interface between the household and the community.** How does the transformation of household functions enabled by information technologies alter an individual's expectations of community?
>
> **Political values.** Does identification with networked communities affect Americans' construction of democratic participation, responsibilities, and obligations? Will Americans devalue political values associated with geographic community as they integrate into networked communities?
>
> **Virtual communities.** Are they communities? In what ways do people enact the rights and responsibilities of citizenship in virtual communities?
>
> **Networked communities and the elderly.** To what extent does participation in networked communities enrich the lives of the elderly and/or contribute to alienation from geographic communities?
>
> **Families.** Does Internet use by families contribute to the establishment and maintenance of family networks? How fragile are these networks?
>
> **Friendship.** Does making friends in cyberspace enrich or fragment emotional life? Does dependence on cyber friends result in lower motivation to develop friendships with those close by?
>
> **Computer networks as social networks.** How social are computer networks? What needs do they meet or fail to meet?

2.1.4 Education

Increased use of computing technologies in K-12 education is giving rise to important new areas for social science research. The Internet has penetrated rapidly and extensively into U.S. public schools. A U.S. Department of Education survey found that as of fall 1996, 65 percent of schools had access to the Internet; penetration had increased by 15 percentage points in each of the prior 2 years (Heaviside et al., 1997). The Office of Technology Assessment (OTA) estimated that in 1995, U.S. schools had 5.8 million computers for use in instruction—about one for every nine students (Office of Technology Assessment, 1995).

However, the presence of computers for instruction does not necessarily translate into student use of computers for instruction. The OTA reported that despite the presence of close to 6 million computers for instruction in the nation's schools (in 1995; presumably there are more now) students spent only about 2 hours a week using them. Like factories at the introduction of the electric dynamo or business at the introduction of computing technology, schools and teachers may not yet have learned how to modify work practices and organizational structures to take advantage of computing and communications technology. Schools have in general not found it easy to use technologies effectively for improving teaching and learning.[1] Nevertheless it is important for policy makers, educators, and parents to understand what could be accomplished with computing technology in schools under optimal conditions.

Although a variety of proposals have been advanced to increase the availability of computers and Internet connectivity, and substantial investment made in purchasing technology, relatively little attention has been paid to how they will be used once they are in place. Because of the decentralized nature of U.S. education, it is difficult to understand for the nation as a whole the breadth and depth of change in educational practice and outcomes associated with the increasing presence of computing and communications technology in schools and classrooms. While many state departments of education and local districts are implementing new programs with a technology component, efforts to design and employ measures of effectiveness that would allow policy makers and parents to compare across projects are generally lacking.

A recent report of the President's Committee of Advisors on Science and Technology, Panel on Educational Technology, stresses the importance of experimental research in exploring what educational approaches are most effective (PCAST, 1997; see Box 2.2). The report notes that research on educational technology has received minimal funding relative to total national spending on K-12 education, and it urges increased investment. One of the major research categories proposed is the need for rigorous empirical study of which approaches to using information technology in schools are most effective.

The starting point for empirical study is descriptive inventories of projects with comparable measures of effectiveness, which would provide an exceptionally useful knowledge base. Such a study can take advantage of natural variation across states and school districts and would not require active intervention.[2]

This mapping of the range of endeavors under way would lay the foundation for the second phase, a more intensive study of how best to use computers in education. It would be worth considering how to organize, fund, and research a small number of schools as demonstration sites where work practices and organizational structures are radically redesigned to improve teaching and learning through technology. To achieve a fair demonstration, schools would have to be paired with a second set of schools matched according to student and staff demographics and capabilities. The second set would receive economic resources comparable to those of the first set that they could deploy in a range of other ways. Although natural variation among schools would be sufficient for the descriptive phase, this active intervention is required for the second phase in order to derive useful conclusions in the short run.

> **BOX 2.2**
> **Research Recommendations of the President's Committee of Advisors on Science and Technology, Panel on Educational Technology**
>
> 1. Basic research in various learning-related disciplines (including cognitive and developmental psychology, neuroscience, artificial intelligence, and the interdisciplinary field of cognitive science) and fundamental work on various educationally relevant technologies (encompassing in particular various subdisciplines of the field of computer science).
> 2. Early-stage research aimed at developing innovative approaches to the application of technology in education which are unlikely to originate from within the private sector, but which could result in the development of new forms of educational software, content, and technology-enabled pedagogy, not only in science and mathematics (which have thus far received the most attention), but in the language arts, social studies, creative arts, and other content areas.
> 3. Rigorous, well-controlled, peer-reviewed, large-scale (and at least for some studies, long-term), broadly applicable empirical studies designed to determine not whether computers can be effectively used within the school, but rather which approaches to the use of technology are in fact most effective and cost-effective in practice.
>
> SOURCE: Reprinted from PCAST (1997), p. 53.

The politics and economics of designing and running such demonstration studies would be enormously complex and contentious. Yet, currently, school districts and teachers are making decisions about how to allocate resources of both money and time for technology-related efforts, without the benefit of good information about the potential consequences of their decisions. A series of discussions is called for that would involve both the public sector and the private sector—and would include educators, parents, technologists, and researchers—in exploring the feasibility and usefulness of such demonstration projects.

A significant opportunity to study the use of information technology in the public schools is presented by the Schools and Libraries Universal Service Fund, which was established as part of the Telecommunications Act of 1996. With funding of up to $2.25 billion per year, the program will provide discounts on telecommunications services, Internet access, and networking, with the largest discounts going to rural and inner-city communities. By enabling a large number of schools to acquire new technology, this program in effect creates a large-scale "laboratory" where the sorts of research described above could be conducted.

2.2 SOCIAL INFRASTRUCTURE: UNIVERSAL SERVICE

Formulating public policy on aspects of social infrastructure such as universal access to telephony and other communications services requires decision making about how large amounts of money are allocated and how broad segments of society are served. Although the debate about such questions may often take on a political cast, both empirical research and the application of social science theory offer much to help guide public policy making and the investment of public resources.

Since the value of a network—such as the public telephone network or the Internet—depends on the total number of people connected to it (a phenomenon known as "network externalities"), it is often argued that access to networks should be universally provided. Universal service has long been part of U.S. telecommunications policy, and there are those who argue that universal service is an appropriate public policy goal for Internet access (see, for example, Anderson et al., 1995).[3]

Whether or not one agrees that universal service for networks is an appropriate objective of public policy, it is worth pointing out that the historical evidence suggests that there would be widespread popular support for applying universal service policies to new networks made possible by advances in technology. Historically, in several instances, the political demand for universal service has repeatedly induced Congress to ensure universal service at uniform rates.

For example, a postal service available to all was established by the Constitution. Initially (in 1792), postal rates for a first-class letter depended on the distance it was to be carried: 6 cents for fewer than 30 miles, 8 cents for 31 to 60 miles, and so on through nine rate classes to the highest rate of 25 cents for more than 450 miles. In 1845 the rate structure was collapsed to only two categories, 5 cents for not more than 300 miles, and 10 cents for more than 300 miles. In 1863 a uniform rate (3 cents) regardless of distance and free intracity delivery were established (U.S. Bureau of the Census, 1975). Rural free delivery began in 1896. Subsidized Parcel Post became effective in 1913, effectively connecting rural residents to the advantages of city department stores through mail-order houses like Sears-Roebuck and Montgomery Ward. A premium for airmail delivery was dropped in 1978.

For services provided by private businesses, government regulation was often used to ensure universal service and nondiscriminatory rate structures. Railroad rates were regulated by the Interstate Commerce Commission (ICC) beginning in 1887. Interstate telephone rates were regulated by the ICC and later the Federal Communications Commission beginning in 1919. Intrastate telephone calls were made subject to state regulatory authority. Telephone companies were required to charge a uniform fee for service connection. Cable television rates and access have also been regulated.

Government ownership, government subsidies and loans, and direct government programs have been used to ensure universal network services. Land grants and other government assistance brought railroads to every city in the country. The Rural Electrification Administration was established in 1935 to extend electrical service to areas where high construction costs and low population density had made private service unprofitable. The federal highway program and later the federal Interstate Highway System connected every congressional district to the national transportation network.

Education can also be thought of as a good with substantial network externalities. In the United States, elementary education has been provided universally (and compulsorily after the 1880s), and secondary education has been provided universally since the mid-1940s. College education has been subsidized by the state and federal governments since the Land Grant Universities were established shortly after the Civil War. Increasing fractions of the population have benefited from government-subsidized higher education. Special programs have been introduced to assist the children from low- and middle-income families to pay the cost of college.

Two points about these government efforts to foster or mandate universality for network goods need to be stressed. First, all of these congressional and state efforts were designed to accomplish (as much as possible) universal geographic connectivity. Thus letters with 32-cent stamps are delivered to remote sites in the Alaskan north, in mountainous wilderness, and on small, but inhabited, islands. Even Hawaii has an interstate highway! Rural residents received telephone and electrical service just as their city cousins did. Second, the principle of universality was to extend to people in all income classes, rich and poor alike. This has often gone beyond establishing uniform rates for service to the creation of subsidized "lifeline" rates for basic service at prices presumably available to even the poorest families.

The political logic behind these moves is threefold. First, they have been defended as required by the principle of democracy. Individuals cannot effectively participate in the democratic process if they do not have *equal* and unrestricted access to the main methods of communication and transportation. Thus as increasing fractions of the population become connected to a network, those left unconnected become an increasing burden on the democratic principle, and the cost of subsidizing their inclusion becomes smaller and smaller. Sooner or later the political calculus tips the balance toward a policy of guaranteeing universal service. The second principle that has been applied is the desirability of equal opportunity. As economic development proceeded, both high-income occupations and low-cost access to the most diverse array of consumer goods being produced became concentrated in the urban areas. Federal action was seen to be required to keep rural Americans abreast of these advances. Farmers, too, it was argued, should share in the opportunities and wealth created by the new technologies. The third argument used to defend special programs for the poor was the argument that connection to a network was essential or at least very helpful for self-advancement. Basic education is necessary to become employable. More education is probably better. Basic telephone and electrical service is probably necessary to hold a good job and to seek out better opportunities. The political fear is that unless government redistributive actions are taken to include the poor in the network, their lack of connectivity will doom them and their children to permanent poverty.

Although it is certainly true that widespread availability may increase the value of a network, it is not necessarily the case that such access will occur only with government provision or subsidies. After all, many goods with network externalities are provided by the private sector, including our fax machines, video player/cassette market, and so on. Indeed, only a couple of years after the Anderson et al. (1995) report, for-profit firms such as Hotmail[4] began offering free e-mail, supported by advertising.

Basic telephone service has long been regarded as a social good that required a deliberate policy effort to achieve universal access. However, a close reading of history suggests another possible conclusion. According to Mueller (1997), penetration of basic telephone service could easily be comparable to today's rates, even if there had been no policies of subsidized access. Various comments to the FCC in its recent docket on universal service reform indicated that the current structure of pricing in telephony is costing the United States billions of dollars, with very little impact on penetration rates for basic telephone service. These deadweight losses arise because the prices of services such as long-distance calling, for which demand is sensitive to price, are set well above cost, and the prices of price-insensitive services, such as basic service, are often below cost, in direct violation of the economic principles of efficient pricing to cover joint and common costs ("Ramsey pricing"; see Kahn, 1970).

Advocates of universal service for the Internet or telephony typically make their case on grounds of geography or of income. One can well see why interested parties might argue for geographic subsidization: economic theory suggests that most of the benefits of providing services to isolated areas will be captured by those who own land in those areas. Land with electricity, telephone, and road service is certainly more valuable than land with none of these features, and it is, of course, appealing to those who own the land to have someone else pay for such improvements.

Geographical concerns also flow from the interest in social and economic development in rural areas. This was a past concern in the United States for telephony, and it remains an issue for expansion of new broadband services to rural areas. Rural access to even basic telephony remains a major issue in many developing countries. Whether cross-subsidies are the appropriate means to fund the expansion of rural telecommunications services is an area of ongoing public policy debate.

With respect to income arguments for universal service subsidies, it is also important to understand clearly that cost may not be the only reason that the poor do not have access to goods such as telephone service. Mueller and Schement (1996) found that a higher fraction of households below the poverty line in Camden, New Jersey, had cable TV service than had telephones. The most important reason for people choosing not to have telephones was that their friends and relatives would make long-distance calls and leave them liable for paying the bill. According to this study, the monthly charge for basic access was not a significant factor in their choice of whether or not to purchase telephone service.

Public policy debate surrounding the 1996 Telecommunications Act raises new and unresolved research questions. For example: Is special funding for schools and libraries necessary, and if so what is the most efficient means for providing it? Should "carrier-of-last-resort" obligations be allocated via auctions (see section 2.4.8, "Auctions")? Some studies that might shed light on this last question include international comparative studies of the effects of various policy approaches and the impact of subsidies in these policy regimes on consumer behavior.

2.3 BUSINESS, LABOR, AND ORGANIZATIONAL PROCESSES

2.3.1 Location: Internationalization and Telecommuting

One important way in which information technology is affecting work is by reducing the importance of distance.[5] In many industries, the geographic distribution of work is changing significantly. For instance, some Silicon Valley firms have found that they can overcome the tight local market for software engineers by sending projects to India or other nations where the wages are much lower. Furthermore, such arrangements can take advantage of the time differences so that critical projects can be worked on nearly around the clock. As the day ends in San Jose it is just beginning in Bangalore, India, and so the teams can hand off their work electronically to colleagues thousands of miles away (*Economist*, 1996). Firms can outsource their manufacturing to other nations and rely on telecommunications to keep marketing, R&D, and distribution teams in close contact with the manufacturing groups. Thus the technology can enable a finer division of labor among countries, which in turn affects the relative demand for various skills in each nation.

Although there are a number of case studies examining this phenomenon, quantitative evidence is desirable. For example, how many programmers are there in India who are actually working for Silicon Valley firms? And to what extent is this phenomenon of redistribution of employment linked specifically to information technology as opposed to other factors?

While the international redistribution of work is clearly significant, an equally important, if less obvious, effect of the technology is in enabling a redistribution of work within countries such as the United States. This shift began with the advent of inexpensive telephony, nationwide toll-free telephone numbers, and the ability to network dispersed call centers to corporate databases (CSTB, 1994a). For instance, technology has also enabled many financial services firms to move jobs out of lower Manhattan. Some of the data entry work is being shifted to New Jersey while large call centers are being set up in North Dakota and other midwestern states. Other industries are similarly affected. A majority of the large national hotel chains have set up their reservations centers in Omaha, Nebraska, leveraging large computer databases and cheap long-distance telephone service.

Even as it becomes easier to transmit data across both state and international borders, tracking or regulating these activities remains very difficult. A given collection of bits being sent from the United States to India may encode a child's drawing being sent to a proud grandmother or the latest version of a million-dollar software program. Furthermore, as discussed above, the technology enables various types of work and employment to be decoupled from one another. The net result is that the firms have greater freedom to locate their economic activities, creating greater competition among regions in infrastructure, labor, capital, and other resource markets. Most interestingly, it also opens the door for more "regulatory arbitrage": firms can increasingly choose which tax authority and other regulations apply. The emergence of a significant Web-based off-shore gambling industry is only one example of this phenomenon.

That the importance of distance will be reduced by computers and communications technology also has implications for the residence patterns of Americans and the demand for transportation services. Telecommuting is being touted in California as a way to ease traffic congestion (Smart Valley, 1994; see also CSTB, 1994c). Telecommuting may significantly reduce the need for workers to locate their residence within automobile or public transit range of their employer's workplace.

As creative workers of all types and service workers ranging from telephone receptionists and data entry operators to management consultants, accountants, and lawyers find that they can realistically do most of their work at home rather than in a centralized workplace, the demand for homes in climatically and physically attractive regions could increase dramatically. Box 2.3 discusses possible consequences of such a shift.

The ability to do most of one's work at home will reduce but not eliminate the need for face-to-face meetings with fellow employees and customers. Telecommuters are likely to need to travel more for business meetings than are similarly employed office workers. Typically these trips will be long distance. This is not just because the favored residential locations of telecommuters are likely to be remote, but also because the enterprise employing the telecommuter is likely to be less centralized than under the current system. The demand for business travel and accommodations should increase. The location of these periodic business meetings will increasingly be urban areas such as Boston, New

> **BOX 2.3**
> **Telecommuting Scenario: Employment Shifts to Rural Areas**
>
> One can anticipate a shift of population away from the metropolitan areas to bucolic agricultural settings (rural Vermont, the California wine country, fishing villages), to resort areas (Aspen, Monterey, Sedona), and to the sunbelt and beachfront. Just as the automobile, superhighways, and trucking helped shift population out of the central city to the suburbs in the 1950s, the computer, the information superhighway, and modems will help shift population from the suburbs to more remote areas.
>
> The consequences of a shift in employment from the suburbs to more remote areas would be profound. Property values would rise in the favored destinations and fall in the suburbs. Individuals and groups interested in preserving the rural, or historical, or charming aspects of life and the environment in the newly attractive areas could face new pressures. Since most of those able to relocate with the advent of realistic telecommuting would be among the better educated and higher paid, the demand for high-income and high-status services in these areas should soar. Gourmet restaurants, clothing boutiques, high-income grocery stores, office supply depots, topflight medical services, and venues for artistic and cultural events should thrive. But so, too, would there be an expansion of services of all types. These new magnet areas would need more gas stations, gardeners, churches, housekeepers, construction workers, and postal employees. This would create new and expanding job opportunities for the local population, but more significantly the telecommuters would bring with them many others from the cities and suburbs who would not be telecommuting. This economic boom for rural and resort communities would be mirrored by a decline in property values and population in the least attractive areas of the central cities and suburbs. The exodus and the resulting decline in the tax base would reduce local government revenues, perhaps leading to a decline in governmental services, and would exacerbate the economic differences between the mobile segment of the population and those who remain in the older suburbs.

York, Washington, New Orleans, Chicago, Los Angeles, San Francisco, and Seattle and quite possibly resort business centers. Those urban centers should thrive, while smaller or less attractive cities will share the fate of the older suburbs and struggle with declining populations, jobs, and property values.

Telecommuting will enable not only shifts of hundreds or thousands of miles, but also shifts of only a few miles within cities. Information technology could also create employment opportunities for people in the inner city who may lack adequate means of transportation to the outlying areas where new jobs are being created.

There is a need for interdisciplinary research to further examine the impacts of widespread telecommuting (see Box 2.4). The political, social, and economic consequences seem likely to be quite significant, and the potential for a sudden rise in telecommuting within the next few years seems high. Insights might well

> **BOX 2.4**
> **Telecommuting Scenario: Increased Employment Flexibility**
>
> By reducing the fixed cost of employment, widespread telecommuting should make it easier for individuals to work on flexible schedules, to work part time, to share a job (perhaps with their spouse), or to hold two or more jobs simultaneously. Since changing employers would not necessarily require changing one's place of residence, telecommuting should increase job mobility and speed career advancement. Some think that this increased flexibility will reduce job stress and increase job satisfaction. That would be a welcome outcome in itself, and since job stress is a major factor governing health there may be additional benefits in the form of reduced health costs and mortality rates. These impacts also seem ripe for research by social scientists, particularly demographers, and medical researchers.
> If the increased flexibility of work schedules is great enough, there may be some profound effects on retirement and saving behavior has well. With a reduced and less stressful work load, the elderly may wish to continue working well past the conventional retirement age. If so, they may choose to save less during their peak earning years because their need for asset income in late life would be reduced. Those who enter telecommuting early enough to purchase or build residences in remote areas before property values rise in those areas will experience substantial capital gains on their home and for this reason also might feel less need to save from current income. The implications of such developments for company pension systems and the social security system need study.

be gained by a renewed study of the causes and consequences of urbanization and suburbanization in our past.

It is clear that widespread use of telecommuting, even in its nascent stages, will have a major impact on how organizations function. The evolution of organizational forms in response to increased use of networking needs detailed study. For example, how is work being done at a distance monitored and evaluated? One implication is that work tasks could be designed in such a way that there is an identifiable output that the home worker or the telecommuter is delivering.

2.3.2 Labor and Information Technology

Labor Market and Information Technology

The popular press is filled with anecdotal evidence about the negative effects of information technology on employment. However, relatively few attempts have been made to address these issues scientifically.

Wolff (1996) conducted a careful analysis of the effect of computerization on the composition of the labor force during the period from 1950 to 1990 using U.S. census data.[6] The first step in his analysis was to classify the census data into

267 occupations and 64 industries, which were then further refined into the categories "knowledge workers," "data workers," and "goods and service workers." "Information workers" refers to the sum of knowledge and data workers.

Wolff (1996) found that from 1950 to 1990, employment of knowledge workers grew at 3.1 percent a year, while that of data and service workers grew at 2.6 percent a year. Employment of goods producers increased at a rate of only 0.3 percent per year. Overall, in 1950, 37 percent of the employed labor force was information workers; by 1990, 55 percent of the labor force was information workers.

What accounts for this dramatic change in labor market structure? Wolff (1996) showed that the total growth in employment could be decomposed into three effects: a "substitution effect" that describes the extent to which industries have substituted information labor for other types, a "productivity effect" that accounts for changes in productivity growth among different industries, and an "output effect" that accounts for the change in the composition of final output.[7]

Wolff (1996) found that the substitution effect accounted for about half of the growth of the share of knowledge workers in employment. Almost none was due to output effects. In other words, most of the increase in knowledge workers was due to the fact that employers substituted knowledge workers for other kinds of labor, coupled with the fact that industries that used knowledge workers intensively (e.g., service industries) had lower rates of growth in labor productivity than did goods-producing industries. Analysis of this sort is very important in understanding labor force changes and can be a significant input into policy analysis.

Wage Inequality and Information Technology

One of the most striking changes in the economic landscape of the United States over the past 20 to 30 years has been a dramatic increase in inequality of earnings. A growing number of researchers suspect that technological change in general, and computerization in particular, may be part of the explanation.

Although there was relatively little change in the dispersion of wages in the 1950s and 1960s, starting in the 1970s wage inequality increased rapidly. Per-capita income and family income show similar patterns. Interestingly, the changes in inequality are evident across virtually every income subgroup: the wages for those at the 95th percentile increased relative to those at the 90th percentile, which in turn outpaced those at the 85th percentile and so on down to the poorest people in the country (see Figure 2.2).

Although the rise in inequality has been well documented in the academic literature (see Levy and Murnane, 1992, and Gottschalk, 1997, for reviews), there is not yet a consensus as to its causes. However, much of the increase in inequality seems to be related to a growing premium for skilled workers throughout the economy. For instance, the premium paid to college-educated workers and those with more experience has grown significantly. Since skilled workers were al-

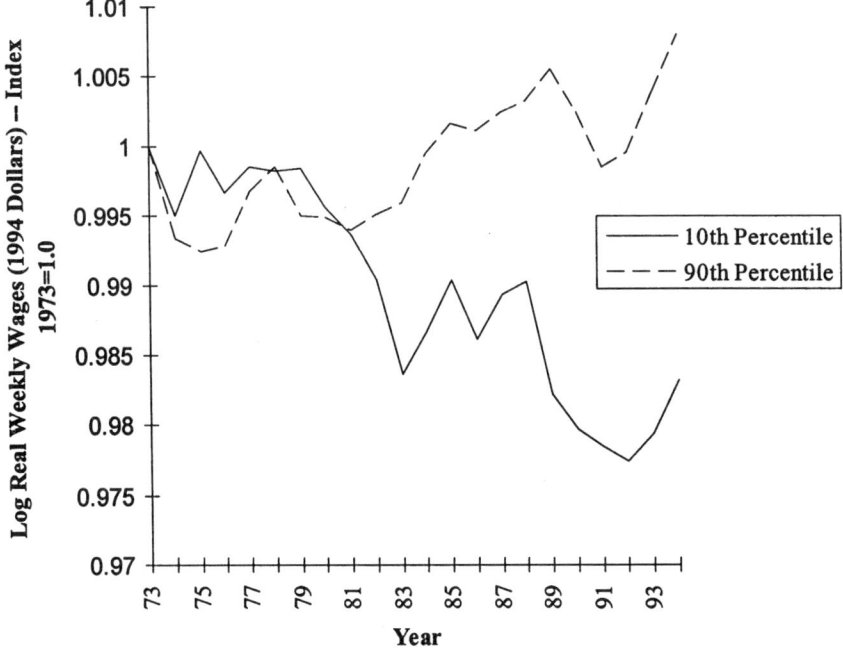

FIGURE 2.2 Wage inequality in the United States, 1973 to 1994. SOURCE: Adapted from Gottschalk (1997), p. 27.

ready at the top of the wage distribution, any increase in their relative wages will tend to increase overall inequality. Furthermore, because the supply of college-educated workers has grown over the past several decades, the fact that their relative wages have increased indicates that the demand for such workers has grown even faster.

The increased demand for these workers cannot easily be explained by changes in the composition of industry output or other observable factors. "Technical change," typically a residual in wage equations, has been left as the best explanation. More direct evidence that technical change is behind the growth in inequality was provided by Berman et al. (1994). They found that the rate of investment in computers was positively correlated with higher demand for skilled workers relative to less skilled workers. This finding clearly runs counter to the claim that computers "deskill" work, as some have claimed. Although this is clearly the case in certain applications, the findings of Berman et al. suggest that it is not true on average.

The mechanism by which computers increase the relative demand for skilled work is still not well understood. There are at least five distinct possibilities:[8]

1. Computers may be disproportionately automating routine, rote jobs, thus reducing the demand for low-skill workers, but not much affecting high-skill workers. Indeed, Mark (1987) found that industries with significant changes in technology typically experienced significant reductions in the number of basic production workers but not in the number of more skilled workers.
2. Computers may complement highly skilled work, making it more valuable. For instance, after controlling for observable characteristics, Kreuger (1993) found that workers using a computer were paid, on average, 20 percent higher wages.
3. The direction of causality could instead go in the opposite direction, with high-paid workers getting computers first, as a signal to their colleagues of their skills. Feldman and March (1981) put forth such a thesis years ago.
4. Computers may facilitate a winner-take-all effect by reducing communications and search costs. As a consequence, the "best" experts in each field can compete over broader geographic regions, displacing the local expert and capturing higher earnings in the process. This explanation seems most applicable to the few "superstars" at the top of the earnings profile.
5. Computers may enable broader reorganization of work, which may change the relative demand for various skills. For instance, decentralization of decision making, use of lateral communications, and greater outsourcing of activities may reduce the need for people who can follow instructions carefully and increase the need for people who can solve problems independently.

Existing measures of income inequality do not consider the nonmarket goods and services that people consume. However, a significant share of an individual's well-being may be derived from factors that are not counted in traditional income. For instance, if employees find that work done with computers is more (or less) enjoyable than it was before the work was computerized, then this perception may exacerbate (or mitigate) the increase in inequality. Unfortunately, there is relatively little data on the extent to which people value nonmarket services and virtually none on how computerization might affect such services.

Effects of Information Technology on Labor and Skill Demand

The evidence on information technology and wage inequality suggests that computers may be partly responsible for the relative increase in the demand for skilled, educated workers. However, thus far, the measures of "skill" and "education" are fairly coarse. Further research is needed to enhance understanding of what skills information technology complements (Levy and Murnane, 1997). Traditional skills, such as math and reading skills, appear to be important, but other skills, such as the ability to work well with others, may also be significant factors.

If computers increase the demand for educated workers, then a national policy of increasing investment in education, especially at the bottom of the educational scale, will help with two national goals that historically have been in opposition: increasing economic output and decreasing inequality. Simply spending more on education or requiring students to spend more time in school may help with these problems, but a major research gap exists in understanding how to make education more efficient. Relatively little is known about what types of courses and what methods of instruction are most effective in providing the education and skills sought by the marketplace. One does not have to believe that economics is the only driver of educational choice by policy makers and students to believe that it is one important consideration. (See also the discussion of the role of information technology in education in section 2.1.4.)

2.3.3 Organizations and Processes

Measuring Productivity

As noted in Chapter 1, while the rapid pace of technological change in computing and communications has been astounding, it has been hard (at least until very recently) to find evidence for improvements in productivity as a result of these dazzling technological innovations.[9] A fundamental problem is that many of the variables typically measured are becoming less relevant in the emerging information economy. For instance, Walter Wriston, the former chief executive officer of Citibank, has quipped, "When I was a kid in the bank, the key economic indicator we looked at was freight-car loadings. Who the hell cares about them now?" (Stewart, 1997).

In today's economy, technology, knowledge, skills, and organizational competencies are often more important resources than land, labor, and traditional capital. Economic output is becoming increasingly "unmeasurable" as gross domestic product shifts from mining, manufacturing, and agriculture to services (Griliches, 1994). Even in manufacturing, intangible components of value, such as product variety, customization, timeliness, and quality have become more important. Similarly, intangible assets, ranging from software, copyrights, and patents to worker skills, customer relationships, and organizational knowledge, are increasingly recognized as important inputs.

Direct measurement of these intangible assets remains elusive, but one indicator is the substantial increase in the ratio of the financial valuation of firms (stock market equity and value of outstanding debt) to the book value of these firms (plant, property and equipment, cash, inventories, and other measured assets) over the past decade. Apparently, investors in the financial markets believe that an increasingly small fraction of firms' true assets are accounted for by traditional metrics. Interestingly, a recent study (Brynjolfsson and Yang, 1997) found that changes in the value of firms' computer assets correlated strongly with changes in the implied extent of intangible assets.

However, there is no reason that the "unmeasurable" outputs and inputs must remain so. As the benefits to businesses of intangibles such as those mentioned above have grown, and as the costs of overhead have come to dominate direct labor and materials costs, researchers such as Robert Kaplan have helped transform managerial accounting to better reflect these realities (Kaplan, 1989). A similar rethinking of our national economic accounts is in order.

The issue of unmeasured improvements in quality—of particular importance in evaluating the output of services—has also received considerable attention from economists. Section 1.1.1 describes how improvements in computing technology have reduced the real cost of computing. Recently, economists have begun making the same sorts of adjustments in other cases, such as for pharmaceuticals (Berndt et al., 1996), as well as for various particular types of medical care such as heart procedures. When patient survival rates and quality of life are considered, they typically find that "real" medical prices have actually been falling, or at least not rising as rapidly as previously thought, and that "real" output and productivity have been growing impressively (Cutler and McClellan, 1996; Cutler et al., 1996). Similar work could be done for information technology—a task made easier now that advances in IT enable better tracking of quality improvements.

Finally, even as information technologies are helping to make organizations more economically efficient than ever before, many people are questioning whether other important goals and values are being overlooked. For instance, social fragmentation, increased inequality, environmental degradation, and greater emotional stress are sometimes associated with advances in technology. A single-minded focus on economic efficiency, narrowly defined, may come at the expense of other goals valued by society. Indeed, technologies need not serve only as generators of wealth. They also can serve other societal functions such as increased equity.

Further compounding the question, technology is giving us new options by relaxing many long-standing constraints. Thus, there is a strong need today for clear thinking about what goals organizations can and should serve. Perhaps a portion of research funding should be reserved for work that contemplates not only how technology can make our lives better, but also what society means by "better."

Historical Perspective: The Computer and the Electric Dynamo

Although the various scientific and engineering disciplines excel at producing technological developments, understanding how or whether these developments lead to greater productivity is quite a different matter. Replacing old information technology with new while retaining the same work practices and organizational structure may have little impact on productivity. The true measure of the technology's worth can be evaluated only when work practices and organizational structures are revamped to best take advantage of the flexibility and power of today's computing and communications technologies.

The subtle process of extracting productivity gains out of technological advancements has been the subject of much scrutiny by social scientists. One particularly relevant and illuminating study is by David (1990). This historical analysis discusses the electric dynamo and its role in an earlier "productivity paradox." At the turn of the century, electrification was seen, much as computers are today, as a transformational technological advance whose impact would soon be widely felt. However, factory electrification did not have much impact on productivity growth in manufacturing before the 1920s.

> The proximate source of the delay in the exploitation of the productivity improvements potential incipient in the dynamo revolution was, in large part, the slow pace of factory electrification. The latter, in turn, was attributable to the unprofitability of replacing still serviceable manufacturing plants embodying production technologies adapted to the old regime of mechanical power derived from water and steam. (David, 1990)

The first phase of electrification (from the mid-1890s to 1920) mainly utilized the group drive system of power transmission, with one motor powering many pieces of equipment. This way of shifting to electric motors entailed minimal changes to the basic factory design, and essentially replaced the old mechanical power system with an electric one. However, in the 1920s, the "unit drive" approach, with individual motors powering each piece of equipment, was widely adopted. The benefits of this approach were not limited to the immediate savings associated with greater energy efficiency. In fact, the greatest benefits derived from the ability to build lighter, more modular, single-story factories using this new technology. Learning how best to utilize this flexibility was not immediate:

> Although all this was clear enough in principle, the relevant point is that its implementation on a wide scale required working out the details in the context of many kinds of new industrial facilities, in many different locales, thereby building up a cadre of experienced factory architects and electrical engineers familiar with the new approach to manufacturing. (David, 1990)

The analog of this story for the computer has yet to be written. While there are encouraging reports (see CSTB, 1994a; Brynjolfsson and Hitt, 1996, 1997) that perhaps the productivity paradox is no more, there yet remains substantial work to be done in understanding what work practices and organizational struc-

> **BOX 2.5**
> **The Concept of "Organization"**
>
> Perhaps the most important potential impact of computers and communications on organizations is a shift in the very concept of "organization" as an economic and social entity. Once considered to be semipermanent and routinized by definition, ideal organizations increasingly have come to be seen as flexible, change-oriented, and able to shift their boundaries, alliances, and partnerships rapidly to meet changing conditions. Computers and communication technologies increasingly permit anytime, anywhere communication, synchronous and asynchronous collaboration, and tight linkages in operational processes within and between organizations (e.g., manufacturers and their suppliers and distributors, and manufacturers and the direct buying public). The concept of the "adhocracy"—a fluid organization in which members come and go as interests change—has emerged as competition for the concept of bureaucracy. After many decades of increasing vertical integration of production and growth as a totem of success, many organizations have divested themselves of every function that was not a core competence, and that could possibly be "outsourced" or bought on the market. Small really did become beautiful, at least in principle. Young entrepreneurs who started little companies in their garages built novel ideas into huge companies and fortunes, capturing the imagination of the world. And the mighty such as AT&T, IBM, and GM appeared shaken as the world they had built started to collapse around them.
>
> Yet, as recent history has shown, organizations such as AT&T, IBM, and GM have by no means been pushed aside by the changes of the information age. They have adopted and adapted the technologies and harnessed them in ways that have allowed radical downsizing of work forces while retaining and in some cases enhancing top management control over firms' performance and profitability. And the start-up companies created in garages have found it necessary to adopt time-honored aspects of organizational hierarchy in order to function effec-

tures are optimal in this new computer age. How will the modern counterpart to David's "cadre of factory architects" be developed? That is the challenge facing the social scientists studying the new industrial frontier.

Information Technology and Organizational Structure

Both firms and markets can be thought of as sophisticated institutions for processing information about desires, costs, capabilities, and constraints (Galbraith, 1977; Hayek, 1945; Radner, 1992; Sah and Stiglitz, 1986). Thus, given the fact that the cost of computer processing of information has declined by several thousandfold over the past three decades, it would be surprising if these institutions did not change. Several researchers have developed models that predict how changing information processing and communication costs are likely

> tively. This lesson from recent history reveals an important but frequently overlooked aspect of the information revolution: that its revolutionary character is being channeled through pathways established by powerful social and institutional forces that are not necessarily swept aside by the effects of technology, no matter how powerful those effects are.
>
> Much of the rhetoric about profound change in organizations has been speculative and undisciplined, based more on idealized views of what organizations ought to be rather than on the practical realities that shape organizational form and function. One can construct scenarios of organizational demassing and decentralization, but one also can just as easily construct sound arguments that computer and communication technologies give new life to the traditional bureaucracy. Functions normally carried out by middle managers—information gathering, decision making within directives, communications with lower-level staff, and monitoring and upward-reporting of activities carried on below—can be replaced to some extent with technology. The resulting "flattening" of the organization through the elimination of middle managers has been said to bring greater "empowerment" of remaining employees. But technological change can just as easily allow significant increases in organizational centralization, tighter monitoring of employee activity, more effective enforcement of compliance with the desires of top management, and the redesign of tasks in ways that make it difficult for employees to act outside of prescribed patterns.
>
> There are reasons to be confident about profound changes under way in the character and concept of organizations as a result of new computer and communications technologies. At the same time, it is important not to let ideological enthusiasm substitute for careful reasoning and empirical research.
>
> —John Leslie King and Kenneth L. Kraemer, "Computer and Communication Technologies: Impacts on the Organization of Enterprises and the Establishment of Civil Society" (see Appendix C of this volume)

to affect firms and markets (e.g., Malone, 1987; Brynjolfsson, 1996a; Bakos, 1997).

Not only are markets and firms changing, but new structures, some never before feasible or even imagined, may also emerge. Research is needed to extend existing theories about organizations and to learn from the organizational changes and experiments that are already happening (see Box 2.5). Results of such research would provide a sound basis for corporate "re-engineering" efforts that seek to make better use of information technology.

Recent research on the effects of information systems has highlighted the importance of complementarities. Theory (Milgrom and Roberts, 1980), case studies (Brynjolfsson et al., 1997; Orlikowski, 1992), and econometric/statistical analyses (Brynjolfsson and Hitt, 1997) indicate that the effects of information technology depend significantly on other organizational factors such as organizational form, communications practices, and the education and training of the work force. Therefore, research on the organizational impacts of IT should consider these complementary factors whenever possible. Understanding the nature of the complementarities is critical to being able to make predictions about the social and economic impacts of IT. For instance, if IT is complementary to an organizational structure for which teams and decentralized decision making by workers are important, then as IT becomes cheaper, one would expect that there would be increasing demand for people who work well in teams and who have the skills and education needed to make them effective decision makers.

One of the difficulties researchers face is that the data on the organization of work are fragmented and disorganized. There is a clear need for a compilation of what data already exist in this area. A project that sought to catalog, or better yet, assemble and make available, the key data sets on this topic could reduce duplication of efforts, speed research, and help settle debates that stem from misunderstandings about the basic evidence.

Time series data, even short time series, would be especially valuable in clarifying the role of technology in some of the organizational changes that are observed. For instance, better time-budget studies could help address the ongoing debate as to whether the average worker is spending more hours or fewer hours at work. Data gathered from employers indicate that the work week has shrunk, but employees report that they are working more hours. The discrepancy may be owing to employees working more at home or working for multiple employers, or it may have some other cause.

Another possible source of data is exit interviews, during which workers could be asked how technology has changed the nature of the work they do. Firms and social scientists could collaborate on survey design and data collection; results would benefit the participating companies as well as the broader research community.

Process Handbook

In recent years, a number of striking examples have emerged of how information technology can be combined with the redesign of organizational processes or the invention of new processes to transform the way organizations work. Although initially uncommon and perceived as radical, ideas such as just-in-time inventory control and concurrent engineering[10] have become accepted as "best practice" (Carter and Baker, 1991). How can the new organizational possibilities enabled by the continuing, dramatic improvements in information technology be developed, understood, and exploited? Given time, managers and employees of companies will certainly develop new ways of working that take advantage of these new opportunities. For more rapid progress on these problems, however, it is useful to develop a more systematic foundation for understanding organizational processes. In order to understand successful organizational practices, one must be able to recognize and represent organizational practices that are observed, and imagine alternative ones.

While data sets exist on individuals, firms, industries, and nations, there is a substantial gap in the availability of data at the level of business processes. Business processes are a distinct unit of observation from firms or individuals. Not only does an individual firm involve numerous business processes, but many business processes also cut across the firm's boundaries. The creation of a database with information on business processes that included numerous examples of how different groups and companies perform similar functions could enable new research directions. The database should provide a taxonomy for categorizing business processes, and ideally should be designed in a way that multiple researchers could access, add to, and comment on the data.

In fact, a prototype for such a database—a process handbook—has been created by Thomas Malone and colleagues at the Massachusetts Institute of Technology. The handbook is intended to help people imagine new organizations and organizational practices, redesign existing organizations, share ideas and "best practices" about organizational processes, and generate or select software to support or analyze these processes.

One key feature of this representation technique is that it not only breaks down activities into process subparts ("subactivities") but also adds the concept of specialization—differentiating a process into various specific ways of doing the process ("specializations"). For example, specializations of the process labeled "sell something" include "sell by retail store" and "sell by mail order." The technique's second key feature is that it characterizes dependencies between processes and ways of managing these dependencies, also known as "coordination" mechanisms (e.g., Malone and Crowston, 1994). A dependency exists, for example, when an item produced by one process must be made available to another at the right time. Two alternative coordination approaches to handling this dependency would be to produce the good to order or produce the item to be held in inventory until it is required.

The work provides an approach to analyzing processes at various levels of abstraction, thus capturing both the details of specific processes as well as the "deep structure" of their similarities. A primary advantage of the approach is that it allows people to explicitly represent the similarities (and differences) among related processes and to find or generate sensible alternatives for how a given process could be performed.

Results from this project suggest that such databases are both technically feasible and managerially useful (Malone et al., 1997). The process handbook project has developed a series of software tools for storing and manipulating processes, which have been used to represent more than 2,000 activities of both generic processes and specializations of these processes from specific organizations.

Because empirical research in this area is often constrained by lack of data on organizational processes used by firms, the further development of data sets like the process handbook could engender significant new research on the impacts of information technology that would not otherwise be possible.

2.3.4 Social Science and the Workplace

Differential Impacts Within the Workplace and Professional Communities

Section 2.1.2 discusses the differential impacts of information technology in the home. Not surprisingly, the same phenomenon of differential impacts owing to the use of information technology is also found in the workplace.

Scientists are one set of information technology users for whom the differential impacts in a professional setting have been studied. In structured interviews with 67 scientists in 1991 and 1992, Walsh and Bayma (1997) showed that scientists in four scientific fields—mathematics, experimental biology, chemistry, and particle physics—used computer networks quite differently. They identified four attributes of scientific disciplines that predicted lesser or greater use: (1) size of discipline—smaller disciplines used computer networks more than larger ones; (2) market penetration—disciplines in which property rights and financial rewards to research findings were more closely linked used computer networks more; (3) locus of information—disciplines in which most research findings are produced at the laboratory bench used computer networks less; and (4) technical limitations—disciplines that rely on photographs and drawings used computer networks less.[11]

Even within a single scientific field, e-mail can differentially benefit scientists who otherwise could be at an information disadvantage. For example, according to one study, physical oceanographers who work at inland universities or laboratories derived more benefit from each additional e-mail message sent or received than did oceanographers who worked at coastal universities or laboratories (Hesse et al., 1993), when standard measures of scientific productivity were considered such as number of journal articles published.

Differential impacts have been observed for shift workers as well. Shift workers in a municipal government derived more benefit from each additional message sent (although not received) than did day workers, as gauged by standard measures of organizational commitment and well-being (Huff et al., 1989).

Because e-mail omits direct information about social status—such as age, physical appearance, and gender—that inevitably accompanies face-to-face communication, it can differentially benefit people who otherwise could be socially marginalized. Younger oceanographers derived more benefit from each additional e-mail message than did older, more established ones (Hesse et al., 1993). Physically disabled members of a multiyear program of computer communication derived more benefit than did nondisabled members (Earls, 1990). Members of a retirement-planning task force who were themselves recent retirees derived more benefit from use of e-mail than did their still-employed counterparts (Bikson et al., 1991).[12]

Romm and Pliskin (1997) have examined the use of e-mail in the workplace. They suggest that several characteristics of e-mail—speed of delivery, ease of sending to a large number of addressees, ease of adding commentary to messages and forwarding them on, and ease of control over which versions of messages are sent to which recipients—make it a powerful political tool. Used deliberately in this way as a tool for "virtual politicking," e-mail can increase the power of employees relative to that of management. The adoption of information technology to improve the performance of organizations will also have significant, differentially distributed impacts on the individuals within those organizations.

Technical Support Communities

Social science methodology associated with the study of communities has proven useful in improving business performance. In the mid-1980s, anthropologist Julian Orr conducted extensive field work among Xerox Corporation service repair technicians (Orr, 1990). One of his findings was that technicians never relied exclusively, or sometimes even at all, on the company-provided service manuals when troubleshooting machine problems. Often the manuals were out of date or did not address local, idiosyncratic problems. Rather than using manuals, or in addition to using them, they relied on war stories passed from technician to technician in an oral storytelling culture. Orr pointed out the value of these stories to corporate management, noting that they represented an important intellectual resource that the company should capitalize on.

Partly inspired by Orr's work, a team of Xerox developers spent a long time observing and talking with service technicians, learning what would be useful to them from their point of view. Based on their fieldwork they built a system to leverage technicians' local knowledge through a community-validated "tips" database. A "tip" is a problem-cause-solution case that is voluntarily written and submitted by anyone in the field service organization and validated by technical specialists. When the tip is released to the field, it carries in it the name of both the submitting technician and the validator. In one field trial of the tips system with 1,300 field support people, Xerox found that about 15 percent of the employees submitted tips and that the tips database was accessed more than 1,000 times a day (Bell et al., 1997).

The technology per se in this system is not at the forefront of computer science. Both developers and managers attribute the success of this system in part to the effort to take seriously social science ideas about community. They learned that local knowledge conveyed in the community vernacular by community members is useful to technicians troubleshooting unfamiliar problems. And so the system was designed to support vernacular content. They learned that community knowledge could spread much more rapidly than standard corporate publication or validation cycles. And so the system was designed to include many human validators in order to ensure very short validation cycles. Initially, developers and managers worried that they might have to provide economic incentives for technicians to contribute tips. But they learned that technicians value the social validation that comes from other community members who appreciate their tips. And so the system was designed to ensure that people contributing tips could be maximally visible to others in their community. In the first deployment of the tips system, the corporation collected data suggesting that use of the tips database was responsible for a significant improvement in this group's service performance. The corporation has subsequently begun deploying variants of this system in many of its service organizations.

2.4 INFORMATION ECONOMY AND SOCIETY

Advances in information technology raise a number of research issues involving the economic, social, and cultural aspects of how society accesses, uses, and values information. For example, the ability to store and distribute more information more rapidly is leading to concerns about information overload and raising new questions about how information is evaluated by users. Increasingly, information is exceeding the bounds inherent in the written and printed word. New types of media and new technologies for accessing information pose challenges to educators, creators and distributors of information, and policy makers, among others.

2.4.1 Protection of Intellectual Property

Increasing representation of a wide variety of content (e.g., text, images, video, audio) in digital form has resulted in markedly easier and cheaper duplication and distribution of information—with mixed effects on the provision of content. On the one hand, content can be distributed at a dramatically lower unit cost. On the other hand, distribution of content outside of channels that respect intellectual property rights can reduce the incentives of creators and distributors to produce and make content available in the first place. Information technology has raised a host of questions about intellectual property protection, and quite a number of solutions have been proposed. Making appropriate choices requires attention to a range of considerations and perspectives and can be informed by economic and historical analysis.

Economic Analysis of Intellectual Property Rights

The classic economic study of the trade-off between innovation and intellectual property protection is that of Nordhaus (1969), who examined the optimal length of a patent. Longer-lived patents give producers more incentive to innovate but also lead to longer periods of monopolization. Using a simulation model, Nordhaus studied the benefit-cost trade-off between these two effects and concluded that a patent life of around 20 years was a reasonable middle ground. Subsequently, economists have examined other dimensions of patent policy, such as the scope of patents, the standard for novelty, and so on.

Whereas patent rights apply to inventions, copyright applies to artistic or literary expression (be it in print, audio, or visual form) and is the dominant form of intellectual property protection for electronic content. Numerous studies have looked at the economic impact of patents, but far fewer such studies have been done on copyright, even though there is currently much legal and policy activity in this area. In part this discrepancy reflects differences in data availability: patent data is available electronically in a centralized database, whereas copyright is granted automatically and does not require the copyright holder to register formally in all instances.[13]

Even relatively simple cost-benefit examination of some of the issues would contribute to a better understanding of the effects and implications of particular approaches raised in policy debates about intellectual property rights—for example, a new form of copyright protection for data in databases that the Europeans are asking the United States to consider.

Economic considerations are also important in evaluating methods for enforcing requirements attached to the use of copyrighted materials, including technological approaches. One specific approach is the use of secure hardware that enforces specific terms and conditions (Stefik, 1995). However, both theoretical examination (Shy, 1998) and practical experience with devices that provide protection against unauthorized copying suggest that this strategy is problematic in a highly competitive environment. If copy protection imposes inconvenience on users, then new products that do not incorporate copy protection can successfully compete against those that do. This occurred with spreadsheets during the mid-1980s when a rash of new entrants caused Lotus to remove its key-disk copy protection scheme. Knowing how intellectual property protection strategies and market structure interrelate is clearly important for understanding how secure hardware might work in protecting intellectual property rights.

Among the variety of alternatives for protecting intellectual property are fixed licensing rates, media taxes, and statistical sampling. The costs and benefits of these approaches clearly depend on the costs of monitoring use, but little theoretical or empirical work has been done that examines this issue in detail.

Historical Perspectives on Copyright

The challenge of setting appropriate intellectual property policy is not new. Indeed the history of copyright's use is filled with examples that are relevant to today's concerns. Now, as in the past, there are those who question whether copyright is appropriate at all in the information age. Some would argue that "information wants to be free." But what would be the consequences of all information being free? Hesse (1991) examined experiences following the elimination of copyright in post-revolutionary France.

The French monarchy used copyright as a tool for censorship. Just as in England, the French kings granted monopoly rights to publishers in exchange for the right to censor publications. One of the first acts of the French revolutionaries was to eliminate copyright in 1789. The revolutionaries thought that all people would then be free to publish whatever they wanted without government censors looking over their shoulder.

The consequences were disastrous: literature, especially serious literature, disappeared. The only material published was newspapers, pornography, scandal sheets, and seditious tracts. These were printed on cheap paper suitable to be read only once and then thrown away. In 1789 more than 100 French novels were published; in 1794 only 16 were published. The elimination of French culture was enough to frighten even the revolutionaries, and the government quickly reinstituted copyright and initiated a program to subsidize the production of cultural works.

But within a few years budget cuts forced the elimination of the subsidies. The French government had set the term of copyright to run for 10 years after the author's death. But given the short life span typical of the period, this term generally allowed for only a single edition to be published. Publishers therefore gravitated toward works in the public domain, according to a then-contemporary observer:

> Modern publishing consists of all the books that are reprinted endlessly, which are no one's property, and which anyone can make use of . . . [The publishers] all print the same works . . . and end up remaindering them. But the public does not even profit from the low prices because the editions are abridged, inaccurate, and poorly produced, which harms the art and the honor of French publishing in the eyes of Europe. (Pierre-Cesar Briand, 1810, as quoted in Hesse, 1991)

The treatment of copyright immediately after the French Revolution shows that the absence of copyright protection can be disastrous. But there are also cases in which information providers have been too conservative in the management of their intellectual property.

Rise of the Novel. The first modern libraries for middle-class readers were created in the late 1700s, soon after the invention of the English novel. English bookstores could not keep up with the demand for novels and romances, and so they started renting them out. These circulating libraries, as they were called, were denounced by the literate classes as "slop shops of literature." They were also unpopular with publishers and booksellers, but for a different reason. As an observer put it at the time:

> ... when circulating libraries were first opened, the booksellers were much alarmed; and their rapid increase added to their fears, and led them to think that the sale of books would be much diminished by such libraries. (Knight, 1854)

However, in the long run there is no doubt that the sale of books was not *diminished* by the circulating libraries, but rather was much enhanced. Before the advent of the circulating libraries there was no low-cost, entertaining literature—and so the common folk had little reason to learn to read. In 1800 there were only 80,000 readers in England. By 1854, that number had increased more than 60-fold to 5 million readers (Knight, 1854). The publishers who served the new mass market for books thrived, while those who sold only to the elite disappeared.[14]

As the market for books grew, people started to buy rather than rent. As Knight reported:

> ... thousand of books are purchased each year by such as have first borrowed them at those libraries, and after reading, approving of them, have become purchasers. (Knight, 1854)

The presence of the circulating libraries did kill the old publishing model—but at the same time it enabled the creation of the new model of mass-market books. The publishers and booksellers who recognized this causality prospered; those that continued to push for the old model went out of business.

The for-profit, circulating libraries continued to survive in England well into the 1950s. What ended them was not a lack of demand for reading material, but rather the paperback book—an even cheaper way of providing literature to the masses.

Rise of the Video. The pattern seen in the rise of the novel occurred also in the market for prerecorded videos in the 1980s. Initially the video machine was no threat to the film industry because it was so expensive. In the early 1980s video machines cost more than $1,000, and video tapes sold for around $100. Videos were a medium only for the rich—just as books were in 1800.

The video rental stores changed all that. Like the circulating libraries 200 years earlier, they brought a new form of entertainment to the masses. The rental market broke out of the low-level equilibrium. If an ordinary family could *rent* the video machine and *rent* the cartridge, the industry could get enough cash flow to invest in new production technologies. By the mid-1980s the average middle-class family could afford a video machine, and video rental stores were thriving.

Hollywood did not like the video rental business. Studios tried to get around the first-sale doctrine with various leasing arrangements, but these schemes were not acceptable to the video store owners. But despite Hollywood's objections to video rentals, they ended being very profitable for the movie studios. The availability of inexpensive videos meant that people watched many more movies. By the 1990s, video machines were selling for less than $200 and 85 percent of U.S. families owned one.

Eventually the Hollywood producers realized that people would actually *buy* a video if the price was right. Since 1990, the video *rental* market has been flat, and all the action is in the sales market. In the last 15 years, video purchase prices have dropped more than 90 percent—and Hollywood is making money like never before.

Far from killing Hollywood, video was Hollywood's savior. Just as in the case of circulating libraries, video rental created a huge new market for both renting and buying the product. The companies that recognized the implications of the new technology succeeded beyond their wildest dreams, and those that did not have vanished.[15]

2.4.2 Free Speech and Content

Many contentious issues surround free speech and regulation of content on the Internet, and there continue to be calls for mechanisms to control objectionable content. Since the Communications Decency Act was struck down by the Supreme Court in 1997, many groups have become interested in developing other ways of rating or labeling content. Emotions run high on both sides of this issue, but attention to several empirical questions would be of use in finding a sensible solution.

First, very little objective information is publicly available on the kinds of content accessible on the Web, even though content-monitoring software companies such as Surfwatch and CyberPatrol[16] are in a position to have such data. Little is known about how much access children have to "objectionable" sites. Certainly some surveys are in order.

Second, definitions of "unacceptable" content are subjective. Dealing with indecent material involves understanding not only the views on such topics but also their evolution over time. What are institutional and individual attitudes toward filtering? What do parents, schools, libraries, and other institutions want? In the case of the Internet—where content flows globally—it is important to understand how different localities define objectionable content.

There are larger political issues involved as well. The same technology that allows for content filtering with respect to decency can be used to filter political speech. In some countries (e.g., Germany), hate speech and Nazi symbols are outlawed. Approaches designed to limit indecent content could be used to restrict access to political material as well. How effective would such approaches be? How desirable would they be?

Since censorship of indecent material does not appear to be an option in the

United States, a well-known policy response is labeling. The idea is that consumers will be better informed in their decisions to avoid (or seek out) objectionable content. An interesting question is what constitutes the "best" form of such labels from the viewpoint of cognition and use. The considerable debate about the type of labels used for the V-chip, for example, encompasses whether they should be based on age or type of content, whether they should be one dimensional or multidimensional, whether they should employ three levels of rating or seven, and so on. The debate has been conducted with little in the way of scientific investigation of alternatives to inform the participants.

One interesting proposal is the Platform for Internet Content Selection (PICS; Resnick and Miller, 1996). PICS is a set of protocols that defines the communication of "ratings." The protocol set is very broadly designed so that any site can declare itself a "rater" and provide ratings to the public.[17] PICS provides an open standard that may be very helpful in dealing with the issue of content in a flexible way, but there are many questions about how this technology might be used.

For one thing, some incumbents in the industry already have proprietary labeling schemes. What are their incentives to move to the PICS standard? The literature on economic considerations in standards setting (see Besen and Farrell, 1994, for a survey) would be useful in stimulating careful thinking about this issue.

What is the cost recovery model for labeling services? Is there any reason to believe that competitive forces will yield an appropriate social outcome, or are the opportunities for "free riding" (enjoying the benefits without incurring the costs) so strong that a market for labeling cannot be sustainable? How frequently is material added to or updated on the Internet, so that reexamination is appropriate?

2.4.3 Privacy

The rapid increase in computing and communications power has raised considerable concern about privacy (Box 2.6 discusses one aspect). Privacy issues arise in the public and private sector as well as in the conduct of social science itself.

An initial set of questions concerns public attitudes toward privacy. Classic studies of this subject include Baker and Westin (1972) and Westin and Louis Harris & Associates (1981). A recent survey of Web users included several questions measuring the view of survey respondents on such issues as the need for new laws to protect privacy on the Internet and the rights of content providers to resell information about users (Kehoe et al., 1997). Kang et al. (1995), which provided an overview of issues relating to the Internet, also called for better data.[18] A more recent study looked specifically at the privacy concerns and experiences of computer users (Louis Harris & Associates and Alan F. Westin, 1997).[19] This survey found that while many people are concerned about the confidentiality and security of personal information online, there are very few

> **BOX 2.6**
> **The Argus State: Technological Advances and Individual Privacy**
>
> Decreases in the cost of video, audio, and other sensor technology, as well as cheaper data storage and information processing, make it likely that it will become practicable for both governments and private data-mining enterprises to collect enormously detailed dossiers on all citizens. This prospect raises a host of issues requiring research and debate. Among them:
>
> - Who currently collects what data about individuals? How is it used? How is it shared? What are the trends?
> - What are the existing default rules in different jurisdictions relating to the collection of information? Does the nature of default rules meaningfully alter outcomes? Do prohibitions on data collection (e.g., data protection laws) affect outcomes? To what extent are existing rules vulnerable to foreign "data havens" and other regulatory arbitrage? To what extent do/will consumers choose alternatives to the default rules when such an option is available?
> - What are the possible political, social, and economic consequences of extensive individual profiling? Is extensive profiling likely? Is the absence of a great deal of the privacy now taken for granted compatible with freedom? What difference does it make if the profiling is undertaken by (or available to) democratic governments? Non-democratic governments? Private industry? What would the economic and social consequences be of making profiling data available to some? To all? At a cost? At no cost? Would it be socially valuable to prohibit the creation of individualized dossiers? In an era of distributed databases, would it be technically practical to enforce such a prohibition?
> - To what extent do different types of electronic cash and electronic commerce enable or disable profiling? To what extent do concerns about the control of electronic money laundering imply the power to restrict free speech or anonymous commerce? To what extent does the protection of free speech and a private social and economic space require the protection of anonymous speech and/or anonymous commerce? What are the current national policies regarding anonymous speech and commerce? In a networked world, what are the external and extraterritorial effects of one nation's policies regarding anonymous speech and commerce?
>
> —Michael Froomkin, "Five Critical Issues Relating to Impacts of Information Technology" (see Appendix B of this volume)

reports of actual breaches of confidentiality. Whereas only 5 percent of Internet users said that they had been a victim of what they regarded as an invasion of their privacy, 54 percent of Internet users reported that they were concerned that information about which sites they visited would be linked to their e-mail address and disclosed without their consent or knowledge. The report also found lower trust in online institutions and communication: computer users had less confidence in online businesses than in other institutions and were more concerned about the confidentiality of e-mail than that of other common means of communication. However, with increasing familiarity comes greater trust: those who used e-mail regularly were less than 50 percent as likely to be concerned about the confidentiality of this form of communication.

Absent better understanding of the nature and extent of public concern, the public debate appears to rest on assertions by vocal advocates. More data and analysis would support more effective debate and decision making.

The ease of dissemination afforded by new technologies such as the Internet is raising privacy issues related to the release of government-collected information about individuals. As an illustration of the delicate nature of privacy policy, consider the issue of tax assessments. In most local communities, these are publicly available in City Hall. The public purpose served is that individuals can compare their own assessment to the assessment of similar properties and file a protest if they believe that their property has been unfairly valued. Victoria, British Columbia, put its tax-assessment rolls on the Internet in order to make it easier for residents to access this information. However, many residents thought that the assessed value of their property was now too accessible. Ultimately, Victoria had to close down the Web site, under pressure from British Columbia's Information Commissioner, who believed that the site violated Canadian privacy laws (Colebourn, 1996).

In a related example, a computer consultant in Oregon paid the state $222 for the complete motor vehicles database, which he then posted to a Web site. The database allows anyone with knowledge of a particular Oregon license plate number to look up the vehicle owner's name, address, birth date, driver's license number, and vehicle title information (McCall, 1996).[20] Also, state and local governments are themselves finding that their data can be a source of revenue, through the sale either of customized search services or entire databases (Chandrasekaran, 1998). Already, regulations and legislation that address concerns about personal dossiers are emerging at both state and federal levels for the specific case of medical records. A recent CSTB report (CSTB, 1997a) examines trends and issues relating to the protection of medical information.

"Informed consent" in surveys and experiments is a dimension of privacy that strikes close to home for social scientists. Quite strong safeguards are in place for social science work involving human subjects, but in some ways it is difficult to apply some of these practices to the Internet. For example, the fact that data is being collected can easily be concealed from subjects. One source of useful data comes from retrospective examination of existing records such as server logs or "Usenet" postings where a social science experiment was not the original intent of the data collection. Just as in the case of private data, cross-tabulation of innocuous data sets can identify seemingly anonymous subjects. Certainly, social scientists must develop a code of practices, ethics, and perhaps regulations that will help deal with these issues.

Another dimension of privacy is "annoyance." A recent report on junk e-mail by World Research, Inc. (1997) announced that half of the more than 1,000 respondents in a voluntary online survey said that they "hate" junk mail, and another quarter said that they found it "bothersome." Three-quarters of the respondents felt it should be regulated. The interesting question is what form of regulation (if any) would be appropriate. A number of congressional bills have been introduced to address this issue, such as S.771, which proposed requiring that advertisements be self-labeled. It would be interesting to investigate how effective such solutions have been in controlling physical junk mail, magazine ads, "infomercials," and so on.

There have been suggestions that industry self-regulation could be an effective tool for protecting privacy. A National Telecommunications and Information Administration report contains a number of papers exploring the prospects for and limitations of self-regulation (NTIA, 1997). One approach, offered by Laudon (1996), proposes a market for personal information in which individuals would have the right to sell or prevent the sale of information about themselves. Varian (1996a) has examined some economic aspects of such a market, but much work remains to be done.

Cryptography is a technological approach to protecting privacy. Cryptography policy is being widely debated; see CSTB (1996b) for a thorough study. The online Information Economy Page on Security, Privacy, and Encryption[21] is also a valuable resource. However, there are comparatively few studies of the implications of cryptography policy. One area where social science can contribute is in characterizing the role of encryption in the commission and detection of crime. For example, it has been claimed that use of cryptography presents a serious barrier to criminal investigations. Yet a study by Denning and Baugh (1997) found that use of encryption was not currently obstructing a large number of investigations. However, it also found that the use of encryption by criminal elements was growing rapidly and could become a problem in the future, suggesting the need for further study.

2.4.4 Information Use and Value

Information Overload

It is popular wisdom that people today suffer information overload. If true, overload has implications for those studying such issues as the value of information. Characterizing and quantifying overload also can shape the design of new information technology tools. Several questions need answering to determine the truth of this assertion. In what particular sense are people dealing with more information than in the past? Is digital information more complex, harder to apprehend, less compressible? Are there new social or psychological phenomena emerging?

One issue is whether in fact more information is being produced. A line of studies going back through Pool (1984) and Machlup (1982) looked at production of information, but there seems to be a shortage of current data on measures of production, particularly in the electronic environment. It would be useful to update the Pool and Machlup studies.

Second, people may be spending more of their time absorbing information. There is certainly a need for detailed studies of how people spend time with regard to various information sources, and in particular what they are doing with these sources. Are they using them as a basis for decision making or are they collecting largely irrelevant information just because it is available and they think they should know about it?

Use of the Internet is a prime example of where research into time use is valuable. A 1997 Price Waterhouse Consumer Technology Survey (Price Waterhouse, 1997) polled 1,010 American consumers via telephone and found that 43 percent of the time spent accessing the Internet from home was used for obtaining information, and 34 percent was used to send or receive e-mail. This categorization is a start, but clearly it is important to know what kind of information people are accessing on the Internet and how it is being used. Time-use diaries (see section 3.1.3) are another important source of information.

There is also the issue of how individual differences, expertise, and intent may determine how much information is selected and extracted. These questions need to be examined in comparative studies of changing uses of information and effects on productivity within specific contexts and domains. For example, comparative studies to determine the effects of the availability of electronic preprints in particular scientific disciplines as well as other information-sharing and dissemination practices of various disciplines could yield useful insights.

Further elucidation of questions concerning information overload can come from microlevel studies of technology, information viewing practices, and information-seeking behavior. Collecting better information on the use of library materials in the electronic environment could represent an important opportunity. However, it is worth noting that most online systems are not instrumented to allow such data collection, except for a few locally developed systems like the University of California library information system, UC MELVYL.[22] The paper by Amy Friedlander, "Impacts of Information Technology: Behaviors and Metrics," in Appendix B describes additional approaches to the question of library information use.

Current use is not the only measure of value in a library context. There is also value associated with future, potential use such as having access to archival material and preserving the scholarly record. The paper in Appendix B by Alexander Field, "Critical Issues Relating to Impacts of Information Technologies," raises questions about what is needed to ensure retrievability of material in archives in the information age.

Branding, Credibility, and Authority

Branding[23] and authority—the credibility associated with the name of a publisher or author—are interrelated in critical ways with the information overload question and with user strategies to manage it. Authority is also critical in social and societal uses of information. Little is understood about where authority comes from and how it operates in the information context. How do people assign credibility, and how is this changing, in an increasingly information-rich and competitive environment? What kinds of credibility systems could be invented or developed? How does branding work in the digital environment, and how do brand identities transfer from other media? How does the credibility established by peer review conducted prior to publication in scientific journals translate to the digital environment where researchers can reach a wide audience without publishing in traditional journals?

In a highly competitive environment, the costs for information production and distribution are sometimes driven to the lowest possible level. To understand how authority works in this situation requires comparative data on the quality and cost of information. Also, research is needed to develop a theory of production and publishing strategies in the new Web environment that includes both "push" and "pull" technologies,[24] micropayments, advertising support, and other alternatives. Together, these constitute a much richer set of options than that provided by current media. It is also important to understand interactions affecting how people search for information. For example, a CommerceNet/Nielson survey in the spring of 1997 found that 71 percent of frequent users found Web sites through search engines, 9.8 percent used friends and relatives, 8.5 percent used newspapers and magazines, and 8.4 percent used links from other sites (CommerceNet/Nielsen Media Research, 1997).

On the question of authority, a candidate for case study is legal information, which formerly was a monopolistic market but now is fragmenting as new players become involved. A baseline needs to be established, followed by studies of how authority changes with fragmentation into competitive marketplace (see Berring, 1995, which describes authority in legal information). How does the market structure affect the creation of authority? Is it better to have a single, authoritative source (and pay monopoly prices) or to have competing authorities and face problems of choice and accuracy? The paper by Michael Froomkin in Appendix B discusses some additional questions about the economics of trust.

Medicine and finance offer two opportunities to study credibility and how it is established. In both cases, changes in technology and government policy have made a great deal of data available to the public (via MEDLINE[25] and EDGAR[26]). At the same time many nontraditional sources of information can be found via the Web and other media—some very good and some very much outside the mainstream, if not downright fraudulent. How are people using these information sources, and how do they assign credibility to them? A recent study of credibility in Usenet groups for the support of people with medical or psychological ailments or disorders found that members relied on predictable strategies to establish the legitimacy of their questions and the authority of their replies. Members (or interlopers) who did not use these strategies were either ignored or censured by the group (Galegher et al., 1998).

How does technology change relationships with professionals, for example, physician-patient relationships? What are the costs of errors in judging credibility? One study of the effects of an e-mail "listserve" support group found that members who reported the greatest benefits were those who were also using professional medical services (Cummings et al., 1998).

On the Internet there is a growing range of sources of information whose credibility varies. How does this variability change social behavior? Does it contribute to social fragmentation? Does this variability when combined with the global nature of the Internet reinforce fringe beliefs that would not be self-sustaining in an environment determined by geography? Are there indicators of the current level of common knowledge or experience (beyond viewing of network television) that can be tracked to gain insight into these changes? How will people recognize and manage bias in information, such as that which may be present in advertiser-sponsored content?

The Information Gap

The typical formulation of the gap separating information "haves" and "have-nots"[27] is highly biased toward a definition of literacy as the ability to read and write written text, and even somewhat biased toward scholarly communication. Vast amounts of audio and video information are becoming available, searchable, and retrievable. Currently the enabling technologies for these activities are expensive and are not available as consumer products. However, at some point the infrastructure necessary to support the transmission of digital multimedia information, such as broadband networks to the home, will be available.

It is important to characterize more general forms of literacy and relate these to the educational process. How is the definition of literacy changing? How is the value of different forms of literacy (e.g., the ability to facilitate a discussion, or create slides for a presentation) shifting? Television has been a pervasive medium of communication for several decades. What new questions do novel, more interactive media present that television did not? It is probably necessary to go beyond using such terms as "literacy" or "numeracy" to indicate a wider set of skills, and instead characterize the skills specifically.

What part can the educational system and universities play in serving the information poor? How should this change models of distance learning and distance education? It would be useful to establish a baseline on current distance education practices and effectiveness by careful studies of the National Technological University in the United States, the Open University in the United Kingdom, and other similar organizations. Can distance learning be used to narrow the gap between the information "haves" and "have nots," or will it only widen it? What would be some of the characteristics of a system of distance education targeted toward the information poor?

How are differences in wealth related to possession of needed skills or access to information? Should the focus be on increasing skills or on reducing the need for skills by providing more accessible technologies and content? For example, what happens if and when people move away from text-dominated computing and communication? It is important to understand and establish the validity of interrelationships among access to information, the characteristics of the technology used to access the information, and economic opportunities.

2.4.5 Pricing Models and Content

Different approaches to paying for information often involve different incentives for what types of information are created and sold. For instance, Spence and Owen (1977) showed that when television was paid for by advertising as opposed to pay-per-view fees, there was an incentive to develop more programs that would appeal to a wide audience, rather than programs that were intensely valued by a small group of people. The reason was that advertising rates are based on the size of the audience and not on how much enjoyment each viewer gets from a show. In contrast, a highly focused show that appeals to a narrow audience might be able to recover its costs more easily in a pay-per-view system because it could charge a higher price per viewer. Quite diverse content distributed by cable television, such as the History Channel, the Cooking Channel, and the like, is supported by finely tuned advertising. This line of reasoning helps to explain why broadcast television, which until recently depended almost exclusively on advertising revenues, is often perceived to appeal to the least common denominator. Similar trade-offs are likely to apply in other product markets such as the market for content on the Internet. For example, if online content is supported primarily by advertising, one might expect that it will devolve to the lowest common denominator. Compared with broadcast television, the Web offers much greater opportunity for niche markets, analogous to specialized cable channels, and perhaps niche advertising. A model to describe the quality and diversity of possible content when cost-recovery is generated by such niche advertising would be quite interesting.

Furthermore, even when goods are supported by direct consumer payments, different incentives arise depending on whether the payments are for individual goods and services or for bundles of goods and services. Information goods that are profitable as part of a bundle may be unprofitable when sold separately, and vice versa.

2.4.6 Pricing Information

The emergence of the Internet as a way to distribute digital information such as software, news stories, stock quotes, music, photographs, video clips, and research reports has created new opportunities for the pricing of information goods. Providers of digital information goods are unsure about how to price them and are struggling with a variety of revenue models (CSTB, 1996c). Because perfect copies of these goods can be created and distributed at virtually no cost, some of the old rules, such as "price should equal marginal cost," do not apply, as noted by Varian (1995a,b).

The Internet has also created new opportunities for repackaging content through bundling, site licensing, subscriptions, rentals, differential pricing, and per-use fees. All of these schemes can be thought of as either aggregating or disaggregating information goods along some dimension. For instance, aggregation can occur across products, as when software programs are bundled for sale in a software "suite" or when access to the full contents of an online service is provided for a fixed fee. Aggregation can also occur across consumers, as when a site license is provided to multiple users for a fixed fee, or over time, as when subscriptions are made available.

Many observers have predicted that software and other types of content will be increasingly disaggregated and metered, as on-demand software "applets" or as individual news stories and stock quotes. For instance, Robert Metcalfe has written: "When the Internet finally gets micromoney systems, we'll rent tiny bits of software for seconds at a time. Imagine renting a French spelling checker for one document once" (Metcalfe, 1997). The main rationale for this prediction is that the current advantage obtained from bundling many goods to save on transaction and distribution costs will no longer apply, given that both of these types of costs are often much lower on the Internet.

However, recent theoretical work suggests that in some cases aggregation can also be a surprisingly effective pricing strategy (Bakos and Brynjolfsson, 1997a,b). Not only can it increase the seller's profits from a set of digital information goods, but it may also benefit the consumer as well. As a result, instead of subdividing goods into smaller pieces to be rented separately to individuals, it is sometimes more efficient to bundle many digital goods together. The reason is that by enabling a form of price discrimination—the charging of different prices to different consumers based on their valuation of the quantities they consume—aggregation can make it easier for the seller to extract value from a given set of goods (Box 2.7). For the case of bundling, this type of aggregation has been studied in a number of articles in the economics literature (e.g., McAfee et al., 1989; Schmalensee, 1984). The analysis shows that the benefits of aggregation depend critically on the low marginal cost of reproducing digital information and the nature of the correlation in valuations for the goods: aggregation is less

BOX 2.7
Economics of Bundling: Graphical Intuition

The impact of aggregation on the profitability of selling information goods can be illustrated by graphically analyzing the effect of bundling on the demand for information goods. Consumers will choose either 0 or 1 unit of an information good, such as a music video or a journal article, depending on how their valuation of the good compares to its price. A possible aggregate demand curve for such a good is depicted in Figure 2.3.

Perfect price discrimination—charging different prices to different consumers, based on their valuations of a good—will maximize the seller's profits and will eliminate the deadweight loss shown in Figure 2.3 (Varian, 1995a). If the seller cannot price discriminate, however, the only single price that will eliminate the inefficiency from the deadweight loss will be a price equal to the marginal cost, which is close to zero. Such a low price will not generate sufficient revenues to cover the fixed cost of production and is unlikely to be the profit-maximizing price.

Aggregation can sometimes overcome this dilemma. Consider again a journal article and a music video, and suppose that each is valued by consumers at between $0 and $1, generating linear aggregate demand curves like the one in shown Figure 2.3. Suppose further that a consumer's valuation of one good does not correlate with his or her valuation of the other, and that access to one good does not make the other more or less attractive.

What happens if the seller aggregates the two goods and sells them as a bundle? Some consumers—those who valued both goods at $1—would be willing to pay $2 for the bundle; others—those who valued both goods at almost $0—would not be willing to pay even a penny. The total area under the demand curve for the bundle of the two information goods, and hence the total potential surplus, is exactly equal to the sum of the areas under the separate demand curves. However, most interestingly, bundling changes the shape of the demand curve, making it flatter (more elastic) in the neighborhood of $1 and steeper (less elastic) near either extreme, as shown in Figure 2.4. As more goods are added, this effect becomes more pronounced. For example, Figure 2.5 shows the demand curve for a bundle of 20 information goods, each of which has an independent, linear demand ranging from $0 to $1.

A profit-maximizing firm selling a bundle of 20 goods will set the price slightly below the bundle's mean value of $10, and almost all consumers will find it worthwhile to purchase the bundle. In contrast, only half the consumers would have purchased the goods if they had been sold individually at the profit-maximizing price of 50 cents each, and so selling the goods as a bundle leads to a smaller deadweight loss and greater economic efficiency. Furthermore, the seller will earn higher profits by selling a single bundle of 20 goods than by selling each of the 20 goods separately. Thus, the shape of the bundle's demand curve is far more favorable both for the seller and for overall economic efficiency.

Why does the shape of the demand curve change as goods are added to a bundle? The law of large numbers implies that the average valuation for a bundle of goods with valuations drawn from the same distribution will be increasingly concentrated near the mean valuation as more goods are added to the bundle. For example, some people subscribe to America Online for the news, some for stock quotes, and some for horoscopes. It is unlikely that a single person places a very high value on every single good offered; instead most consumers will assign high values to some goods and low values to other goods, leading to moderate values overall. However, if some consumers tend to have systematically higher valuations for all types of goods, then the moderating effect of bundling will be muted and, in some cases, unbundling will be preferred. In general, a strategy of mixed bundling, which involves offering both the complete bundle and various subbundles, can be shown to be the dominant strategy.

Similar effects result in other types of aggregation, such as aggregation across consumers, as in the case of selling a single site license for use by multiple consumers. The law of large numbers, which underlies these aggregation effects, is remarkably general. For instance, it holds for almost any initial distribution with a finite variance—not just the linear demand assumed for the examples above. Furthermore, the law does not require that the valuations be independent of each other or even that the valuations be drawn from the same distribution.

However, theoretical analysis shows that when marginal costs are high, then disaggregation may be more profitable than aggregation. Because the marginal costs of reproducing goods are so much lower on the Internet than they are in most other contexts, bundling may become much more attractive as Internet commerce grows. The policy implications of such changes, including their potential effects on competition and innovation, remain issues for future research.

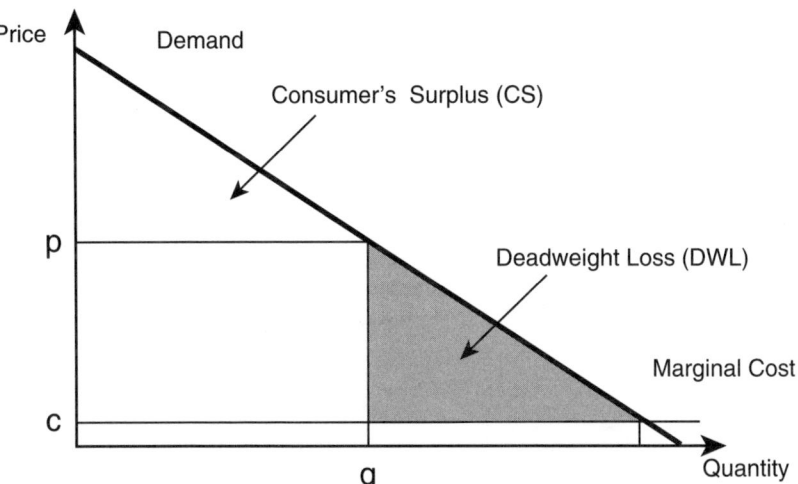

FIGURE 2.3   Deadweight loss from sales of a zero-marginal-cost information good. Assume that after the first unit, marginal production costs, denoted by c, are close to zero. At price p, the number of units purchased will be q, resulting in profits of $(p-c)q$. However, as long as $p > c$, some consumers who value the good at more than its production costs c will not be willing to pay the going price p. As a result, these consumers do not get access to the good, creating a deadweight loss for society, denoted by the shaded region.

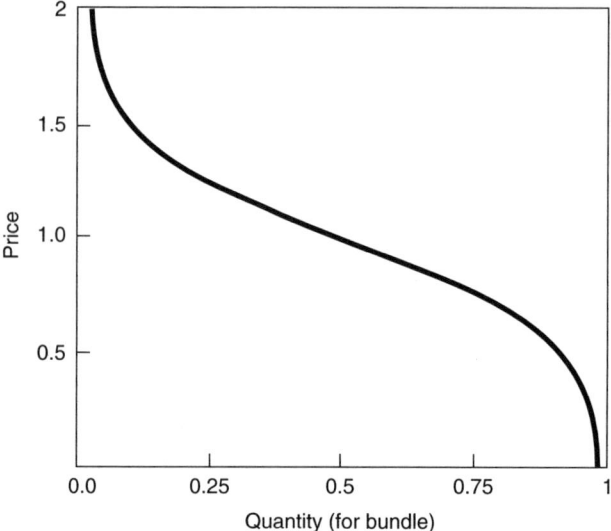

FIGURE 2.4 Demand curve for bundle of two information goods with independent uniform demand.

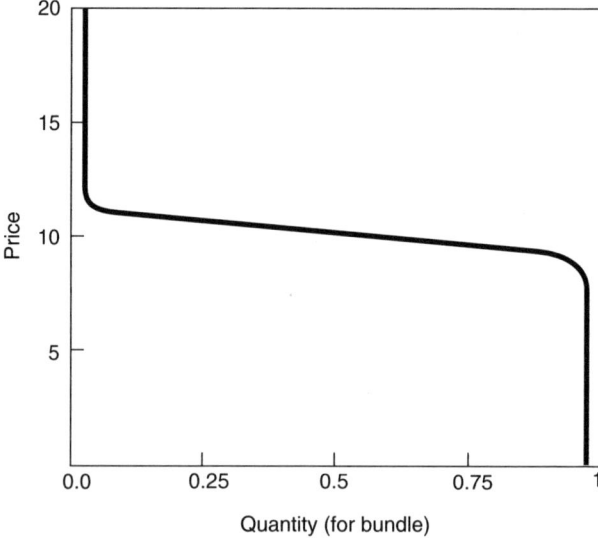

FIGURE 2.5 Demand curve for a bundle of 20 information goods with independently distributed uniform valuations.

ILLUSTRATIVE EXAMPLES AND UNANSWERED QUESTIONS

attractive when marginal costs are high or when valuations are highly correlated (Bakos and Brynjolfsson, 1997a,b).

Thus, strategies involving bundling, site licensing, and subscriptions can each be understood as responses to the radical decline in costs for the reproduction of information made possible by digitization and distribution through the Internet. Increased use of micropayments can be seen as a consequence of radically lower transaction and distribution costs. Information goods that had previously been aggregated to save on transaction or distribution costs may be disaggregated as predicted by Metcalfe (1997), but new aggregations of goods may emerge to exploit the potential for price discrimination.

Experimentation with various approaches continues, and it is premature to conclude that one approach such as microcharging is best, or to try to predict even in what circumstances it may be preferred. Collection of data, analysis, and further theoretical work would all be helpful.

2.4.7 Network Externalities

Economists say that a *network externality* exists when one consumer's demand for a product or service depends on how many other consumers purchase that service. For example, consider a consumer's demand for a fax machine. People want fax machines so that they can communicate with each other. If no one you communicate with has a fax machine, it certainly is not worthwhile for you to buy one. Modems have a similar property: a modem is useful only if there is another modem somewhere that you can communicate with.

Network externalities are ubiquitous in computing and communications. The demand for e-mail depends on how many other users there are; the demand for a Web browser depends on how many servers there are; and even the demand for a word processing package will depend on how many other users of that package there are.[28]

Network externalities were first modeled by Rohlfs (1974) in an attempt to understand why AT&T's Picture Phone was not successful. However, there is little interest in failures, and Rohlfs's article did not attract wide notice until almost 10 years after it appeared. Today much more is known about this phenomenon. Nicholas Economides has studied network economics extensively and maintains a Web site that contains a bibliography of his and other work on this topic.[29] Also see Katz and Shapiro (1994) for a nice overview of network externalities and their implications.

In each of the examples above (fax, e-mail, Web, word processing), the use grew slowly at first and then suddenly surged ahead. Figure 2.6 shows the price and number of fax machines shipped over a period of 12 years.

This qualitative behavior can be reproduced by some very simple economic models whose essential feature is multiple equilibria. If everyone expects a product to be a failure, then no one will buy it and the product will fail. But if

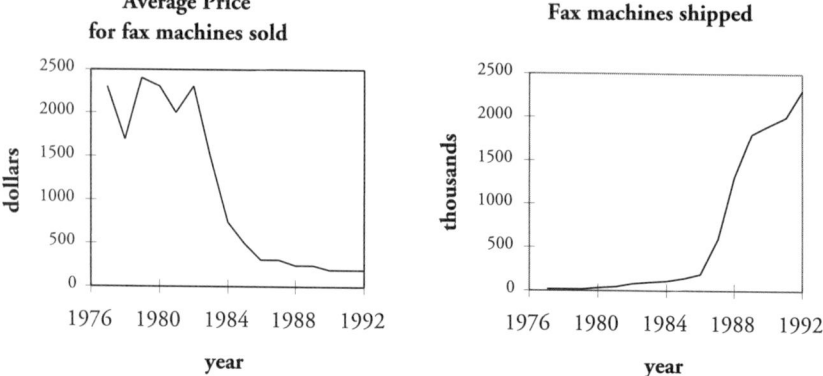

FIGURE 2.6 Average price of fax machines sold (left) and number of units shipped (right). SOURCE: Adapted from Economides and Himmelberg (1995).

everyone expects a product to succeed, many people will want to buy it and the product will succeed. Which of these outcomes occurs depends on whether the number of early adopters exceeds a particular critical mass that is a function of the parameters of the model. In a stochastic model, the probability that this will happen depends on the magnitude of the random fluctuations in the number of adopters.

Because of the phenomenon of critical mass, it is very important to try to stimulate growth early in the life cycle of a product. Today it is quite common to see producers offering very cheap access to a piece of software or a communications service in order to create a new market where none existed before. A critical question is how big the market has to be before it can take off on its own. Theory can provide little guidance here; the appropriate strategy depends on the nature of the good and the costs and benefits that users face in adopting it.

2.4.8 Auctions

Auctions, one of the oldest market institutions,[30] have played an important role in the development of wireless communications. The modern study of auctions by economists dates back to Vickrey (1961), whose work, which was later awarded a Nobel prize, was little read until the early 1970s, when the U.S. Department of the Interior auctioned off the right to drill for oil in offshore tracts. Following the auction, several economists became interested in the optimal strategies associated with such auctions and examined ways that auctions might be designed to achieve some given end (e.g., profit maximization, or efficient allocation of resources).

In recent years Congress has authorized the Federal Communications Commission (FCC) to allocate the radio spectrum via auction—a policy recommended by economists Leo Herzl and Ronald Coase over the period from 1957 to 1959

(Coase, 1959). These auctions are generally regarded as having being quite successful.[31] See McMillan (1994) for a readable introduction to how the FCC auctions were conducted.

The economic analysis starts by considering two sorts of auctions: common-value auctions and private-value auctions. In a common-value auction, such as the auctioning of offshore oil drilling rights, the item that is being bid for is worth some particular amount, but the bidders may have different opinions about how much that amount is. In a private-value auction, the item in question is worth different amounts to different people. Most auctions of ordinary consumer goods such as works of art and antiques are of the private-value type. For more on the theory and practice of auctions, see the survey by Milgrom (1989) and the references cited therein. See also the discussion in Box 2.8.

2.4.9 Electronic Commerce

Electronic commerce is different from physical commerce because technology changes the modes of communication, ultimately affecting the flow of information. The reduced cost of communicating, transmitting, and processing information is at the core of these differences. The marginal cost of disseminating information electronically to new or existing customers is lower than with more conventional methods, since the cost of an additional Web query or e-mail message is close to zero. Similarly, customers can use the Internet to search across competing sellers—which can be done directly by visiting various sellers' Web sites and inquiring about prices, products, and availability. Increasingly, searches can also be facilitated by using "intelligent agents" or intermediaries that can gather and aggregate the necessary information on behalf of the customer. As a result, geographic and informational barriers that dampen competition among sellers may become increasingly irrelevant.

Bakos (1997) has analyzed the implications of reduced search costs for competition, efficiency, and the division of surplus between buyers and sellers. His model indicates that when electronic marketplaces reduce the costs to the consumer of searching for the lowest price, there will be (1) an improvement in overall economic efficiency and (2) a shift in bargaining power from sellers to buyers. As a result buyers will be strictly better off, but the effect on sellers is ambiguous. A change from very high to moderate search costs will tend to make sellers better off, as new markets emerge. For instance, a market for specialty car parts might be unsustainable without a technology like the Internet to lower the transaction costs involved in finding buyers and sellers. The creation of such a market provides new opportunities for sellers. However, Bakos's model indicates that if search costs continue to fall, sellers may be made worse off since buyers can more easily find the seller that offers the lowest price. Since all sellers charging more than this lowest price will lose business, competition will tend to drive down prices until they reach the marginal cost of the product, leaving no

> **BOX 2.8**
> **Simple Insights Learned About Auctions**
>
> *Common-value Auctions*
> A sensible strategy in a common-value auction, it would seem, would be to estimate the value of the item in question, add on a profit margin, and then bid that amount. However, if everyone uses such a procedure, it follows that the winner will tend to be the bidder with the highest estimate—which then is likely to be an overestimate of the true value. Hence the "winner" will usually end up overbidding, a phenomenon known as the *winner's curse*.
> Avoiding the winner's curse involves bidding down from one's estimated value, with the reduction depending on the number of other bidders. If one's estimate is higher than the estimates of 2 other bidders it may be reasonably close to the true value; but if it tops the estimates of 100 other bidders, it is almost certainly an overbid!
> Economists have developed a number of statistical and game theoretical models of bidding behavior in such markets that have been applied successfully in practical contexts such as auctions of parts of the radio spectrum.
>
> *Private-value Auctions*
> The most common form of private-value auction is the *English auction*, in which bids are successively raised until only one bidder is left who then claims the item at the last price bid. In this kind of auction, the person who is *willing* to bid the highest gets the item, but the price paid will generally be slightly above the bid of the second-highest bidder.
>
> *Sealed-bid Auctions*
> In a *sealed bid* auction, each consumer submits a bid sealed in an envelope. The bids are opened and the item is awarded to the highest bidder at the price he bid. The optimal strategy in the sealed-bid auction is to try to guess the amount the other consumers will bid, and then enter a bid slightly above the highest of these, assuming that the item is attractive to the bidder at that price. Thus bidders will not, in general, want to reveal their true valuation for the item being auctioned off. Furthermore, the outcome of the sealed bid auction will depend on each bidder's beliefs about the others' valuations. Even if these beliefs are correct on average, there will be cases in which the bidders guess incorrectly and the item is not awarded to the person who values it most.
>
> *Vickrey Auctions*
> A variation on the sealed-bid auction—known as the "Vickrey auction," after the economist who first analyzed its properties—eliminates the need for strategic play. The Vickrey auction simply awards the item to the highest bidder, but at the second highest price that was bid. It turns out that in such an auction, there is no need to play strategically—the optimal bid is simply the true value to the bidder.[1]
> It is also worth observing that the revenue raised by the Vickrey auction will be essentially the same as that raised by the ordinary English auction, since in each case the person who assigned the highest value gets the item but only has to pay the second highest price. (In the English auction, the person *willing* to bid the highest gets the item, but he or she has to pay only the price bid by the person with the second highest value, plus the minimal bid increment.)
>
> ---
>
> [1]The essence of the argument can be seen in a two-bidder example. Let v_1 be the true value of bidder 1, and let b_1 and b_2 be the bids of the two bidders. Then the expected payoff to consumer 1 is
>
> $$\text{Prog}\left[b_1 > b_2\right]\left[v_1 - b_2\right].$$
>
> If $v_1 > b_2$ then bidder 1 would like the probability to be equal to 1—which he can assure by reporting $b_1 = v_1$. If $v_1 < b_2$, bidder 1 would like the probability to be zero—which he can ensure by reporting $b_1 = v_1$. Either way, it is optimal for bidder 1 to report the true value.

surplus for the sellers (Bakos, 1997). The dynamics of "friction-free" capitalism are not attractive to sellers of commodity products who had previously depended on geography or customer ignorance to insulate them from the low-cost seller in the market. As geography becomes less important, new sources of product differentiation, such as customized features or service or innovation will become more important, at least for those sellers who do not have the advantage of the lowest cost of production.

Is this kind of dynamic already emerging in Internet commerce? Although there is much speculation about the effect that the Internet will have on prices, thus far there has been virtually no systematic evidence obtained or analysis done. However, one exploratory study by Bailey and Brynjolfsson (1997) did not find much evidence that prices on the Internet were any lower or less dispersed than prices for the same goods sold via traditional retail channels. Their analysis was based on data from 52 Internet and conventional retailers for 337 distinct titles of books, music compact disks, and software. Bailey and Brynjolfsson provided several possible explanations for their unexpected findings, including the possibility that search on the Internet during the sample period was not as easy as is sometimes assumed, that the demographics of the typical Internet user encouraged a higher price equilibrium, that many of the Internet retailers were still experimenting with pricing strategies, and that Internet retailers were differentiating their products (e.g., by offering options for delivery or providing customized recommendations), which added value. Because of the rapid pace of change in Internet commerce, it is not clear whether their findings will apply to current and future periods. However, they have suggested the need for close examination of the common assumption that the Internet will be simply a "friction-free" version of the traditional retail channels.

Despite the uncertainties about electronic commerce and relatively few attempts to look at the broad picture, there is a great deal of private-sector interest. Electronic commerce is also receiving increasing attention from policy makers. The Clinton Administration's *Framework for Global Electronic Commerce* (1997; available online at <http://www.whitehouse.gov/WH/New/Commerce/index.html>) highlights both the economic potential of electronic commerce via the Internet as well as the need for government to avoid undue regulatory restrictions and to not subject Internet transactions to additional taxation.

Right now society is in a period of intense speculation and experimentation. Experimentation involves a risk owing to path-dependence—technological choices made in the past may constrain what technological options will be compatible in the future. Standards developed now for electronic payment may remain in use well into the future, and careful thought should be given to their implications. For example, some of the architectural design of the Visa-MasterCard "Secure Electronic Transactions (SET)" technical standard was necessitated by the need to conform with current cryptographic export control policies. Yet these policies are today very much in flux and may be entirely different in a few years. Migrating the SET standard so that it is consistent with these new policies could be very costly, if not impossible.

Even if cryptography policy changes, society may be locked into design choices already made. Thus it is critically important that any such standards be examined by those with expertise in technology, economics, business, and law— no one discipline suffices to provide the necessary expertise.

One important insight about electronic commerce that follows from a legal and economic analysis has to do with assignment of liability, that is, with who ends up bearing the costs of unexpected outcomes. If the goal is to minimize overall transaction costs, liability should be assigned most heavily to those who are best placed to reduce the costs of transactions.

Consider, for example, the rule in the United States that the consumer is liable for only the first $50 in losses from fraudulent credit card use. This assignment of liability has led to the development of highly sophisticated statistical profiling of consumer purchases that allows companies to detect fraudulent activity, thereby reducing the total costs of transactions. If the liability had instead rested entirely with consumers, one might have expected to see them being more careful in protecting their credit cards, but there would have been little reason for banks to invest in risk management technology. Another example is the difference between U.S. and U.K. assignment of liability for automatic teller machine (ATM) fraud. In the United States the burden of proof lies with the bank; in the United Kingdom it lies with the customer. This has led U.S. banks to invest in video cameras at ATM machines, whereas U.K. banks typically have not made such investments.

The issue of liability is critical for electronic commerce. A survey released in March 1997 by CommerceNet/Nielson Media Research (1997) found "a lack of trust in the security of electronic payments as the leading inhibitor preventing people from actually purchasing goods and services online." This is remarkable considering the fact that the standard $50 limit still applies to online credit purchases. One might conjecture that credit card companies are not interested in a marketing effort to educate the public on this issue until they understand their own potential liabilities for fraud and misuse. There is also a need to understand the psychological and social dimensions of "trust," since trust is a critical component of any sort of commercial transaction.

The information economy calls for new economic institutions such as "certificate authorities" that certify the connection between legal identities and possession of cryptographic keys—a public-key infrastructure. Large certificate issuers include Versign, which has close ties to the credit card issuer Visa, and GTE, which has close ties to MasterCard. The economics of this industry are uncertain and clearly depend critically on the issue of liability assignment.

Another factor that is potentially delaying the growth of electronic commerce is intellectual property protection. Some of the broader issues are dealt with in section 2.4.1, "Protection of Intellectual Property," but some of the specifically commerce-oriented issues are mentioned here.

The first such issue is the role of copy protection, which is a technical means for making it more difficult to create additional functional copies of software in a competitive environment. Copy-protected mass-market software was effectively competed away during the mid-1980s. Any copy protection that inconveniences users is difficult to maintain in a highly competitive market. See Shy (1998) for an economic analysis.

More generally, numerous copy protection schemes have been proposed to help safeguard intellectual property, suggesting that there will almost certainly be a standards battle for supremacy in this market. Besen and Farrell (1994) have provided a survey of economic analysis with regard to conflicts about standards that sets forth the current state of the art in this area. More work in this area would be valuable.

Electronic commerce also raises significant antitrust issues. There are large economies of scale in distribution—a single general-purpose online bookstore or CD store can serve a very large market. There are also potential demand-side economies of scale in payment mechanisms and software, which leads to a winner-take-all market structure with a single firm (or small set of firms) dominating the market.

There have been a number of interesting studies of market structure in this context (see, e.g., Katz and Shapiro, 1994, for a survey); however, much more work is needed. The role of antitrust policy in an industry with strong network externalities and standardization issues is especially important to understand. A dominant firm brings the benefits of standardization, but presumably also imposes inefficiencies due to its monopoly position. The social trade-off between these benefits and costs is critically important and is the subject of much current debate. Some dispassionate analysis would be highly welcome.

There has been much speculation about the macroeconomic effects of electronic commerce, such as the loss of economic sovereignty. Most economic analysis has focused on moving from multiple currencies to a single currency (as in the European Union context), but the emergence of currencies issued by private companies and barter arrangements is a distinct possibility. Economic monetary history would likely shed some light on how an economy functions in the presence of multiple private currencies, since that circumstance was common up until the turn of the last century.

There is also the question of who will appropriate the benefits of electronic commerce. Varian (1996a) has argued that price discrimination will become a widely used approach to selling information. (One form of price discrimination is enabled by bundling, discussed in section 2.4.6, "Pricing Information.") He cites earlier studies that suggest that the welfare effects of price discrimination will be benign from the viewpoint of overall welfare, but price discrimination may certainly affect the division of economic gains between consumers and firms. These earlier studies typically assumed a monopolistic market structure, which may or may not be appropriate for electronic commerce. Thus extending these models to more competitive market structures would enhance understanding of the likely impact of electronic commerce on consumers.

2.5 ILLUSTRATIVE BROAD TOPICS FOR ONGOING RESEARCH

Workshop discussions and position papers yielded numerous suggestions for research topics, a number of which are discussed above. From these topics—spanning a wide range of interdisciplinary subjects from economic productivity to communities in the information age—the workshop steering committee selected an illustrative set of promising areas for research, listed below.

- **Interdisciplinary study of information indicators.** The idea of developing a method for quantifying certain aspects of society in the United States is as old as the Constitution. Over the last two decades, researchers have recognized and begun to analyze the increasing role that information plays in all aspects of society. These efforts have proved most fruitful when measuring the contribution of information to the economy,[32] the size of the information work force,[33] and the level of penetration of the information infrastructure.[34] In most of these analyses, the conclusions drawn have been consistent with the view that society is in the process of a fundamental change through the rapid development and implementation of information technologies and the products and services associated with them.

Some of these studies raise the indirect question of the value of attempting to use a set of indicators to represent the information activities of society, such as public discourse and democratic processes, to improve understanding. This approach was first pioneered by Borko and Menou (1983). In essence, looking at society from an *information* perspective leads us to perceive society as composed of information structures and communication behaviors. In other words, those activities that lead to the construction of environments for producing, receiving, distributing, and processing information reflect the creation of information structures, while those activities that involve transmission of information reflect communication behaviors. Box 2.9 lists some notional indicators.

The dramatic information-centric changes that have occurred across all societies in recent decades suggest that the social forces enabled by the development of information structures and the prevalence of communication behaviors be measured. More fully developed, a set of quantitative information indicators offers opportunities for comparatively measuring community information assets, public participation, interconnectedness, social capital, information poverty, and universal service.

It would be useful for the nation to invest in an interdisciplinary study of information indicators. The perspectives of many disciplines come to bear on the question of measuring impact. An exploration of how different disciplines do or do not reach consensus about how to measure impacts, and the extent to which consensus is desirable, is called for. From such an exchange can come broadly

> **BOX 2.9**
> **A Primitive List of Information Indicators**
>
> *Information Structures*
> Books produced (general/textbooks)
> Cable TV access/trunk lines
> Number of cinema seats
> Number of computer systems/databases
> Number of database subscribers
> Number of journal articles/technical reports
> Number of libraries/archives
> Number of modems
> Number of movies released
> Number of newspapers
> Number of online subscribers
> Number of personal computers
> Number of registered computer users
> Number of satellite dishes
> Number of telephones
> Number of TVs/radios
> Number of periodicals published (general/scientific)
> Number of public telephones
> Number of radio/TV channels
> Number of telephone access/trunk lines
>
> *Communication Behaviors*
> Circulation of library volumes
> Domestic/international mail traffic
> First-class letters mailed
> Hours spent accessing the Internet
> Hours spent listening/viewing radio/TV

accepted measures of access, use, and the impact of information and information technology. One particular outcome could be the aggregation of the kinds of microindicators listed in Box 2.9 into broadly accepted macro information indicators such as the following:

—**Interconnectivity index.** A measure of the facility of electronic communication, and an evaluation of the development of this dimension of the information infrastructure;

—**Information quality of life index.** Similar to an index produced by the Organisation for Economic Cooperation and Development, an index that would attempt to evaluate the qualitative levels of communication available to individuals;

—**Leading information indicators.** An index that would attempt to predict the growth of the information infrastructure;

—**Home media index.** An index of the state of penetration of communications technologies in the home that might qualify as a leading index of the potential for future consumption of information; and

—**Marginalization index.** An index that would measure the extent to which specific populations are excluded from participation in the information infrastructure.

Were such a set of indicators developed, funding agencies like the National Science Foundation might have a standardized tool in hand through which to assess the outcomes of the research that they sponsor.

- **Impacts of information technology on labor market structure.** Information technology has been linked to wage inequality and other changes in the structure of the labor market (more detail is provided in section 2.3). Understanding the extent to which and the mechanism by which computers may affect increased wage inequality is important in determining the nature and extent of public policy responses. This research should acknowledge that computers, by themselves, are not causal agents. Rather it is the entire constellation of economic and organizational strategies, managerial perspectives, and work practices within which computing technology is embedded that affects wage inequality.

One possible response is improved training of workers for IT-related jobs. Understanding the needs for education and training requires better definition of the skills required to make use of IT. Results from such research would benefit both policy makers and the private sector as they seek to better match education and training to workplace skill requirements.

- **Productivity and its relationship to work practices and organizational structures for the use of information technology.** Extracting the benefits of new technologies depends in part on organizational adaptation to them. As discussed in more detail above, industrial exploitation of the benefits of the electric dynamo in the early part of this century required new approaches to manufacturing. Organizations using information technology today are at a similar learning stage.

A major impediment to determining optimal work practices and organizational structures has been the lack of a clear picture of what data already exist. Developing such a list would help speed up research in this area. There are a number of places where specific research needs are already apparent, such as the collection of time series data to help clarify the role of technology in organizational changes.

Understanding the productivity benefits of information technology—illuminating the so-called productivity paradox—also is worthy of continued research. Important questions include how to better quantify what have been considered "unmeasurable" economic inputs, such as organizational knowledge, and "unmeasurable" outputs, such as product quality, associated with computers.

As recognition grows that productivity gains from information technology increasingly depend not just on the introduction of new technology but also on finding new ways and organizational structures to use it, it is worth noting that advances in the technology have owed much to government-supported computer science research. Advances in economic productivity would benefit from analogous research on how to better use information technology in the workplace. This is one facet of the broader question of learning how to better use information technology to achieve a host of social and economic goals. There are already moves to increase research in this domain; one example is the National Science Foundation's interdisciplinary Knowledge and Distributed Intelligence initiative.

- **Intellectual property issues.** Information technology raises many new questions about optimal protection of intellectual property rights, posing challenges to policy makers revising intellectual property law or international agreements as well as to commercial interests considering particular intellectual protection schemes. Many new schemes have been advanced for protection of intellectual property, and more needs to be known to choose among them. While considerable research has been conducted on the effect of different patent regimes on innovation, little has been studied regarding the consequences of different copyright protection schemes (see section 2.4.1). Theoretical work and empirical research on different copyright protection regimes will help inform future actions to protect intellectual property.

- **Social issues addressed at the protocol level.** The Internet has given rise to many new social issues in intellectual property, privacy, and data filtering. Addressing these social issues at the protocol level—through policies, rules, and conventions for the exchange and use of information—is a promising area for interdisciplinary research. Examples include:
    —PICS, the Platform for Internet Content Selection, which implements a set of protocols for rating Web sites (Resnick and Miller, 1996);
    —P3P,[35] a project for specifying privacy practices;
    —Language specifying the terms and conditions by which intellectual property is managed; and
    —Open Profiling Standard,[36] a method for individual users to selectively release information about themselves under specific conditions.

Each of these projects involves both technological and social dimensions. For example, PICS raises issues not only about how best to encode ratings for Web sites, but also about how to represent them; cognitive issues about how elaborate the rating schemes should be; and economic issues about how rating bureaus can recover costs. Another issue is how users can evaluate the trustworthiness of the labels provided by ratings services.

NOTES

1. See Tyack and Cuban (1995) for an analysis of why earlier technologies for improving teaching and learning never achieved their promise. See also references in CSTB (1994b, 1996c).
2. "Active intervention" refers to deliberate intervention—such as the introduction of new technology or educational practices—for the purposes of research.
3. While this discussion focuses on this question in a U.S. domestic context, in much of the rest of the world, socioeconomic disparities and the gap between urban and rural access are much greater.
4. See <http://www.hotmail.com>.
5. Note, however, that not all forms of communication necessarily reduce localness. For example, Wiley and Rice (1933) postulated that the telephone, a point-to-point medium, reinforces locality whereas broadcast media tend to diminish the importance of locality.
6. This work updated earlier work conducted at a time when computing was less prevalent.
7. The "output effect" also includes changing tastes or desires, e.g., the changes in preference for cars rather than horses or for word processors rather than typewriters.
8. One might expect software development to contribute to increased demand for skilled work, but recent work by Brynjolfsson (1997) found that it was not a major factor, at least not in most industrial countries. Although the U.S. software industry is fairly large and growing, it is still not large enough to explain any significant share of the effect.
9. See Brynjolfsson (1993), Attewell (1994), Sichel (1997), and CSTB (1994a) for empirical studies of the productivity paradox. See CSTB (1994a), Baily and Chakrabarti (1988), Brynjolfsson (1993), Wilson (1995), and Brynjolfsson and Yang (1996) for reviews.
10. Concurrent engineering refers to the practice in which personnel from every phase of product development—e.g., from design to production engineering, quality control, and service—collaborate in product development beginning at the earliest stages.
11. Note that improvements in the technology for transmitting and manipulating image data increasingly remove this limitation.
12. With the exception of the retirement-planning task force, the studies of differential benefits cited in this section used survey analysis of naturally occurring differential use. Statistical techniques were used to control for the effects of other variables, but because people were not randomly assigned to the use (or nonuse) of technology, strict causal claims are not warranted. In the retirement-planning study, still-employed and recently retired people were randomly assigned to task forces with and without access to technology. Because of the random assignment, causal claims are warranted.
13. U.S. Copyright Office records on documents registered for copyright are available via the Library of Congress Information System (LOCIS) for 1978 onward.
14. Figures on literacy are not always reliable, in part because the definition of literacy is somewhat vague. The numbers given in this discussion were taken from contemporary accounts.
15. Early expectations were that interactive cable services providing video on demand (VOD) or near-VOD would be lucrative and popular. However, early experiments by the cable industry showed that consumer response to VOD was unlikely to generate sufficient revenue to justify investment in interactive cable systems. Investment in two-way capabilities in the cable industry today is predicated on a market for broadband data delivery (including Internet as well as telephony and video conferencing) to both the home and small businesses, in addition to video programming.
16. See <http://www.cyberpatrol.com/>.
17. This set of protocols was adopted as a standard by the consortium that sets standards for the World Wide Web.
18. EPIC (see <http://www.epic.org/privacy/privacy_resources_faq.html>) contains an extensive list of online resources on privacy issues.

ILLUSTRATIVE EXAMPLES AND UNANSWERED QUESTIONS 77

19. This study is based on a sample of 1,009 computer users derived from a sample representative of 2,204 persons, age 18 or over, living in households with telephones and located in the 48 contiguous states.
20. Note that federal legislation passed in 1994 (which did not come into effect until 1997) allows people to restrict the release of personal information from state motor vehicle records.
21. See <http://www.sims.berkeley.edu/resources/infoecon/Security.html>.
22. See <http://www.melvyl.ucop.edu/>.
23. Branding is an effort to transform something perceived as generic into something with which people associate a brand name. A recent example is the "Inside Intel" campaign, which built up significant brand awareness for CPUs, something that the average individual cared little about.
24. "Push" technologies send information to an intended consumer without that consumer having requested it, while "pull" technologies send information only in response to a specific request. Radio and television broadcasting and e-mail are examples of push technologies, because they both transmit information regardless of whether or not anyone specifically requested it; the World Wide Web is an example of pull technology since a page must be requested before it is sent. Note that push technologies can be used over the Internet as well; examples include the PointCast system, which delivers customized news to users' computer desktops.
25. The National Library of Medicine's MEDLINE system makes extensive bibliographic information covering the fields of medicine and health care available free of charge to the public through a Web site.
26. The Electronic Data Gathering, Analysis, and Retrieval system makes available to the public through a Web site much of the information companies are required to submit to the U.S. Securities and Exchange Commission.
27. Such a gap exists, for example, between various socioeconomic groups, between urban and rural areas, and between industrialized and developing countries.
28. Also see Markus (1987) on the theory of critical mass for interactive media.
29. See <http://raven.stern.nyu.edu/networks>.
30. Herodotus describes the use of auctions in Babylon as early as 500 BC. It is remarkable that a venerable economic institution like an auction has found a receptive audience on the Internet. The Internet Auction List (<http://www.usaweb.com>) lists more than 50 sites that have regular online auctions, and more are being added every day. Computer equipment, air tickets, and Barbie dolls are being bought and sold daily via Internet auctions. Even advertising space is being sold via auction on AdBot (<http://www.adbot.com>).
31. There have, however, been problems due to overbidding (the so-called "winner's curse" phenomenon, described in Box 2.8) and signaling. Signaling can occur in multiround auctions when the bid values are used to signal the intent of the bidder, in violation of the rule against there being any collaboration or collusion between auction participants. For example, a bid of $1,000,202 might indicate that a bidder has a particular interest in the market with telephone area code 202.
32. See Jussawalla et al. (1988); Machlup (1962); and Porat (1977).
33. See Bell (1973); Katz (1988); Machlup (1962); and Schement (1990).
34. See Dordick and Wang (1993); Ito (1981); and Kuo (1989).
35. See <http://www.w3.org/Privacy/Overview.html>.
36. See <http://www.w3.org>.

3

Data—The Basis for New Knowledge

As the basis for exploration and rigorous analysis of observed phenomena, systematically collected data are critical to investigations of the economic and social impacts of information technology. Moreover, more timely data collection and analysis are likely to be useful in informing future policy decisions. Several data-related issues arise for researchers working at the intersection of information technology and socioeconomic issues. As discussion at the workshop made clear, among the most important is the need for more extensive, more timely, and new sources of relevant data.

3.1 TYPES AND USES OF DATA

Social scientists collect data from and about a variety of social units, ranging in degree of aggregation from individual human beings to corporations, economies, and nations (Box 3.1). Their time perspective may be historical or longitudinal (Box 3.2). The kinds of data collected and the methods of collection also depend on the overall purpose of the study. Special-purpose data sets are generally constructed by researchers to address a particular question—such as the extent to which information technology contributes to economic productivity. Multipurpose data sets can be used to study a wide variety of issues in a range of social science disciplines. As such, multipurpose data sets are part of the infrastructure of social science research.[1] The scope and range of such data sets are illustrated by the top-level categories of the data in the archives maintained by the Inter-university Consortium for Political and Social Research (see Box 3.3).

> **BOX 3.1**
> **Some Major Sources of Social Science Data with Examples of Types of Data Collected**
>
> *People*
> • As personal observers (e.g., verbal "think-aloud" responses gathered in studies of decision making and problem solving; responses to interviews and questionnaires)
> • As corporate or community representatives (e.g., descriptions of corporate deployment of information technology elicited in interviews with chief information officers)
> • As performers (e.g., scores from educational testing; patterns of participation in groups)
> • As decision makers (e.g., data revealing consumer preferences or choices)
>
> *Documents and Records—Historical and Contemporary*
> • Diaries (e.g., details of personal situations)
> • Media content (e.g., indicators of cultural themes)
> • Commercial records (e.g., data on the diffusion of the telephone)
> • Public records (e.g., data from birth and death records indicating population changes over time)
>
> *Organizations*
> • Performance measures collected from publicly reported data such as earnings reports; other financial measures
> • Personnel statistics
> • Product performance data
>
> *Communities*
> • Data on voter turnout or library circulation rates as indicators of citizen participation
>
> *Governments*
> • Labor market statistics
> • National and regional economic statistics

3.1.1 Data from Experiments

Experiments involve setting up control and experimental groups that differ only with respect to the presence or absence of the effect being studied and thus permit researchers to conclude that a difference in outcomes in the two groups is actually due to the difference in treatment. The HomeNet project is an experiment that examines the impacts of computers in the home (see section 2.1.1, "Computer Use in the Home"). The Internet Demand Experiment (INDEX) at the University of California, Berkeley, is attempting to measure user demand for Internet "quality of service" by offering different price-quality combinations and observing what users choose.[2] Offering an actual choice is likely to lead to more accurate results than is asking hypothetical questions.

BOX 3.2
Some Major Study Designs for Collecting Data

Case study: in-depth study of one social unit—a family, a school, an organizational work group, or a political campaign. The researcher uses multiple means of data collection (observation, interviews, document analysis) to develop a rich understanding of the interplay of factors operating in a single social setting.

Cross-sectional study: study in which data are collected on a relatively small number of variables from a relatively large number of social units at one point in time, often from questionnaires or existing records. The researcher often uses statistical techniques to characterize how variables are associated with one another.

Panel study: study in which data are collected on the same variables from the same social units at repeated points in time; supports investigating the impact of particular events that occur over the time course selected (e.g., the impact of a presidential candidate's debate on a panel of voters or the impact of an advertising campaign on a panel of consumers) as well as trends over time.

Experimental study: study in which the researcher uses random assignment techniques to allocate social units to different treatment regimes or experiences. Experiments establish control groups and experimental groups that differ only with respect to the presence or absence of the effect being studied. When random assignment is achieved, and social units have the same experiences in all ways except for the experimental treatment, and there is a measured difference in outcomes associated with the different treatments, then the researcher has evidence for concluding that the difference in treatment actually caused the difference in outcomes.

BOX 3.3
Top-level Categories of Data in the Archives of the Inter-university Consortium for Political and Social Research

- Census Enumerations
- Community, Urban Studies
- Conflict, Aggression, Violence
- Economic Behavior, Attitudes
- Education
- Elites and Leadership
- Geography and Environment
- Government Structures, Policies
- Health Care, Facilities
- Instructional Packages
- International Systems
- Legal Systems
- Legislative, Deliberative Bodies
- Mass Political Behavior, Attitudes
- Organizational Behavior
- Social Indicators
- Social Institutions, Behavior

3.1.2 Panel Data

Panel data is especially valuable because it enables answering questions about both cross-sectional and time-series variations. For example, a panel study of families can address such cross-sectional questions as how children's access to computers in the home is related to their educational performance in school (holding constant other factors). It also can address such time-series questions as whether high school students' educational performance in school is related to their access to computers in the home (holding constant other factors) and how this relationship is affected by the age at which students first had home access. Panel data also allows application of statistical techniques to control for unobserved effects that vary across a population. For example, the kinds of software and hardware available in the home have changed substantially over the past 15 years and are continuing to do so. An analysis of how the age at which students first had home access to computing affects later educational performance in school must take into account changes over time in the particular computing resources available.

A number of these multipurpose sets of panel data are collected by both private research groups and the federal government. Federal longitudinal studies include the Current Employment Statistics program[3] and the National Longitudinal Surveys (Bureau of Labor Statistics, 1998).

The versatility and potential range of uses of multipurpose longitudinal studies are illustrated by the Panel Study of Income Dynamics (PSID) administered by the Institute for Social Research[4] at the University of Michigan. The original purpose of the PSID, a longitudinal study begun in 1968 of a representative sample of U.S. individuals and the family units in which they reside, was to study factors influencing economic variables such as income, wealth, and earnings. Recently the PSID undertook five major key initiatives: (1) studies of data quality; (2) a re-contact initiative; (3) coding of data on census tract, mortality, and relationships; (4) supplements on wealth and health; and (5) early file release through the Internet. These initiatives have increased the cumulative response rate of the PSID; shown its continuing value as representing the U.S. population; added enormously to the stock of knowledge about important areas such as health and wealth; added detailed information on the residential areas in which respondents live, on mortality, and on relationships among family members; and increased the accessibility of the data to users. As a consequence of low attrition rates and the success of re-contact efforts, the sample size grew dramatically over the period, from about 7,000 core households to almost 8,700.

An extension of the PSID—the new parent-child survey component that will include time-use questions covering use of computers by children both at home and in school—illustrates the sort of valuable information on use and impacts of information technology that these extensive surveys can provide (see Box 3.4).

> **BOX 3.4**
> **Computer Use by Children: The PSID Parent-Child Survey**
>
> The Panel Study of Income Dynamics (PSID) is currently supplementing its core data collection with data on parents and their 0- to 12-year-old children—the PSID Parent-Child Survey. The objective is to provide researchers with a comprehensive, nationally representative, and longitudinal database of children and their families that will enable study of the dynamic process of childhood development.
>
> The additions to the core data set include the following: (1) reliable, age-graded assessments of the cognitive, behavioral, and health status of 3,500 children (including about 550 immigrant children) in 2,500 families, obtained from the mother, a second caregiver, an absent parent, the teacher, the school administrator, and the child; (2) a comprehensive accounting of parental and caregiver time inputs to children as well as other aspects of the way children and adolescents spend their time; (3) teacher-reported use of time in elementary and preschool programs; and (4) measures of use of resources other than time—for example, the learning environment in the home, teacher and administrator reports of school resources, and decennial census-based measurement of neighborhood resources. (The survey questions may be found at the PSID Web site at <http://www.umich.edu/~psid/>.)
>
> The data include those entered in two home-based time diaries for each child age 0 to 12, covering both school and nonschool days. There are also data from teacher-reported school-day diaries for about 75 percent of the children. The home-based and school-day diaries include a special coding for computer-related activities. In the home-based diary children can report time spent with TV, video games, or computers. In the school-day diary children's use of time can be reported on in terms of their having had computers as the instructional mode. Among the parameters considered in the class time segments are the length of time spent; who was present; whether the teacher was with the child; whether the activity involved groups, the whole class, or only the individual; and the teacher's assessment of the level of the child's involvement. Collection and analysis of data on time use entered in a diary have been established as a valid method for measuring actual time use. This approach gives more accurate results than do respondents' reports about their allocation of time to different activities over a week.
>
> The Parent-Child Survey data will be released to the public in fall 1998, as soon as they are cleaned (erroneous or nonsensical data eliminated) and documented. The data collection will support studies of the ways in which time, money, technology, and social capital at the family, school, and neighborhood levels, as well as parental psychological resources and sibling characteristics, are linked to the cognitive and behavioral development of children. The researchers plan to reinterview the children in 1999, again including time diary measures of computer use.

3.1.3 Data from Time-Use Studies

Data obtained from time-use studies, which can take the form of cross-sectional, panel, or experimental studies, can help answer questions such as what people do with computers. Current information on that and related topics is rather limited. One source of such data is a 1997 Price Waterhouse Consumer Technology Survey (Price Waterhouse, 1997), which asked 1,010 consumers how they spent their time using computers. Twenty-five percent of the consumers had Internet access from the home. On average, 43 percent of their time using computers was spent accessing the Internet for research; 34 percent for e-mail; 9 percent for game playing; 5 percent for reading online magazines and newspapers; 4 percent for online chat; 2 percent for online banking; and 1 percent each for two-way voice communications and online shopping.

Although these numbers are suggestive of how computers are used by consumers, they certainly are not definitive, given that they describe computer use only by adults at a particular point in time. Ongoing studies that examine users of different ages and from different population groups, along the lines of the parent-child time-use studies referred to above, would be very helpful. It might also prove useful to use cluster analysis to discover patterns of usage that do not emerge from averages over predetermined income, class, age, or population groups.

3.1.4 Metadata

"Metadata" are data about data, such as compendia or collections of data sets. The *Statistical Abstract of the United States* (U.S. Bureau of the Census, 1992) and *Historical Statistics of the United States: Colonial Times to 1970*, Bicentennial Edition (U.S. Bureau of the Census, 1975) are two well-known examples. A vitally important part of the research infrastructure, these publications as well as metadata sites on the World Wide Web such as STAT-USA (<http://www.stat-usa.gov>) are enormously helpful to researchers, teachers, journalists, and policy makers even though they generally do not present new data (Box 3.5).

Metadata are valuable because they are selective and authoritative, and, moreover, they provide a context that assists users in interpreting the data se-

---

BOX 3.5
The Enduring Value of Compilations of Data

There are some who suggest that compendia of data will no longer be useful or necessary in a computer-intensive future, when anyone with a computer and a modem will be able to download whatever data series is of interest nearly instantaneously and often without charge. These commentators may be correct about the future ease of access to data in digital format, but they are surely wrong to suggest the imminent obsolescence of compendia. Collections of compiled data will not become redundant when the entire Internet in effect becomes one gigantic repository for statistics. Indeed, with the decline in the cost of computer power one can expect the volume of available data to reach unprecedented levels. This avalanche of alternatives will make research tools like compendia more valuable, not less so.

lected together with warnings about pitfalls and possible misinterpretations and references to the debates and sources containing alternative measures. Compilation of metadata requires exacting research, intensive review, and refereeing by the nation's and the world's best experts.

Unfortunately, in recent years government statistical agencies, operating under severe financial constraints, often have given the development of new compendia or the maintenance of existing metadata sets a low priority. The *Historical Statistics* volume, for example, has not been updated or revised for a quarter-century; several years ago the Bureau of the Census abandoned its plans to take on this effort. Instead, the project has been taken up by a private publisher (Cambridge University Press) in collaboration with a team of more than 70 scholars whose volunteer contributions of time and expertise indicate how important the revision of *Historical Statistics* is to the research community.[5]

Both public and private foundations devoted to funding research have tended to resist underwriting the costs of preparing metadata sets, perhaps because they view such projects as mere digitizing and collating efforts requiring little or no scholarship or research.[6] Although the *Historical Statistics* project may prove to be commercially viable, efforts to revise and update other less widely used data compendia may not be able to attract the aid of a private-sector sponsor. Collaboration between government statistical agencies and experts in academia and industry in preparing these resources might be facilitated by direct contracts and grants or through informal partnerships between the agencies and experts from the scholarly and business communities.

3.2 AVAILABILITY OF AND ACCESS TO DATA

In general, researchers must conduct their work within limited budgets and also face the need to preserve long-term continuity in studies while capturing rapidly changing phenomena. Owing partly to constraints on federal data gathering (see section 3.2.3 below), government and academic researchers have been relatively slow to refocus their data collection efforts on the emerging social and economic impacts of information technology. Myriad private-sector groups have responded more quickly to businesses' appetite for timely information about the technological challenges they confront. For example, private-sector market research organizations run household or consumer panels that administer monthly surveys. Particularly given the time lag required for careful analysis, investigation of rapid changes in peoples' responses to technology requires that social scientists have better access to data from a variety of sources. Social scientists need better access to each other's data as well as to information that is collected by the private sector and government.

3.2.1 Data Collected by the Private Sector

The significant private-sector resources devoted to data collection could be of great value to researchers and policy makers if properly leveraged. Trade associations such as the Semiconductor Industry Association gather detailed data on industry output, prices, employment practices, demand forecasts, and managers' key concerns. Rather than attempting to duplicate or replace these efforts, it would be useful to coordinate collection of data for research with the data gathering of industry groups. Resources could be pooled and greater cooperation fostered among participants. Respondents to surveys are most diligent, for example, when they can expect some return on their efforts. The prospect of obtaining feedback, typically in the form of aggregate results, is often an important incentive.

The fact that a private group is interested in gathering, or already has gathered, certain data suggests that the information is perceived by managers as having real value. Indeed, in some cases private-sector client groups may be interested in helping to disseminate the results of research to at least a selected audience, thus increasing the overall impact of the research. Often a consulting firm will broadly release at least a summary of a research study in order to bolster the firm's reputation, although the proprietary nature of the results may inhibit wide dissemination in their full form.

A major concern associated with the use of data collected by the private sector is that private firms often lack academic standards of quality control such as peer review. Consultants, trade magazines, and industry groups may be less than rigorous about survey design, sample selection, or other biases in the data, and as a result their data may be unreliable or misleading.

One approach to improving the reliability of findings is to use data from multiple independent sources to the extent possible. For instance, in his study of information technology and productivity, Lichtenberg (1995) drew on data from two distinct private-sector sources on firms' capital investment in information technology. Although the correlation was far from perfect, the overall econometric results were quite similar regardless of which data source was used, making the results more credible.

Another possible approach to ensuring quality is to work closely with private data-collection firms, although private groups generally want to keep data and results private and available for the exclusive use of clients. Nevertheless, in at least one instance, a team of researchers struck a bargain with a media group, according to which the research team was to design several annual surveys, supervise the sampling and data collection, and then conduct the analysis itself. The media group paid all the costs of this undertaking and turned the data over to the research team; in exchange, the researchers wrote a sequence of articles summarizing the latest publishable findings, which were then presented each year in a special issue based on the surveys. Such collaboration is currently the exception, as is private-sector commitment to these sorts of long-term research endeavors.

Indeed a difficulty in working with private-sector groups is that they are often focused on whatever topic is currently "hot," and yesterday's news, it seems, is of only academic interest. The practical result is that time series of more than a few years are difficult to obtain, which makes it difficult to conduct statistical analysis. Another drawback is that private-sector data collectors may well change the definitions used in surveys and the nature of the groups sampled; again, the focus is often how new data relate to the latest management question, and not how recently collected data relate to past data. In fact, many such firms do not even attempt to preserve data for more than a year once it has been collected, as Brynjolfsson and Kemerer learned when they sought to estimate the value that consumers placed on various software features so that they could determine how the quality-adjusted price of spreadsheets had evolved over time (Brynjolfsson and Kemerer, 1996).[7]

3.2.2 The Need for Firm-level Data

As observed by Ronald Coase more than 50 years ago, firms are the dominant way of organizing economic activity (Coase, 1937). Any complete understanding of the economic and social impacts of information technology requires examining activities at the level of individual firms. Unfortunately, there are significant gaps in the available data that describe this level, forcing researchers to make extrapolations from other types of data to try to answer important questions about the effects of technologies' use. For instance, one recent research study developed a theory of how companies' growth would be affected by new technologies but could only test it using industry-level data. As the authors lamented: "Each industry contains thousands to tens of thousands of firms, so it may seem odd to take industries as firms. Unfortunately, there are no firm-level data sets that span the economy" (Basu et al., 1997).

Although important insights can be gained from assessing industry-level data, trends at this level of aggregation may be quite different from trends at the level of the firm. For instance, income inequality could be increasing overall in the economy even if gaps in wage levels within every individual firm were being reduced—if, for example, firms "outsourced" noncore work while specializing in narrower functions. In fact, important questions about causality, learning, and lags in observed effects are best analyzed by studying a cross section of firms over time. One-time cross-sectional studies of firms will not suffice.

A few firm-level longitudinal data sets do exist, such as Standard and Poor's Compustat databases, which provide extensive financial data on publicly traded firms, including their sales, stock prices, and employment statistics. More detailed firm-level data sets have been assembled in Europe, such as the data set assembled by the Industriens Utrednings Institut (Industrial Institute for Economic and Social

Research) in Stockholm, Sweden, and data sets collected by the Institut für Wirtschaftsforschung (Institute for Economic Research) in Munich, Germany.

Many more finely focused firm-level data sets also exist for specific industries and purposes in the United States and abroad. One is the data set derived from a minimum wage survey of U.S. firms. Each of these data sets has proven useful for addressing certain research questions. However, very few of the firm-level panel studies include data on information technology or important organizational variables. In addition, the results of studies that examine smaller, more focused samples of firms within specific industries cannot be readily generalized to other industries or the broader economy.

An economical approach to assembling a broader firm-level data set is to build on existing data sets and link them together. For instance, to address questions about information technology and productivity, Brynjolfsson and Hitt (1996) combined data from Compustat with private-sector data from International Data Corporation as well as data obtained in their own surveys. This approach enabled them to identify a significant correlation between use of information technology and firm-level productivity that could not be discerned from conflicting case studies or coarser, economy-wide data.

A number of lessons can be learned from prior work with firm-level data:

- Firms or business units are always changing and reorganizing, thus posing challenges for measurement and data collection parallel to those arising from changes in the set of individuals that constitute a household in studies such as the Panel Study of Income Dynamics. Of course if they are followed, the spinoffs of changes are also potentially very interesting (e.g., in the study of the formation of new enterprises).
- Firms need feedback. For instance, most firms greatly value information that enables benchmarking: knowledge of where one's own firm stands in relation to an aggregate of anonymous peers. The opportunity to obtain such information was the main incentive provided for respondents in the case of the Institute for Economic Research study. Respondents in such data collection surveys could even be given access to the database itself, although this approach can substantially increase the workload associated with maintaining the data.[8]
- Firms are often very heterogeneous. As a result, for some purposes it makes sense to focus on firms that have something in common, such as an industry group. In other cases, it may be best to seek multiple respondents from the same firm, each of whom may have a different perspective. Even when one individual is compiling the data for a firm, it must be understood that the information may derive from a set of individuals with knowledge of different functional areas of the enterprise.

Once firm-level data are compiled, they can often be usefully linked to data at other levels of aggregation, both higher and lower. For instance, industry- and firm-level data can be combined to address such questions as whether productive use of information technology correlates with one type of organizational structure in retailing and a different one in high-technology manufacturing.

In other cases additional insights may be gained by combining firm-level data with finer-detail information about individuals in those firms. This approach—constructing a study covering a sample of firms that also includes data on a sample of individual employees in those firms—was used with remarkable success by Greenan and Mairesse (1996) to measure the correlation between computerization and productivity in firms. Although Greenan and Mairesse had complete production data for a large sample of French firms that enabled them to estimate a variety of productivity measures, they did not have any direct data on the extent of computerization at those firms. Instead, they combined data from a separate survey of individuals, which asked whether they used a computer at work and what the name of their employer was, with the firm-level production data. They found that many of the firms in their first data set matched with one or more individuals in the second data set. If the sampled employee used a computer at work, this was evidence that the firm was more computerized than its competitors. Although matching the data in this way was very difficult and provided a fairly weak indication of the effects of computerization, the researchers were able to establish an overall positive correlation between computerization and productivity for the French firms.

3.2.3 Data Collected by Government

The federal government collects a vast amount of data, much of which is readily available via printed or computer-accessible media. Among the advantages of federally collected data are its high quality and objectivity, its accessibility for use by the public, and its free availability as material in the public domain that can be used without raising intellectual property concerns. The FedStats Web site (<http://www.fedstats.gov>), launched in 1997 by the Federal Interagency Council on Statistical Policy, is a directory of data collected by the U.S. federal government and available online.

Nevertheless, the availability of data has been curtailed in recent years due to budget cuts, government reforms, and policy changes. Overall federal government collection of data is restricted by both the statutory goals of the Paperwork Reduction Act of 1995 and Administration targets for reducing the burden of collecting information. Structural and regulatory changes have also reduced the availability of standardized, public data describing the telecommunications sector. For example, deregulation of the telecommunications industry has reduced the quantity and availability of data on telephony, and deregulation of terminal equipment (e.g., telephone instruments) led the FCC to stop collecting data on such equipment. In addition, following privatization of the Internet and the end of government funding for the NSF-run Internet backbone, data were no longer available on the size and characteristics of Internet traffic.[9] It is ironic that the communications industry, an object of intense scrutiny by policy makers, is more poorly measured now than in the past.

In ways that are important to setting communications policy, efforts to reduce the data collection burdens imposed by the federal government and to reduce the role of regulation in telecommunications are at odds with the need for good data on the telecommunications infrastructure and the changing nature of consumer use of new technologies. If social science researchers are to gain insights into what information technology-related changes are taking place within the home, how Americans invent ways to interconnect, and how access to new communications media can affect economic growth and civic participation, then more, not less, statistical data on the penetration and uses of media needs to be collected, starting with use of the telephone (Box 3.6).

3.3 NEW TYPES OF DATA

3.3.1 Documenting the Effects of Technology Deployment

Many social institutions—schools, libraries, hospitals, municipalities—are going online. Institutions may collect and report basic measures of use, such as the number of times their online resources are accessed ("hits"), but often local resources are not devoted to using such information to systematically document the dynamics and the social and individual effects of system deployments.

Individual institutions typically lack the time, expertise, motivation, and perspective to document the dynamics and effects of change resulting from the use of information technology. Indeed even the first step, measuring access to and use of online resources, is a nontrivial problem. Since each component of a Web page (a graphic, text, or other item) will result in a separate hit, hits as a measure of use will give different counts depending on the details of the content's design. Collecting meaningful data on use, especially where cross-comparisons are to be made, depends on systematically defining such things as visitors, users, and the like.[10]

Externally supported comparative research projects exploring the effects of technology deployments could be enormously useful to at least four audiences. Policy makers and citizens would be able to understand the benefits (and costs) of online access to information and online interactions with social institutions. Technologists and managers would be able to understand the effects of different technology configurations and deployment strategies. Scholars would be able to test and revise existing theories of institutional participation with new kinds of data. Future generations of scholars and citizens would be able to study this transition period, as institutions experiment with different modes of online service.

Consider a specific example. The Gates Library Foundation, established by Microsoft Chief Executive Officer Bill Gates, will provide $200 million, matched

BOX 3.6
Challenges of Collecting Data on the Use of Information Technology: Telephones, the Census, and the Current Population Survey

To understand the difficulties in answering the simplest questions about the use of information technology, consider basic data on household use of telephony. Households that have telephone service constitute the conceptual basis for all measures of universal service. The most widely used measure is the percentage of households with telephone service—sometimes referred to as telephone "penetration."[1] Yet this measure, though seemingly straightforward, can harbor multiple definitions, and studies designed to measure it are subject to errors.

Prior to the 1980 census, precise calculation of telephone subscribership—i.e., one definition of penetration—was of little concern. In the days of one phone, one household, one service provider, telephone penetration was traditionally measured by dividing the number of residential telephone lines by the number of households. As households added second lines and as the number of second homes increased, measurement based on the number of residential lines became subject to a large margin of error. By 1980, the penetration according to the traditional measure (residential lines divided by the number of households) reached 96 percent in the United States, whereas the number of households that reported having telephones in the 1980 census lagged at 92.9 percent.

In 1980, the Federal Communications Commission (FCC) requested that the Bureau of the Census include questions on telephone penetration as part of its Current Population Survey (CPS), which monitors demographic trends between decennial censuses. For national studies, use of the CPS has several advantages: (1) it is conducted every month by an independent and expert agency, (2) the sample is large, and (3) the questions are consistent. Thus, changes in the results can be compared over time with a great deal of confidence.

Unfortunately, however, the telephone penetration results of the CPS cannot be directly compared with the figures on telephone penetration obtained in either the 1980 or 1990 census. Differences in the sampling and survey methodologies are a source of discrepancies.

Although the CPS is conducted every month, not all of the questions are included every month. Since the sample is staggered, the information that is reported for

---

[1] According to the Bureau of the Census, "A household includes the related family members and all the unrelated persons, if any, such as lodgers, foster children, wards, or employees who share the housing unit. A person living alone in a housing unit, or a group of unrelated persons sharing a housing unit as partners, is also counted as a household. . . . The figures for number of households are not strictly comparable from year to year. In general the definitions of household for 1790, 1900, 1930, 1940, 1950, 1960, and 1970 are similar. Very minor differences result from the fact that in 1950, 1960, and 1970, housing units with 5 or more lodgers were excluded from the count of households, whereas in 1930 and 1940, housing units with 11 lodgers or more were excluded, and in 1790 and 1900, no precise definition of the maximum allowable number of lodgers was made." (U.S. Bureau of the Census, 1975)

According to the CPS, "A household consists of all the persons who occupy a house, an apartment, or other group of rooms, or a room, which constitutes a housing unit. A group of rooms or a single room is regarded as a housing unit when it is occupied as separate living quarters; that is, when the occupants do not live and eat with any other person in the structure, and when they have direct access from the outside through a common hall. The count of households excludes persons living in group quarters, such as rooming houses, military barracks, and institutions. Inmates of institutions (mental hospitals, rest homes, correctional institutions, etc.) are not included in the survey." (U.S. Bureau of the Census, 1993)

> any given month actually reflects responses over the preceding 4 months. Aggregated summaries of the responses are reported to the FCC, based on the surveys conducted through March, July, and November of each year. Also, the questions in the CPS were written long before the breakup of AT&T and reflect realities of the monopoly era, when having a telephone also meant having service. But in the post-divestiture era encompassed by the 1990 census, the question, Is there a telephone in this house/apartment? inadvertently focuses on the telephone as an instrument. Instead the real issue is the presence of telephone service. Therefore, one potential for statistical bias stems from a literal response to this question. In the case of the census, the respondent could truthfully answer yes to the question and confound the results with an upward bias; and since there is no follow-up to the census, the upward bias would go uncorrected. In the case of the CPS, follow-up questions and surveys may correct for this bias;[2] however, they contain the potential for a downward bias. The follow-up, a telephone call repeated in subsequent months, will catch a household that originally had telephone service and lost it, but will not catch a household that did not originally have telephone service but subsequently received it—thus, the downward bias.
>
> For the researcher, another difficulty is that the census is not strictly comparable with the CPS. The differences—some correctable, some inherent—result in a gap in the final numbers. According to the 1990 census, 94.8 percent of all households in the United States had telephones. However, CPS data showed penetration at 93.3 percent for 1990. This difference, which represents nearly 1.4 million households, is statistically significant and appears to indicate that the CPS may be on the low side of the actual penetration rate, whereas the census may be on the high side.
>
> Collecting comparable data on the use of the Internet, e-mail, or other new information technology, and measuring the penetration of telecommunications in an increasingly heterogeneous environment, clearly present a substantial challenge. For example, reliance on CPS data would carry with it an inherent bias against the use of wireless and mobile services for telecommunications purposes. Address-based measurement excludes the presence of new wireless technologies if they are used as substitutes for wired service to the home.
>
> ---
> [2] The Current Population Survey includes households in the survey for the same 4 consecutive months in 2 consecutive years.

by $200 million in software provided by Microsoft, to connect the nation's public libraries to the Internet (Lohr, 1997). Since not all libraries will go online at the same time, the program offers the opportunity for a range of comparisons. Longitudinal studies could document changes in a variety of social welfare indicators (perhaps, for example, changes in circulation rates, civic participation, and consumer awareness) as a function of Internet access and use. More pragmatically, they could document how different deployment strategies (e.g., location of Internet stations; access and use policies; tie-ins with school, civic group, or municipal government programs) were associated with patterns of use and effects. These findings would be extremely useful to the later-deploying libraries.

Similar longitudinal comparative studies should be designed and conducted to understand the dynamics and effects of increasing numbers of other social institutions going online. Projects that deploy new technologies, especially prototypes, should be encouraged to build in the capture of such data. Digital libraries, distance learning, and efforts to use information technology to enhance government services ("digital government") would all be valuable areas in which to incorporate study of the sociological and economic impacts of information technology.

3.3.2 Data on Social Interactions from the Internet

A great deal of social behavior is visible on the Internet. For example, one can see how many Usenet groups or public distribution lists exist on what topics, and what the level of activity is on each. Snapshots of publicly accessible social behavior could be captured and made available to social scientists studying group behavior on the Internet.[11] It might even be possible to study the complete corpus of communication within a group of Usenet news or e-mail "listserves." However, collecting data from the Internet presents technological difficulties and may also raise legal questions.[12]

In addition to Usenet groups and e-mail lists, another source of data is illustrated by Kaminer (1997), who has used the UNIX logs of natural scientists to obtain data on their use of a variety of Internet features (telnet, FTP, and so on). Using a multivariate approach, he has shown that increased use of the Internet increases a scholar's research productivity (publications per year), other things being held constant.[13]

Systematic longitudinal data on group behavior on the Internet would be a valuable resource for social scientists studying the formation and diffusion of electronic communities. Such data are in some measure the electronic equivalent of the town records that historians have used to document and understand 19th-century community formation and development. But these electronic data on Internet behavior are ephemeral. Unless they are collected and archived now, they will disappear, and researchers will have no systematic record of how group behavior on the Internet is growing and evolving over time. What databases should be developed to support research in these areas?

Tools used to analyze Usenet and e-mail data might also be applied to Web-based systems and emerging software systems for collaboration. Application of these approaches to new technologies will in some cases require a new focus on data collection methodologies. For example, methods are needed to factor out distorting artifacts such as the use of proxies to access Web resources or the activities of indexing robots.

3.3.3 The Internet as a Window into How Commercial Transactions Are Conducted

In his position paper "Electronic Interactions" in Appendix B of this volume, Paul Resnick suggests that the Internet would also permit study of a number of interesting topics in how commercial transactions are conducted. For example:

- Recommendations and referrals can help people to find interesting information and vendors. There is a need for continued research on techniques for gathering and processing recommendations (this is sometimes called collaborative filtering). Compilation of "grand challenge" data sets of recommendations would help this field advance.
- The structure of negotiation protocols and the availability of information about past behavior of participants will affect the kinds of outcomes that are possible. Economists have theoretical results regarding many simplified negotiation scenarios, but there is a need for interdisciplinary research to apply and extend these results to practical problems of protocol design.
- In the transaction consummation phase, much effort has focused on secure payment systems. Some transactions, however, require a physical consummation (mailing of a product, for example) and hence must rely on trust in some form. Research can explore the role of reputations in creating trustworthy (though not completely secure) contract consummation. Such transactions may also have lower transaction costs than secure payment systems, even in the realm of purely electronic transactions.

3.4 TIME AND TOOLS FOR GATHERING AND INTERPRETING DATA

3.4.1 The Time Required to Do Good Social Science

It is important to recognize that systematically gathering and analyzing social science data are very time-intensive tasks. The need for time can lead to difficulties in synchronization of attention to the object of study, information technology effects, and ways of studying information technology. Although information technology is developing at a very rapid pace, the speed at which social science data have been acquired has changed little in the last few decades. Analysis of quantitative data, after it has been acquired and prepared, has certainly been speeded up by the widespread use of computers, but analysis of qualitative data has been much less affected.

A few examples illustrate the time required for data collection and analysis.

- As previous research efforts have shown (see, e.g., Orr, 1990), it can take significant time for a researcher to enter a community, gain the trust of its members, and begin to understand how community members interact with one another and with technology.

- The Homenet field experiment to understand how families use Internet technology was begun in 1994 and is still under way (Kraut et al., 1996; Kiesler et al., 1997). It has taken significant time to recruit families (both those who will receive technology and those who will serve as a control group), to acquire and deploy technology and train people to use it, and to administer questionnaires and conduct interviews and home visits. Data collection must be repeated at regular intervals in order to investigate changes over time. The systems that are deployed in the Homenet study are not yet obsolete, but they are aging. If researchers give participants newer technology, they compromise their understanding of how peoples' use of a particular technology changes over time. If they do not give participants newer technology, their findings, particularly any negative ones, can be dismissed because they were based on old technology.
- It takes at least 6 months after an interface is implemented, debugged, and regarded as stable to conduct a laboratory study of peoples' social behavior in responding to that interface (e.g., Sproull et al., 1996). Thus interface designers can develop new interfaces more rapidly than researchers can collect data on social responses to each particular interface.

These observations suggest that some mismatch is unavoidable between technology development and social science research. Researchers studying the effects of widespread deployment of a new technology must wait for widespread deployment to occur. By that time, however, the technology is no longer new. For example, although electronic mail was invented in the 1960s, the first research on e-mail's effects on patterns of organizational communication was not published until 20 years later, when noticeable numbers of organizations were beginning to use it routinely.

In addition to lags imposed by the need to wait until technology is widely deployed, there are the normal delays inherent in social science research. Data collection and careful data set preparation take time, especially for large data sets.

Sometimes the mismatch between development of technology and research on its effects can lead to criticism of studies for relying on older data, even though more recent data of equivalent quality was not available. Examples include the RAND Corporation's analysis of home access to computing, which is based on the 1989 and 1993 Current Population Survey data (Anderson et al., 1995), and Attewell's analysis of the effects of home computers on educational performance, which is based on data from the 1988 National Educational Longitudinal Study (Attewell and Battle, 1997). However, in many cases the mismatch does not matter. For example, researchers investigating the impacts of alternative models of investment in technology would find data on corporate expenditures on information technology enormously useful—such data would certainly be treated as proprietary when current but after a relatively brief time would be considered obsolete for corporate decision-making purposes. In some cases, such as historical studies, older data is better. For instance, data about early adopters of technology can certainly be useful in better exploring advantages that may accrue to early entrants in an industry (the so-called first-mover advantage).

3.4.2 Appropriate Subject Pools and Instrumentation

In addition to benefiting from improved access to data (see section 3.2 above), social scientists exploring the impacts of information technology also would benefit from better access to appropriate subject pools for behavioral studies. Most university-based subject pools, which do not operate during exam periods and breaks, are best suited to short-term studies of the behavior of individuals. To study the effects of technologies designed for groups, researchers need access to groups. Creating groups composed of strangers in an experimental laboratory will not allow researchers to understand the long-term effects of technologies that require or cause substantial changes in organizational procedures governing how people work together.

In addition, social scientists need new instrumentation for more rapid data collection. Data collection may be an area for fruitful collaboration between social scientists and technologists exploring, for example, Internet-based survey and interviewing technologies. Use of these new sources of data would also require attention to the privacy concerns they raise.

3.5 APPROACHES TO MEETING REQUIREMENTS FOR DATA

Based on discussions at the workshop and in position papers submitted by workshop participants, the workshop steering committee developed a set of approaches to meeting requirements for data needed to advance research on the impacts of information technology. Listed below, these approaches are intended as illustrations of ways to enable researchers—in concert with government and the private sector—to address the need for more extensive, more timely, and new sources of data.

- **Making data related to the social and economic impacts of computing and communications available to the research community through a clearinghouse.** A clearinghouse would provide documentation and archiving of data sets (but not an evaluation of data quality). It might be necessary to develop incentives for researchers to contribute data to this archive. Journals could make submission of data to an appropriate clearinghouse a requirement for publication. For example, journals publishing research in the biological sciences typically require authors to deposit genetic sequences and similar data in publicly accessible databases such as the National Institutes of Health genetic sequence database, GenBank.[14] The terms of federal research funding could also support efforts for a clearinghouse. For example, the National Science Foundation expects grantees to share research data with other researchers (with safeguards in place for the rights of experimental subjects and the like). Depositing research data in a clearinghouse could be an efficient way for researchers to satisfy this expectation. An explicit expectation that data be deposited in appropriate data banks could also be added as a condition of receiving grants.

In addition, a clearinghouse could encourage comparability—in both format and research methodology—across data sets and the reuse of data, especially if academic researchers and also commercial data sources were to collaborate on defining standards.

A possible model for such a clearinghouse is the Inter-university Consortium for Political and Social Research located within the Institute for Social Research at the University of Michigan. Funded by subscribing member institutions, it provides access to a large archive of computerized social science data. A clearinghouse could also derive support from grant funding and charges for access to data sets.

Both the archiving and standards-setting functions would enable increased secondary use of data sets, which would of course depend on the social science community's ease of access to data in a clearinghouse. Joint work between social scientists and technologists could lead to building new kinds of data clearinghouses and new tools and techniques for making use of them.

- **Exploring ways for researchers to gain access to private-sector data.** Commercial data on firms' capital investment in information technology is of considerable value to researchers examining the social and economic impacts of computing and communications. Consultant, trade magazine, and industry group data is another valuable resource (see section 3.2.1).

Overall, however, several factors impede collaboration between researchers and the private sector. First, data on individual firms is often protected because of competitive concerns. One remedy is for social scientists and the commercial sector to explore aggregation and other ways of hiding individual corporate identity. Second, incentives for collaboration by private-sector firms typically are lacking, although one way of providing them is to establish an agreement whereby researchers who use private-sector data then make research results available in a useful form to the firm or organization that supplied the data. To both protect proprietary interests and increase incentives, strengthened institutional relationships between the research community and industry associations would be valuable.

It is important to note that private-sector sources of data may have a number of possible limitations, including a lack of consistent definitions and methods over time and the tendency of private-sector firms to preserve only the current information. In many of these cases closer working relationships between researchers and the private sector can provide solutions (see section 3.2.1 for examples).

- **Increasing data collection efforts by government.** As described in section 3.2.3, deregulation and privatization can reduce the quantity and availability of data on telecommunications and computing at a time when more, not less, information is needed to guide policy decisions. Budget constraints and government reforms to reduce information gathering burdens also have reduced data collection. In addition, fewer resources have been available for analyzing data and for making the data publicly available.

Workshop participants noted that loss of such data sources inhibits social science explorations of the social and economic impacts of computing and communications. At a minimum, government decision makers need to be aware of the cost of losing such data. In some cases they may be able to find other ways to gather valuable information. For example, additional questions might be added to the Census Bureau's Current Population Survey (CPS) to measure wireless phone or Internet use (see Box 3.6), as was done by the National Telecommunications and Information Administration and described in the report "Falling Through the Net" (NTIA, 1995), which reported on computer and modem use and explored the demographics of telephone, computer, and modem use in terms of population density, ethnicity, age, and economic status. However, this approach has been taken only once, because it is expensive to add supplemental questions to the CPS.

- **Exploring the development of new multipurpose data sets by the research community.** To what extent can multipurpose data sets based on such techniques as user diaries prove helpful to researchers examining the social impacts of information technology? Careful observational methods have been critical to specific deep organizational studies in such areas as computer-supported cooperative work (e.g., the study of Xerox technicians described in section 2.3.4). However such research has not typically relied on multipurpose public data sets. As the body of observational data grows, it may be possible to start development of such nonquantitative multipurpose data sets. A precedent is the Human Relations Area Files at Yale University, which consist of ethnographic extracts organized in various categories. Given a rich enough corpus of observational data in a given domain, it may prove both possible and valuable to invest in the creation of new, qualitative multipurpose data sets.

- **Establishing stronger ties with industry associations to facilitate collaborative research.** In general, proprietary concerns are likely to impede collaboration between academic researchers and private-sector firms. Yet to explore topics such as the relationships among organizational structure, the use of information technology, and productivity, researchers need access to firm- and process-level data that typically is not public. Nonpublic data relevant to other social and economic research includes details of pricing, employment, demand forecasts, and the like. Lack of experience in collaborative work between the two communities is another barrier.

Industry associations are a possible bridge between the communities, to allow each to benefit from the resources of the other. One approach might involve sponsorship of forums where academics and industry people can meet to discuss common interests. These events can create serendipitous opportunities for cooperation that could not have been predicted or planned in formal brokering. Industry associations might also help connect the academic and industry communities in more formal roles such as the following:

—As an intermediary that aggregates or otherwise makes proprietary data anonymous so that firms will be more comfortable about providing it to outsiders;

—As a matchmaker in bringing together industry and the research community to work on projects of mutual interest;

—As a depository for research results based on industry-provided data (if research reports are readily available to them, industries may be more willing to provide data); and

—As a sponsor of research on topics of interest to the membership.

Note that limited financial resources may place constraints on such collaboration. Since trade associations are unlikely to have in-house resources to cover the administrative costs of a research study collaboration, it may prove necessary to structure such a project on a break-even basis for the association.

- **Exploring, in workshop sessions, uses of the Internet as a source of data on social interactions.** As described in section 3.3.2, the Internet can provide a wealth of information on group and community behavior. It would be very useful to convene a workshop of technologists, social scientists, academics, and representatives of commercial interests to discuss and resolve such issues as the following:

—How to develop indicators of group behavior that are publicly available on the Internet;

—The feasibility of commercial services providing data such as those on use of their forums and chat rooms;

—Appropriate sampling and estimation procedures;

—Appropriate publishing and archiving procedures;

—Standards for data collection and exchange; and

—How to establish relationships with possible providers of information (e.g., search engines or newsgroup archives).

Such an endeavor would also need to address ethical and privacy issues associated with data collection, archiving, and reporting as well as the proprietary interests of commercial Internet services.

NOTES

1. Many of them were developed for other users, but some have been able to provide useful input to social science studies of information technology. Multipurpose data sets are often collected by organizations dedicated to this task such as the Institute for Social Research (ISR) at the University of Michigan (see <http://www.isr.umich.edu/>), the National Opinion Research Center at the University of Chicago (see <http://www.norc.uchicago.edu>), and several other research organizations. Many such multipurpose data sets are maintained by organizations like the Inter-university Consortium for Political and Social Research (ICPSR, see <http://www.icpsr.umich.edu/>), which is supported by member-university subscriptions. ICPSR, located within the Institute for Social Research at the University of Michigan, is a membership-based, not-for-profit organization serving member colleges and universities in the United States and abroad. Data sets can be found online at <http://www.isr.umich.edu>.
2. For details see the project description and related documents available online at <http://www.INDEX.berkeley.edu>.
3. Data sets and reports are available online at <http://stats.bls.gov/cesprog.htm>.
4. Information on the Institute for Social Research can be found online at <http://www.icpsr.umich.edu>.
5. Work to prepare the new edition (Susan Carter, Scott Gartner, Michael Haines, Alan Olmstead, Richard Sutch, and Gavin Wright, editors, *Historical Statistics of the United States from Colonial Times to the Present*, Millennial Edition, Cambridge University Press, in preparation, scheduled for publication in 2000) has received partial support from the National Science Foundation and the Alfred P. Sloan Foundation.
6. A workshop participant noted that university and college promotion committees seem to give little weight to faculty contributions to such projects, perhaps because they, too, share the widespread misunderstanding of the value of metadata and the scholarly research required to create a metadata set.
7. Brynjolfsson and Kemerer knew that *Software Digest*, published by National Software Testing Labs (NSTL), a private firm, had regularly reviewed all the major spreadsheet products and conducted detailed feature evaluations. By matching these data with price data from Dataquest, another private firm, they could estimate the values that consumers placed on various software features.

    The difficulties came in trying to get historical data. Only intervention by the president of Dataquest following a chance meeting at an industry dinner finally led the researchers to historical data on prices. Obtaining data on software features required a different sort of intervention. To save on storage space, NSTL had simply erased all information regarding previous years' spreadsheet products because there was no market for that information. Repeated queries to various managers of the firm, as well as efforts to find the back issues in libraries, were unsuccessful. Finally, a mid-level employee of the firm came to the rescue. On his own initiative, he had stockpiled back issues of *Software Digest* in the basement of his home, along with thousands of other magazines. He agreed to ship several large boxes with the relevant issues to Brynjolfsson and Kemerer, where they were duly re-entered into a computer database.
8. Dealing with people's inquiries for data can be time consuming because people often need different data formats, more detailed documentation, and follow-up explanations of what the variables mean; make requests for related data; and have other requirements that need attention. At a minimum, such database support activities involve one or more conversations with people at each participating company.

9. The NSFNET backbone was originally the core of the Internet, and thus much of the total Internet traffic passed through it, making useful measurement of total Internet traffic possible. When this backbone was replaced by a new architecture, data on total traffic became harder to acquire. Also, the architecture of the backbone had been designed to allow more measurements than are now possible with the off-the-shelf router components that were used post-NSFNET, in order to satisfy deliverables of traffic measurement in the agreement with NSF.

10. Web advertising is one area where an effort has been made to develop useful definitions of access and use (Novak and Hoffman, 1997).

11. For several years in the early 1990s Brian Reid, an employee of the Digital Equipment Corporation, collected and posted on the Internet data on Usenet groups. Each month he used a sampling plan to report estimates of Usenet readership and message traffic for all Usenet groups. Researchers were able to use Reid's data to track growth in overall group membership over time, track the relative popularity of different groups at any one point in time, or identify groups worthy of further study (e.g., Sproull and Faraj, 1995). Reid stopped collecting and reporting Usenet data in June 1995.

12. Reid's study of Usenet traffic is a case in point. One reason Reid stopped collecting Usenet data was that its relevance declined when the World Wide Web was invented and the ratio of quality material to junk declined markedly. Another reason was the evolution of the way Usenet data was distributed, which made the study's measurement techniques increasingly statistically meaningless. However, the ultimate reason for ending the study was not technological, but rather was related to the threat of legal challenges over privacy issues surrounding collection, analysis, and publication of the Usenet data (personal communication, Brian Reid, Digital Equipment Corporation, 1998).

13. This work replicated findings by Hesse et al. (1993) derived from analysis of electronic survey data.

14. GenBank, an annotated collection of publicly available DNA sequences, is part of the International Nucleotide Sequence Database Collaboration, which comprises the DNA Data Bank of Japan, the European Molecular Biology Laboratory data library, and GenBank. More information on GenBank may be found online at <http://www.ncbi.nlm.nih.gov/Web/Genbank/index.html>.

4

Options for Fostering Interdisciplinary Research and Improving Access to Results

Use of information technology within the workplace, the home, and community and other organizations continues to evolve at a rapid pace. Mainframe computers, desktop personal computers, and, more recently, computers linked by both corporate networks and the Internet all have changed the nature of communication. At least in some segments of society, use of computing and communications technology is rapidly becoming a mass phenomenon. The implications are now topics for consideration in a variety of contexts.

Advances in identification and application of social and economic principles basic to understanding interrelationships between information technology and society are important to those who make public policy as well as to those who design, deploy, and use the technology. Yet to help guide such efforts, there is today relatively little interdisciplinary research, as well as insufficient dialog between the technology and social science communities and insufficient contact between the research and public policy communities. Sociologists collaborate relatively infrequently with economists, much less with computer scientists. As interactions at the June 1997 workshop suggested, however, a collaborative approach to problem solving can lead to a clearer understanding of where technology is moving and what the social impacts may be. Few social scientists, for example, possess the detailed technical knowledge required to build useful data sets from the new kinds of data available from the Internet. But social scientists and computer scientists working collaboratively could develop tools and techniques that would make such data logs available to a wider community of social scientists for use in their research.

Based on discussions at the June 1997 workshop and points in the position papers submitted by its participants, the workshop steering committee identified several options for fostering interdisciplinary research and making the results of such research more accessible to the public and policy makers.

4.1 ENCOURAGING INTERDISCIPLINARY STUDIES AND COLLABORATION

Discussion at the June 1997 workshop indicated that there is a great deal of interest in and value to be gained from pursuing interdisciplinary work. Although some regularly held conferences such as the Telecommunications Policy Research Conference or the Aspen Institute Telecommunications Roundtable are essentially interdisciplinary, workshop participants observed that established means of facilitating working relationships among social and computer scientists are currently lacking. Approaches suggested for encouraging fruitful interactions included interdisciplinary workshops, curricula, and fellowships.

- **Interdisciplinary workshops.** Participants in the June 1997 workshop remarked on the value of convening researchers from various relevant field to explore interdisciplinary approaches to studying the impacts of computing and communications. Workshops and summer programs in a number of interdisciplinary areas would be useful in fostering increased collaborative work. At a minimum, workshops bringing together investigators previously funded by the National Science Foundation (NSF) to do joint technology/social science work might be convened. Expanding the focus of such workshops to include people from industry who could comment on non-NSF-funded collaborative research could also prove useful. In addition, it is important for funding agencies to be able to recognize good interdisciplinary work and for industry managers and academic principal investigators to be able to understand some of the management challenges involved—opportunities for cross-communication that interdisciplinary workshops can facilitate.
- **Interdisciplinary curricula.** Workshop participants suggested that serious interdisciplinary work might also be promoted by preparing students directly to engage in it. For example, although computer science curricula already include courses in performance analysis, the systems analyzed are not typically embedded in large-scale social systems, and so joint course development for analysis of the performance of complex systems could produce useful results. This step might be taken initially in the context of postdoctoral training and master's degree programs, given that currently not enough is known to be codified at the textbook level. It was observed that development of interdisciplinary curricula would help to strengthen the interdisciplinary research community as well as raise awareness of interdisciplinary issues in computer science and engineering and social science fields.

- **Interdisciplinary fellowships.** Also noted by workshop participants was the potential value of having graduate or postgraduate fellowships for social scientists interested in becoming familiar with social and economic aspects of information technology and for computer scientists interested in exploring social issues arising from the use of information technology. Such fellowships would encourage the intellectual cross-fertilization and professional networking crucial to fostering productive research relationships.

4.2 FUNDING TO STRENGTHEN INTERDISCIPLINARY RESEARCH

Arising from the June 1997 workshop activities were a number of suggestions for leveraging funding so as to strengthen cross-disciplinary work in computer and social sciences.

- **Evaluation of large technology system research proposals that recognize the value of including an interdisciplinary component.** Some workshop participants expressed the view that behavioral, social, legal, and economic implications of the design and deployment of technology should be considered in evaluating proposals for research on large technology systems. Interdisciplinary research has for some time been a significant component of a number of NSF-sponsored computer science research programs, such as the national supercomputing centers. Increasingly, support for interdisciplinary research has come to include a social science component. For example, the second phase of the multiagency-supported Digital Libraries Initiative[1] includes a "human-centered" research component to investigate both the impacts of digital libraries and ways of enhancing the potential uses of such libraries. Part of this component covers research on the long-term social, behavioral, and economic implications and effects of new digital library capabilities.

- **Synergistic use of major research programs that build or deploy prototypes of computing and communications systems for use by individuals or organizations.** As workshop participants suggested, research programs that field new information technology offer important opportunities to improve understanding of the technology's impacts and to enhance the organizational or societal outcomes of the research. Funding that targets investigating the social impact of new technologies has a precedent in the Department of Energy and National Institutes of Health set-asides of about 3 to 5 percent of the total research budget of the Human Genome Project to fund research and public education on ethical, legal, and social issues (ELSI) related to the project. Although computing and communications research is not centered in a single very large research effort like the Human Genome Project, overall advances in computing and communications are, as workshop participants noted, posing societal challenges of a similar magnitude.

- **Collaboration with private foundations.** In considering ways to strengthen interdisciplinary research, workshop participants observed that government agencies are not the only source of research funding. Private foundations, such as the Kellogg, Markle, Mellon, and Sloan foundations, have become interested in the economic and social impacts of using information technology and have funded some related initiatives. Moreover, important opportunities for collaboration lie at the intersection of basic research questions, which are often addressed by government investment in the development of new scientific and engineering knowledge, and pressing social needs, which the grants and programs of foundations often are designed to address.
- **Collaboration with industry.** Another suggestion arising from the workshop was that researchers increase their collaboration with industry. Industry research covers such social science-related topics as consumer behavior—including who uses computers, how they are used, and related human factors in computer use. Researchers at several major computer companies were asked to estimate the fraction of total research and development spending devoted by their companies to social science research. One researcher separated out social science from other research and development by identifying which units in the research laboratory conducted social science investigations, an approach indicating that about 1 percent of the company's research and development spending was used for social science research. Taking a different approach—conducting a rough assessment of social science content across the research and development portfolio—research managers in two companies estimated spending on social science research there at about 10 percent of the companies' total research budget.

The private sector has funded a number of useful surveys and applied research projects. Several such research programs mentioned in this report are the result of cooperation between private industry and academic researchers. A current example of a major investment in social and economic research, the IBM Institute for Advanced Commerce, was announced in December 1997 and is intended as a research partnership between academia and industry to study electronic commerce and the changing nature of technology, work, and industry structure. The planned partnership, with initial funding of $10 million, stems from IBM's need for more academic research on the Internet's impact on electronic commerce, an area in which IBM is expanding its business (Narisetti, 1997).

As several participants in the workshop indicated, collaboration between industry and academia could benefit both social science researchers and the private sector. For example, industry consortia funding for independent gathering and publishing of basic information and analysis by independent scientists could foster significant advances and ensure fair reporting of results. Pooling of funding through consortia would allow for larger investments than any one corporation might be willing to make on its own. In collaborative projects for development of technology prototypes, both industry and social scientists might benefit from routine inclusion of performance assessment or evaluation up front.

4.3 MAKING THE RESULTS OF INTERDISCIPLINARY RESEARCH MORE ACCESSIBLE

Workshop participants expressed a belief in the need for more effective communication of the results of interdisciplinary social science research on computing and communications issues to both the public and policy makers.

- **Availability of an online guide to current, relevant research.** It was noted that a perceived disconnect between research results and critical legal and policy decision making is perhaps due in part to the dispersed nature of relevant interdisciplinary research. One suggested approach to improving access to pertinent results was to have an online resource (e.g., a Web page) containing headlines and abstracts of policy-relevant social science research, along with pointers to the print and/or online published results. Such a site could also contain regularly updated literature reviews summarizing the state of the art in various areas, as well as directories of specialists in particular areas. With some effort, such a resource could serve as a medium for communication not only among researchers but also with individuals in the policy and business worlds. The bibliography prepared as part of this report could become part of such a resource. An electronic newsletter providing regular updates on research findings would also be useful.
- **Supplemental ways of disseminating research results.** Some at the workshop also pointed out that research results need to be presented in ways that are most useful to policy makers—in some cases written materials alone may not suffice. Interdisciplinary researchers might seek out and take advantage of opportunities to provide testimony at hearings; professional societies might organize specialized briefings for policy makers.

NOTE

1. A research program jointly sponsored by the National Science Foundation, Defense Advanced Research Projects Agency, National Library of Medicine, Library of Congress, National Aeronautics and Space Administration, and National Endowment for the Humanities.

Bibliography

Association for Computing Machinery (ACM), U.S. Public Policy Committee. 1994. *Codes, Keys and Conflicts: Issues in U.S. Crypto Policy.* ACM, New York. Available online from <http://info.acm.org/reports/acm_crypto_study.html>.

Advisory Commission to Study the Consumer Price Index. 1996. *Toward a More Accurate Measure of the Cost of Living: Final report to the Senate Finance Committee, December 4. Advisory Commission to Study the Consumer Price Index.* December 4. Available online from < http://www.stat-usa.gov/BEN/publications.html>.

Aiello, John. 1993. "Computer-Based Work Monitoring: Electronic Surveillance and Its Effects," *Journal of Applied Social Psychology,* 23(7):499-507.

Alberts, David S., and Daniel S. Papp. 1997. *The Information Age: An Anthology on Its Impact and Consequences.* National Defense University Press, Washington, DC.

Allen, Thomas, and Michael S. Scott Morton. 1994. *Information Technology and the Corporation of the 1990s.* Oxford University Press, Oxford, United Kingdom.

American Library Association. 1996. "How Many Libraries Are on the Internet?," technical report, LARC Fact Sheet Number 26. American Library Association, Chicago, IL.

Anderson, Robert H., Tora K. Bikson, Sally Ann Law, and Bridger M. Mitchell. 1995. *Universal Access to E-mail: Feasibility and Societal Implications.* RAND Corporation, Santa Monica, CA. Available online from <http: /www.rand.org/publications/MR/MR650/>.

Arthur, Brian W. 1989. "Competing Technologies, Increasing Returns, and Lock-in by Historical Events," *Economic Journal,* 99(394):116-131.

Arthur, Brian W. 1994. *Increasing Returns and Path Dependence in the Economy.* University of Michigan Press, Ann Arbor, MI.

Arthur, Brian W. 1996. "Increasing Returns and the New World of Business," *Harvard Business Review,* 74(4):100-109.

Attewell, Paul. 1994. "Information Technology and the Productivity Paradox," *Organizational Linkages: Understanding the Productivity Paradox,* Douglas Harris (ed.), National Academy Press, Washington, DC.

Attewell, Paul, and James Rule. 1989. "What Do Computers Do?" *Social Problems,* 36(3):225.

Attewell, Paul, and James Rule. 1994. "Computing and Organizations: What We Know and What We Don't Know," *Social Issues in Computing*, Chuck Huff and Thomas Finholt (eds.). McGraw-Hill, New York.
Attewell, Paul, and Juan Battle. 1997. "Home Computers and School Performance," technical report. Department of Sociology, Graduate School and University Center, City University of New York.
Autor, David, Lawrence Katz, and Alan Krueger. 1997. "Computing Inequality: Have Computers Changed the Labor Market?," NBER Working Paper 5956. National Bureau of Economic Research, Cambridge, MA.
Bailey, Joseph, and Erik Brynjolfsson. 1997. "In Search of 'Friction-Free Markets:' An Exploratory Analysis of Prices for Books, CDs and Software Sold on the Internet," technical report, MIT Internet Commerce Group. Sloan School of Management, Massachusetts Institute of Technology, Cambridge, MA.
Baily, Martin Neil, and Alok K. Chakrabarti. 1988. *Innovation and the Productivity Crisis.* Brookings Institution, Washington, DC.
Baily, Martin Neil, and R.J. Gordon. 1988. "The Productivity Slowdown, Measurement Issues and the Explosion of Computer Power," *Brookings Papers on Economic Activity*, (2):347-431.
Baker, Michael A., and Alan F. Westin. 1972. *Databanks in a Free Society: Computers, Recordkeeping, and Privacy.* Quadrangle Books, New York.
Bakos, Y. 1997. "Reducing Buyer Search Costs: Implications for Electronic Marketplaces," *Management Science*, 42(12):1676-1692.
Bakos, Y., and E. Brynjolfsson. 1997a. "Aggregation and Disaggregation of Information Goods: Implications for Bundling, Site Licensing and Micropayment Systems," *Internet Publishing and Beyond: The Economics of Digital Information and Intellectual Property*, D. Hurley, B. Kahin, and H. Varian (eds.). MIT Press, Cambridge, MA. Available online from <http://ccs.mit.edu/erik/>.
Bakos, Y., and E. Brynjolfsson. 1997b. "Bundling Information Goods: Pricing, Profits and Efficiency," technical report. Massachusetts Institute of Technology, Cambridge, MA. Available online from <http://ccs.mit.edu/erik/>.
Banker, R.D., and R.J. Kauffman. 1988. "Strategic Contributions of Information Technology: An Empirical Study of ATM Networks," *Proceedings of the Ninth International Conference on Information Systems.* Association for Computing Machinery, New York.
Banker, Rajiv, Robert Kauffman, and Mo Adam Mahmood. 1993. *Strategic Information Technology Management: Perspectives on Organizational Growth and Competitive Advantage.* Idea Group Publishing, Harrisburg, PA.
Baruch College-Harris Poll. 1997. "Baruch College-Harris Poll on Internet Advertising," *Business Week*, September 25. Available online from <http://www.businessweek.com/1997/40/b3547025.htm>.
Basu, Susanto, John G. Fernald, and Miles S. Kimball. 1997. "Are Technology Improvements Contradictory?," technical report. Department of Economics, University of Michigan, Ann Arbor.
Baym, Nancy K. 1993. "Interpreting Soap Operas and Creating Community: Inside a Computer-Mediated Fan Culture," *Journal of Folklore Research,* 30:143-176.
Belinfante, Alexander. 1991. "Monitor Report: Telephone Penetration and Household Family Characteristics," Common Carrier Docket No. 80-286. Common Carrier Bureau, Federal Communications Commission, Washington, DC.
Bell, D. 1973. *The Coming of Post-Industrial Society: A Venture in Social Forecasting.* Basic Books, New York.
Bell, David G., Daniel G. Bobrow, Olivier Raiman, and Mark H. Shirley. 1997. "Dynamic Documents and Situated Processes: Building on Local Knowledge in Field Service," *Information and Process Integration in Enterprises: Rethinking Documents*, Toshiro Wakayama, Srikanth Kannapan, Chan Meng Khoong, Sham Navathe, and JoAnne Yates (eds.). Kluwer Academic Publishers, Norwell, MA.

Bender, D.H. 1986. "Financial Impact of Information Processing," *Journal of Management Information Systems*, 3(2):22-32
Benjamin, Robert et al. 1984. "Information Technology: A Strategic Opportunity," *Sloan Management Review*. Massachusetts Institute of Technology, Cambridge, MA.
Berman, Eli, John Bound, and Zvi Griliches. 1994. "Changes in the Demand for Skilled Labor Within U.S. Manufacturing Industries," *Quarterly Journal of Economics*, 109:367-398.
Bernard, H. Russell, Eugene C. Johansen, Peter D. Killworth, Christopher McCarty, Gene A. Shelley, and Scott Robinson. 1990. "Comparing Four Different Methods for Measuring Personal Social Networks," *Social Networks*, 12:179-215.
Berndt, Ernst R., and Zvi Griliches. 1993. "Price Indexes for Microcomputers: An Exploratory Study," pp. 63-93 in *Price Measurements and Their Uses*, M.F. Foss, M.E. Manser, and A.H. Young (eds.). NBER Studies in Income and Wealth, Vol. 57. University of Chicago Press, Chicago, IL.
Berndt, Ernst, and Catherine Morrison. 1995. "High-Tech Capital Formation and Economic Performance in U.S. Manufacturing Industries: An Exploratory Analysis," *Journal of Econometrics*, 65(1):9-43.
Berndt, Ernst R., Iain Cockburn, and Zvi Griliches. 1996. "Pharmaceutical Innovations and Market Dynamics: Tracking Effects on Price Indexes for Anti-depressant Drugs," pp. 133-188 in *Brookings Papers on Economic Activity: Microeconomics*. Brookings Institution, Washington, DC.
Berring, Robert C. 1995. *Finding the Law*, 10th ed. West Publishing, St. Paul, MN.
Besen, Stanley M., and Joseph Y. Farrell. 1994. "Choosing How to Compete: Strategies and Tactics in Standardization," *Journal of Economic Perspectives*, 8:117-131.
Bier, Melinda. 1996. "Personal Empowerment in the Studies of Home Internet Use by Low-Income Families," *Journal of Computing in Education*, 28(5):107-121.
Bikson, T.K., J.D. Goodchilds, L. Huddy, J.D. Eveland, and S. Schneider. 1991. "Networked Information Technology and the Transition to Retirement," technical report. RAND Corporation, Santa Monica, CA.
Bollier, David, and Charles M. Firestone. 1995. *The Future of Community and Personal Identity in the Coming Electronic Culture*. Aspen Institute, Washington, DC.
Bollier, David, and Charles M. Firestone. 1996. *The Future of Electronic Commerce*. Aspen Institute, Washington, DC.
Borko, H., and M.J. Menou. 1983. *Index of Information Utilization Potential: The Final Report of Phase II of the I.U.P. Pilot Project*. UNESCO, Paris.
Bradley, Stephen, Jerry A. Hausman, and Richard L. Nolan. 1993. *Globalisation, Technology, and Competition: The Fusion of Computers and Telecommunications in the 1990s*. Harvard Business School Press, Boston, MA.
Bresnahan, Timothy. 1986. "Measuring the Spillovers from Technical Advance: Mainframe Computers in Financial Services," *American Economic Review*, 76(4):742-755.
Bresnahan, Timothy. 1997. "Computerization and Wage Dispersion: An Analytical Reinterpretation," unpublished technical report. National Bureau of Economic Research Summer Institute, Harvard University, Cambridge, MA.
Brock, Gerald. 1994. *Telecommunication Policy for the Information Age*. Harvard University Press, Cambridge, MA.
Browning, John. 1997. "Cyber View: Universal Disservice," *Scientific American*, 276(February):40.
Bruce, Harry W. 1996. "A User-Oriented View of Internet as Information Infrastructure," Ph.D. dissertation, University of New South Wales, Australia.
Brynjolfsson, Erik. 1993. "The Productivity Paradox of Information Technology: Review and Assessment," *Communications of the ACM*, 36(12):66-76. Available online from <http://ccs.mit.edu/erik.html>.

Brynjolfsson, Erik. 1996a. "Information Assets, Technology, and Organization," *Management Science*, 40(12):1645-1662.

Brynjolfsson, Erik. 1996b. "The Contribution of Information Technology to Consumer Welfare," *Information Systems Research*, 7(3):281-300.

Brynjolfsson, Erik. 1997. "How Do Information Technology and Work Place Organization Affect Labor Demand? Firm-level Evidence," technical report. Sloan School of Management, Massachusetts Institute of Technology, Cambridge, MA.

Brynjolfsson, E., and C. Kemerer. 1996. "Network Externalities in Microcomputer Software: An Econometric Analysis of the Spreadsheet Market," *Management Science*, 42(12):1627-1647.

Brynjolfsson, E., and J.Y. Bakos. 1996. "Bundling Information Goods: Pricing, Profits and Efficiency," technical report. Sloan School of Management, Massachusetts Institute of Technology, Cambridge, MA. Available online from <http://ccs.mit.edu/erik.html>.

Brynjolfsson, Erik, and L. Hitt. 1996. "Paradox Lost? Firm-level Evidence on the Returns to Information Systems Spending," *Management Science*, 42(4):541-558.

Brynjolfsson, Erik, and L. Hitt. 1997. "Computers and Productivity Growth: Firm-level Evidence," technical report. Sloan School of Management, Massachussetts Institute of Technology, Cambridge, MA.

Brynjolfsson, Erik, and Shinkyu Yang. 1996. "Information Technology and Productivity: A Review of the Literature," *Advances in Computers*, 43(February):179-214.

Brynjolfsson, Erik, and Shinkyu Yang. 1997. "The Intangible Costs and Benefits of Computer Investments: Evidence from the Financial Markets," *Proceedings of the International Conference on Information Systems*, Atlanta, Georgia. Available online from <http://ccs.mit.edu/erik/>.

Brynjolfsson, E., A. Renshaw, and M.V. Alstyne. 1997. "The Matrix of Change," *Sloan Management Review*, 38(2):37-54.

Bureau of Labor Statistics. 1994. "Repetitive Tasks Loosen Some Workers' Grip on Safety and Health," technical report. Bureau of Labor Statistics, Washington, DC.

Bureau of Labor Statistics. 1998. "Labor Market Experiences and More: Studying Men, Women and Children Since 1966," technical report, National Longitudinal Surveys. Bureau of Labor Statistics, Washington, DC, January.

Burtless, Gary. 1988. *The Work Response to a Guaranteed Income: A Survey of Experimental Evidence.* Brookings Institution, Washington, DC.

Campbell, Karen E., and Barrett A. Lee. 1991. "Name Generators in Surveys of Personal Networks," *Social Networks*, 13:203-221.

Carter, D.E., and B.S. Baker. 1991. *Concurrent Engineering: The Product Development Environment for the 1990's.* Addison-Wesley, Reading, MA.

Castells, Manuel. 1996. *The Rise of the Network Society.* Basil Blackwell, Cambridge, MA.

Cavoukian, Ann, and Don Tapscott. 1997. *Who Knows: Safeguarding Your Privacy in a Networked World.* McGraw-Hill, New York.

Cerf, Vinton. 1997. "Computer Networking: Global Infrastructure for the 21st Century," *Computing Research: Driving Information Technology and the Information Industry Forward.* Computing Research Association, Washington, DC.

Chandrasekaran, Rajiv. 1998. "Government Finds Information Pays," *Washington Post*, March 9, p. A1.

Chung, Woo Young. 1998. "Why Do People Use the Internet?," doctoral dissertation (in progress), Boston University, Boston, MA.

Coase, R.H. 1959. "The Federal Communications Commission," *Journal of Law and Economics*, 2:26-40.

Coase, Ronald. 1937. "The Nature of the Firm," *Economica*, 4:385-405.

Colebourn, John. 1996. "Net Listings 'Invade Privacy': Victoria Blasted Over Property Info," *Vancouver Province*, September 26, p. A4.

Colwell, Rita. 1996. "Global Climate and Infectious Disease: The Cholera Paradigm," *Science,* 274(December):2025-2031.
CommerceNet/Nielsen Media Research. 1997. "Demographic and Electronic Commerce Study," technical report. CommerceNet/Nielson Media Research, Palo Alto, CA, Spring. Summary available online from <http://www.commerce.net/work/pilot/nielsen_96/press_97.html>.
Committee on Science, Engineering, and Public Policy. National Research Council. 1987. *Technology and Employment, Innovation and Growth in the U.S. Economy,* Richard Cyert and David Mowery (eds.). National Academy Press, Washington, DC.
Computer Intelligence. 1997. "Consumer Technology Index." Computer Intelligence, La Jolla, CA. Available in part online from <http://www.ci.zd.com/news/ctic97.html>.
Computer Science and Telecommunications Board (CSTB), National Research Council. 1991. *Computers at Risk: Safe Computing in the Information Age.* National Academy Press, Washington, DC.
Computer Science and Telecommunications Board (CSTB), National Research Council. 1993. *Computing Professionals: Changing Needs for the 1990s.* National Academy Press, Washington, DC.
Computer Science and Telecommunications Board (CSTB), National Research Council. 1994a. *Information Technology in the Service Society: A 21st-Century Lever.* National Academy Press, Washington, DC.
Computer Science and Telecommunications Board (CSTB), National Research Council. 1994b. *Realizing the Information Future: The Internet and Beyond.* National Academy Press, Washington, DC.
Computer Science and Telecommunications Board (CSTB), National Research Council. 1994c. *Research Recommendations to Facilitate Distributed Work.* National Academy Press, Washington, DC.
Computer Science and Telecommunications Board (CSTB), National Research Council. 1994d. *Rights and Responsibilities of Participants in Networked Communities,* Dorothy Denning and Herbert S. Lin (eds.). National Academy Press, Washington DC.
Computer Science and Telecommunications Board (CSTB), National Research Council. 1995. *Evolving the High Performance Computing and Communications Initiative to Support the Nation's Information Infrastructure.* National Academy Press, Washington, DC.
Computer Science and Telecommunications Board (CSTB), National Research Council. 1996a. *Keeping the U.S. Computer and Communications Industry Competitive: Convergence of Computing, Communications, and Entertainment.* National Academy Press, Washington, DC.
Computer Science and Telecommunications Board, National Research Council. 1996b. *Cryptography's Role in Securing the Information Society,* Kenneth W. Dam and Herbert S. Lin (eds.). National Academy Press, Washington, DC. Available online from <http://www.nap.edu/readingroom/records/0309054753.html>.
Computer Science and Telecommunications Board (CSTB), National Research Council. 1996c. *The Unpredictable Certainty: Information Infrastructure Through 2000.* National Academy Press, Washington, DC.
Computer Science and Telecommunications Board (CSTB), National Research Council. 1997a. *For the Record: Protecting Electronic Health Information.* National Academy Press, Washington, DC.
Computer Science and Telecommunications Board (CSTB), National Research Council. 1997b. *More Than Screen Deep: Toward Every-Citizen Interfaces to the Nation's Information Infrastructure.* National Academy Press, Washington, DC.
Computing Research Association. 1997. "Computing Research: Driving Information Technology and the Information Industry Forward," technical report. Computing Research Association, Washington, DC.

Congressional Budget Office. 1996. *Emerging Electronic Methods for Making Retail Payments.* U.S. Government Printing Office, Washington, DC.
Cook, Thomas. 1975. *Sesame Street Revisited.* Russell Sage, New York.
Costa, Arthur, and Rosemarie Liebmann. 1997. *Supporting the Spirit of Learning: When Process Is Content,* Corwin Press, Thousand Oaks, CA.
Cron, W.L., and M.G. Sobol. 1983. "The Relationship Between Computerization and Performance: A Strategy for Maximizing the Benefits of Computerization," *Information and Management,* 6(3):171-181.
Cuban, V. 1994. "The Promise of the Computer," *Social Issues in Computing,* Chuck Huff and Thomas Finholt (eds.), McGraw-Hill, New York.
Culnan, Mary. 1991. "The Lessons of the Lotus Marketplace: Implications for Consumer Privacy in the 1990's," technical report. School of Business Administration, Georgetown University, Washington, DC.
Cummings, Jonathan, Lee Sproull, and Sara Kiesler. 1998. "Internet Support Groups as an Adjunct to Patient Care," working paper. Boston University, Boston, MA.
Curley, Kathleen, and Philip Pyburn. 1982. "Intellectual Technologies: The Key to Improving White-Collar Productivity," *Sloan Management Review,* 24(1):31-39.
Curtis, Pavel. 1997. "Mudding: Social Phenomena in Text-Based Virtual Realities," *The Culture of the Internet,* Sara Kiesler (ed.). Lawrence Erlbaum Associates, Rahway, NJ.
Cutler, David, and Mark McClellan. 1996. "The Determinants of Technological Change in Heart Attack Treatment," NBER Working Paper 5751. National Bureau of Economic Research, Cambridge, MA, September.
Cutler, David M., Mark McClellan, Joseph P. Newhouse, and Dahlia Remler. 1996. "Are Medical Prices Declining?" NBER Working Paper 5750. National Bureau of Economic Research, Cambridge, MA, September. Available online from <http://www.nber.org>.
Danziger, James N., and Kenneth L. Kraemer. 1986. *People and Computers: The Impacts of Computing on End Users in Organizations.* Columbia University Press, New York.
Danziger, James N., William H. Dutton, Rob Kling, and Kenneth L. Kraemer. 1982. *Computers and Politics: High Technology in American Local Governments.* Columbia University Press, New York.
David, Paul. 1989. *Computer and Dynamo: The Modern Productivity Paradox in a Not-Too-Distant Mirror,* technical report. Center for Economic Policy Research, Stanford University, Palo Alto, CA.
David, Paul A. 1985. "Clio and the Economics of QWERTY," *American Economic Review,* 75(2): 332-337.
David, Paul A. 1990. "The Dynamo and the Computer: An Historical Perspective on the Modern Productivity Paradox," *American Economic Review,* 80(2):335-361.
Denison, Edward. 1985. *Trends in American Economic Growth, 1929-1982.* Brookings Institution, Washington, DC.
Denning, Dorothy, and William E. Baugh, Jr. 1997. *Encryption and Evolving Technologies as Tools of Organized Crime and Terrorism.* National Strategy Information Center's U.S. Working Group on Organized Crime (WGOC), Washington, DC. Available online from <http://www.cosc.georgetown.edu/denning/crypto/oc-abs.html>.
Dertouzos, Michael. 1997. *What Will Be: How the New World of Information Will Change Our Lives.* Harper & Row, San Francisco, CA.
DiNardo, John, and Steve Pischke. 1997. "The Returns to Computer Use Revisited: Have Pencils Changed the Wage Structure Too?," *Quarterly Journal of Economics* 112(1):291-303.
Dordick, H.S., and G. Wang. 1993. *The Information Society.* Sage, Newbury Park, CA.
Drexler, K. Eric. 1991. "Hypertext Publishing and the Evolution of Knowledge," *Social Intelligence,* 1(2):87-120.

Dutton, William. 1996a. *Information and Communication Technologies: Visions and Realities.* Oxford University Press, Oxford, England.

Dutton, William H. 1996b. "Network Rules of Order: Regulating Speech in Public Electronic Fora," *Media, Culture & Society,* 18:269-290.

Earls, John. 1990. *"Social Integration by People with Physical Disabilities: The Development of An Information Technology Model Based on Personal Growth and Achievement,"* Ph.D. thesis, University of Wollongong, Wollongong, Australia.

Eason, Ken. 1988. *Information Technology and Organizational Change.* Taylor & Francis, New York.

Economides, Nicholas, and Charles Himmelberg. 1995. "Critical Mass and Network Size with Applications to the US Fax Market," Discussion Paper No. EC-95-11, Stern School of Business, New York University, New York. Available online from <http://raven.stern.nyu.edu/networks/papers.html>.

Economist, The. 1996. "Bangalore Bytes: Software in India," March 23, Vol. 338, No. 7958, p. 67.

Educational Testing Service. 1997. *Computers and Classrooms: The Status of Technology in U.S. Schools,* policy information report. Policy Information Center, Educational Testing Service, Princeton, NJ.

Eisenstein, Elizabeth L. 1997. "From the Printed Word to the Moving Image," *Social Research,* 64(3):1049-1066.

Electronic Industries Association. 1984-1990. *Consumer Electronics Annual Review.* Consumer Electronics Group, Electronic Industries Association, Washington, DC.

Electronic Industries Association. 1992. *The U.S. Consumer Electronics Industry in Review.* Consumer Electronics Group, Electronic Industries Association, Washington, DC.

Electronic Privacy Information Center. 1996. *Who Owns Personal Information? Anatomy of a Private Case.* Electronic Privacy Information Center, Washington, DC.

Electronic Privacy Information Center. 1997. *Medical Privacy Public Opinion Polls.* Electronic Privacy Information Center, Washington, DC.

Equifax. 1997. *1996 Equifax-Harris Consumer Privacy Survey.* Equifax, United Kingdom.

Feldman, Martha, and James March. 1981. "Information in Organizations as Signal and Symbol," *Administrative Science Quarterly,* 26:171-186.

Finarelli, Margaret. 1997. *GLOBE: A Worldwide Environmental Science and Education Partnership.* GLOBE Program, Washington, DC. Available online from <http://www.globe.gov>.

Finholt, Thomas, and Lee Sproull. 1990. "Electronic Groups at Work," *Organization Science,* 1:41-64.

Fischer, Claude S. 1977. *Networks and Places: Social Relationships in the Urban Setting.* Free Press, New York.

Fischer, Claude S. 1982. *To Dwell Among Friends: Personal Networks in Town and City.* University of Chicago Press, Chicago, IL.

Fischer, Claude S. 1992. *America Calling: A Social History of the Telephone to 1940.* University of California Press, Berkeley.

Forester, V. 1989. *Computers in the Human Context: Information Technology, Productivity, and People.* MIT Press, Cambridge, MA.

Freeman, Chris, Luc Soete, and Umit Efendioglu. 1995. "Diffusion and the Employment Effects of Information and Communication Technology," *International Labor Review* 134(4-5):587-604.

Freeman, Laura. 1996. "Job Creation and the Emerging Home Computer Market," *Monthly Labor Review,* 119(8):46-55.

Friedlander, Amy. 1995a. *Emerging Infrastructure: The Growth of Railroads.* Corporation for National Research Initiatives, Reston, VA.

Friedlander, Amy. 1995b. *Natural Monopoly and Universal Service.* Corporation for National Research Initiatives, Reston, VA.

Friedlander, Amy. 1996. *Power and Light*. Corporation for National Research Initiatives, Reston, VA.

Froomkin, A. Michael. 1996. "Flood Control on the Information Ocean: Living with Anonymity, Digital Cash, and Distributed Databases," technical report. University of Miami School of Law, Miami, FL. Available online from <http://www.law.miami.edu/froomkin/>.

Furlong, Mary. 1989. "An Electronic Community for Older Adults: The Seniornetwork," *Journal of Communication*, 39(3):145-153.

Galbraith, J. 1977. *Organizational Design*. Addison-Wesley, Reading, MA.

Galegher, Jolene, Lee Sproull, and Sara Kiesler. 1998. "Legitimacy, Authority, and Community in Electronic Support Groups," *Written Communication*, forthcoming.

Gay, Martin. 1996. *The New Information Revolution*. ABC-CLIO, Santa Barbara, CA.

Gelsinger, V. 1991. "2001: A Microprocessor Odyssey," *Technology 2000: The Future of Computing and Communications*, Derek Leebaert (ed.). MIT Press, Cambridge, MA.

Glass, G.V., B. McGaw, and M.L. Smith. 1981. *Meta-Analysis in Research*. Sage Publications, Beverly Hills, CA.

Glennan, Thomas K., and Arthur Melmed. 1996. *Fostering the Use of Educational Technology: Elements of a National Strategy*. RAND Corporation, Santa Monica, CA. Available online from <http://www.rand.org/publications/MR/MR650/>.

Goodman, William. 1996. "The Software and Engineering Industries: Threatened by Technological Change?," *Monthly Labor Review*, 119(80):37-45.

Gordon, Robert J. 1990. *The Measurement of Durable Goods Prices*. University of Chicago Press, Chicago, IL.

Gottschalk, Peter. 1997. "Inequality, Income Growth and Mobility: The Basic Facts," *Journal of Economic Perspectives*, 11(2):21-40.

Gottschalk, Peter, and Timothy M. Smeeding. 1997. "Cross-National Comparisons of Earnings and Income Inequality," *Journal of Economic Literature*, 35(2):633-688.

Graham, John. 1976. *Making Computers Pay*. John Wiley & Sons, New York.

Greenan, N., and J. Mairesse. 1996. "Computers and Productivity in France: Some Evidence," NBER Working Paper 5836. National Bureau of Economic Research, Cambridge, MA.

Griliches, Zvi. 1994. "Productivity, R&D, and the Data Constraint," *American Economic Review*, 84(1):1-23.

Harris, Sidney, and Joseph Katz. 1991. "Organizational Performance and Information Technology Investment Intensity in the Insurance Industry," *Organization Science*, 2(3):263-296.

Harris, V. (ed.). 1994. *Organizational Linkages: Understanding the Productivity Paradox*. National Academy Press, Washington, DC.

Hayek, F.A. 1945. "The Use of Knowledge in Society," *American Economic Review*, 35(4):3-17.

Heaviside, Sheila, Tija Tiggins, and Elizabeth Farris. 1997. "Statistics in Brief: Advanced Telecommunications in U.S. Public Elementary and Secondary Schools, Fall 1996," NCES report 97-944. National Center for Educational Statistics, U.S. Department of Education, Washington, DC.

Herring, Thomas. 1996. "The Global Positioning System," *Scientific American*, 274:44-50.

Hesse, Carla. 1991. *Publishing and Cultural Politics in Revolutionary Paris, 1789-1810*. University of California Press, Berkeley, CA.

Hesse, Bradford W., Lee Sproull, Sara Kiesler, and John P. Walsh. 1993. "Returns to Science: Computer Networks in Oceanography," *Communications of the ACM*, 36(8):90-102.

Hitt, L.M., and E. Brynjolfsson. 1997. "Information Technology and Internal Firm Organization: An Exploratory Analysis," *Journal of Management Information Systems*, 14(2):81-101.

Hitt, L.M., and Erik Brynjolfsson. 1995. "Information Technology as a Factor of Production: The Role of Differences Among Firms," *Economics of Innovation and New Technology*, 3(4):183-200.

Hittleman, Daniel R., and Alan J. Simon. 1997. *Interpreting Educational Research: An Introduction for Consumers of Research,* 2nd ed. Prentice-Hall, Englewood Cliffs, NJ.

Hoffman, Donna L., and Thomas P. Novak. 1998. "Bridging the Racial Divide on the Internet," *Science,* 280(5362)(April 17):390-391.

Hoffman, Donna L., Thomas P. Novak, and Alladi Venkatesh. 1997a. "Diversity on the Internet: The Relationship of Race to Access and Usage," technical report. Vanderbilt University, Nashville, TN, October. Available online at <http://www2000.ogsm.vanderbilt.edu/>.

Hoffman, Donna L., Thomas P. Novak, and Marcos A. Peralta. 1997b. "Information Privacy in the Marketspace: Implications for the Commercial Uses of Anonymity on the Web," discussion paper prepared for the conference "Anonymous Communications on the Internet: Uses and Abuses," November 21-23, University of California, Irvine.

Hoffman, Donna L., William Kalsbeek, and Thomas Novak. 1996. "Internet and Web Use in the United States: Baselines for Commercial Development," *Communications of the ACM,* 39(12): 36-47. Available online from <http://www2000.ogsm.vanderbilt.edu/papers/internet_demos_july9_1996.html>.

Howell, David. 1997. "Institutional Failure and the American Worker: The Collapse of Low-Skill Wages," technical report. The Jerome Levy Institute of Bard College, Public Policy Brief, Annandale-on-Hudson, NY.

Howell, David, and Edward Wolf. 1993. "Changes in the Information-Intensity of the U.S. Workplace Since 1950: Has Information Technology Made a Difference?," Technical Report 93-08, C.V. Starr Center for Applied Economics, New York University, New York.

Huff, Charles, Lee Sproull, and Sara Kiesler. 1989. "Computer Communication and Organizational Commitment: Tracing the Relationship in a City Government," *Journal of Applied Social Psychology,* 19:1371-1391.

Huffy, Chuck, and Thomas Finholt. 1994. *Social Issues in Computing.* McGraw-Hill, New York.

Iacono, Suzanne, and Rob Kling. 1996. "Computerization Movements and Tales of Technological Utopianism," pp. 85-105 in *Computerization and Controversy: Value Conflicts and Social Choices,* Charles Dunlop and Rob Kling (eds.). Academic Press, San Diego, CA.

International Data Corporation. 1997a. "Internet Leapfrog: The Impact of the Internet on Global Economic Competition." International Data Corporation, Framingham, MA.

International Data Corporation. 1997b. "New IT Priorities and Technologies for the Year Ahead," technical report. International Data Corporation, Framingham, MA.

Ito, Y. 1981. "The 'Johoka Shakai' Approach to the Study of Communication in Japan," pp. 671-698 in *Mass Communication Review Yearbook,* G.C. Wilhoit and H. de Bock (eds.). Sage Publications, Beverly Hills, CA.

Johnson, Frank, and George Stafford. 1998. "Technology Regimes and the Distribution of Real Wages," *Microfoundations of Economic Growth: A Schumpeterian Perspective,* Gunnar Eliasson, Chris Green, and Charles R. McCann, Jr. (eds.). University of Michigan Press, Ann Arbor, MI, forthcoming,

Jorgenson, Dale, and Kevin Stiroh. 1995. "Computers and Growth," *Economics of Innovation and New Technology,* 3:295-316.

Jussawalla, M., D.M. Lamberton, and N.D. Karunaratne. 1988. *The Cost of Thinking: Information Economies of Ten Pacific Countries.* Ablex Publishing, Norwood, NJ.

Kahin, Brian, and Charles Nesson. 1997. *Borders in Cyberspace.* MIT Press, Cambridge, MA.

Kahin, Brian, and James Keller, eds. 1997. *Coordinating the Internet.* MIT Press, Cambridge, MA.

Kahn, Alfred E. 1970. *The Economics of Regulation: Principles and Institutions. Volume 1: Economic Principles.* John Wiley & Sons, New York.

Kaminer, Noam. 1997. "Internet Use and Scholars' Productivity," Ph.D. dissertation, University of California, Berkeley. Available online from <http://www.sims.berkeley.edu/~noam/>.

Kang, Jerry, Radhika Karmarkar, and Lis Leidig. 1995. *Privacy and the NII*. National Telecommunications and Information Administration, Washington, DC. Available online from <http://www.ntia.doc.gov/ntiahome/policy/privwhitepaper.html>.

Kaplan, R. 1989. "Management Accounting for Advanced Technological Environments," *Science*, 245:819-823.

Karnow, Curtis E.A. 1994. "The Encrypted Self: Fleshing Out the Rights of Electronic Personalities," *Conference on Computers, Freedom, and Privacy*. Artech Publishers, London.

Karunaratne, N.D., and A. Cameron. 1981. "A Comparative Analysis of the Information Economy in Developed and Developing Countries," *Journal of Information Science*, 3:113-127.

Katz, Elizabeth, R. Grant Tate, and William A. Weimer. 1995. *Survey of Telematics for Education and Training: United States, Canada, and Australia, Volume 2*. European Association of Distance Teaching Universities, Heerleen, The Netherlands.

Katz, James E., and Philip Aspden. 1997a. *Internet Dropouts: The Invisible Group*. Bellcore, Morristown, NJ.

Katz, James E., and Philip Aspden. 1997b. *Motivations for and Barriers to Internet Usage: Results of a National Public Opinion Survey*. Bellcore, Morristown, NJ.

Katz, Michael L., and Carl Shapiro. 1994. "Systems Competition and Network Effects," *Journal of Economic Perspectives*, 8:93-116.

Katz, R.L. 1988. *The Information Society*. Praeger, New York.

Kedzie, Christopher. 1997. "A Brave New World or a New World Order?," *The Culture of the Internet*, Sara Kiesler (ed.). Lawrence Erlbaum Associates, Rahway, NJ.

Keen, Peter. 1995. *Every Manager's Guide to Information Technology*, 2nd edition. Harvard Business School Press, Boston, MA.

Kees, C.P., M. Knipscheer, and Toni C. Antonucci (eds.). 1990. *Social Network Research: Substantive Issues and Methodological Questions*. Swets & Zeitlanger, Amsterdam.

Kehoe, Colleen, Jim Pitkow, and Kimberly Morton. 1997. "GVU's Eighth WWW User Survey Report," technical report. Graphics, Visualization, and Usability Center, Georgia Institute of Technology, Atlanta, GA, December. Available online from <http://www.gvu.gatech.edu/user_surveys/>.

Keyes, Robert. 1993. "The Future of the Transistor," *Scientific American*, 268(6):70-76.

Khosrowpur, Mehdi. 1994. *Information Technology and Organizations: Challenges of New Technologies*. Idea Group Publishing, Harrisburg, PA.

Kiesler, Sara, and Thomas Finholt. 1994. "The Mystery of RSI," *Social Issues in Computing*, Chuck Huff and Thomas Finholt (eds.). McGraw-Hill, New York.

Kiesler, Sara, Robert Kraut, Tridas Mukhopadhyay, and William Scherlis. 1997. "Homenet Overview: Recent Results from a Field Trial of Residential Internet Use," technical report. Carnegie Mellon University, Pittsburgh, PA. Available online from <http://homenet.andrew.cmu.edu/progress/research.html>.

King, John Leslie, Rebecca E. Grinter, and Jeanne M. Pickering. 1997. "The Rise and Fall of Netville: The Saga of a Cyberspace Construction Boomtown in the Great Divide," *The Culture of the Internet*, Sara Kiesler (ed.). Lawrence Erlbaum Associates, Rahway, NJ.

Kling, Rob. 1996. "Computerization at Work," *Computerization and Controversy: Value Conflicts and Social Choices*, 2nd ed. Academic Press, San Diego, CA.

Kling, Rob, and Tom Jewett. 1994. "The Social Design of Worklife with Computers and Networks: An Open Natural Systems Perspective," *Advances in Computers*, volume 39, Marshall Yovits (ed.). Academic Press, Orlando, FL.

Kling, V. 1996. "The Centrality of Organizations in the Computerization of Society," *Computerization and Controversy: Value Conflicts and Social Choices*, 2nd ed. Academic Press, San Diego, CA.

Knight, Charles. 1854. *The Old Printer and the Modern Press*. John Murray, London.

Kollock, Peter, and Marc Smith. 1996. "Managing the Virtual Commons: Cooperation and Conflict in Computer Communities," *Computer-Mediated Communication,* Susan Herring (ed.). John Benjamins, Amsterdam.

Korzick Garmer, Amy, and Charles M. Firestone. 1996. *Creating a Learning Society: Initiatives for Education and Technology.* Aspen Institute, Washington, DC. Available online from < http://www.aspeninst.org/dir/polpro/csp/Abstracts/CrLearn.html >

Kozol, Jonathan. 1991. *Savage Inequalities: Children in America's Schools.* Crown Publishers, New York.

Kranerg, Melvin. 1989. "IT as Revolution," *Computers in the Human Context: Information Technology, Productivity, and People,* Tom Forester (ed.). MIT Press, Cambridge, MA.

Kraut, Robert, William Scherlis, Tridas Mukhopadhyay, Jane Manning, and Sara Kiesler. 1996. "The HomeNet Field Trial of Residential Internet Services," *Communications of the ACM,* 39:55-65.

Kreuger, Alan. 1993. "How Computers Have Changed the Wage Structure: Evidence from Microdata, 1984-1989," *Quarterly Journal of Economics,* 108:33-60.

Kulik, Chen-Lin, and James A. Kulik. 1991. "Effectiveness of Computer-Based Instruction: An Updated Analysis," *Computers in Human Behavior,* 7:75-94.

Kuo, E.C.Y. 1989. "Trends of Information in Singapore," *Symposium on International Technology and Singapore Society: Trends, Policies and Applications.* Singapore University Press, National University of Singapore, Singapore.

Landauer, Thomas K. 1995. *The Trouble with Computers: Usefulness, Usability, and Productivity.* MIT Press, Cambridge, MA.

Lardner, James. 1987. *Fast Forward.* W.W. Norton, New York.

Lau, Lawrence J., and Ichiro Tokutsu. 1992. "The Impact of Computer Technology on the Aggregate Productivity of the United States: An Indirect Approach," unpublished paper. Stanford University, Palo Alto, CA, August.

Laudon, Kenneth C. 1996. "Markets and Privacy," *Communications of the ACM,* 39(9):992-104.

Leavitt, Harold J., and Thomas L. Whisler. 1958. "Management in the 1980s," *Harvard Business Review,* 36(6):41-48.

Leebaert, Derek. 1991. *Technology 2001: The Future of Computing and Communications.* MIT Press, Cambridge, MA.

Leiner, Barry M. et al. 1997. *A Brief History of the Internet, Version 3.1,* revised February 20. Available online from <http://www.isoc.org/internet/history/brief.html>.

Lesk, Michael. 1997. *Practical Digital Libraries: Books, Bytes, and Bucks.* Morgan Kauffman, San Francisco.

Levy, Frank, and R. Murnane. 1997. "With What Skills Are Computers a Complement?," technical report. National Bureau of Economic Research, Cambridge, MA.

Levy, Frank, and Richard J. Murnane. 1992. "U.S. Earnings Levels and Earnings Inequality: A Review of Recent Trends and Proposed Explanations," *Journal of Economic Literature,* 30:1333-1381.

Lichtenberg, Frank R. 1995. "The Output Contributions of Computer Equipment and Personnel: A Firm-Level Analysis," *Journal of Economics of Innovation and New Technology,* 3:201-217.

Lohr, Steve. 1997. "Gates to Aid Libraries, in Footsteps of Carnegie," *New York Times,* June 24, p. C1.

Louis Harris & Associates and Alan F. Westin. 1997. "Commerce, Communications, and Privacy Online," American Business Information Service, Hackensack, NJ.

Luker, Jr., William, and Donald Lyons. 1997. "Employment Shifts in High Technology Industries, 1988-96," *Monthly Labor Review,* 120(6):12-25.

Lyman, Peter. 1996. "Books, Bricks, & Bytes," *Daedalus,* 122(4):109-110.

Machlup, F. 1962. *The Production and Distribution of Knowledge in the United States.* Princeton University Press, Princeton, NJ.

Machlup, Fritz. 1982. *Knowledge: Its Creation, Distribution, and Economic Significance*. Princeton University Press, Princeton, NJ.

Malone, T.W. 1987. "Modeling Coordination in Organizations and Markets," *Management Science*, 33(1):1717-1332.

Malone, Thomas W., and Kevin Crowston. 1994. "The Interdisciplinary Study of Coordination," *ACM Computing Surveys*, 26(1):87-120. Available online from <http://ccs.mit.edu/CCSWP157.html>.

Malone, Thomas, JoAnne Yates, and Robert Benjamin. 1987. "Electronic Markets and Electronic Hierarchies," *Communications of the ACM*, 30(6):484-497.

Malone, Thomas W., Kevin Crowston, Jintae Lee, Brian Pentland, Chrysanthos Dellarocas, George Wyner, John Quimby, Charley Osborne, and Avi Bernstein. 1997. "Tools for Inventing Organizations: Toward a Handbook of Organizational Processes," Technical Report 198. MIT Center for Coordination Science, Massachusetts Institute of Technology, Cambridge, MA.

Marien, Michael. 1986. "125 Impacts of New Information Technologies," *Future Survey Annual*. World Future Society, Bethesda, MD.

Mark, Jerome. 1982. "Measuring Productivity in Service Industries," *Monthly Labor Review*, 105:3-8.

Mark, Jerome S. 1987. "Technological Change and Employment: Some Results from BLS Research," *Monthly Labor Review*, 110:26-29.

Markus, M.L. 1987. "Toward a Critical Mass Theory of Interactive Media—Universal Access, Interdependence and Diffusion," *Communication Research*, 14(5):491-511.

Markus, M. Lynne, and Daniel Robey. 1988. "Information Technology and Organizational Change: Causal Structure in Theory and Research," *Management Science*, 34(5):583-598.

Marsden, Peter. 1987. "Core Discussion Networks of Americans," *American Sociological Review*, 52:122-131.

Marsden, Peter V. 1990. "Network Data and Measurement," *Annual Review of Sociology*, 16:435-463.

Martin, Michael. 1996. "When Info Worlds Collide," *Fortune*, 134(8):130-133.

Marvin, Lee-Ellen. 1996. "Spoof, Spam, Lurk and Lag: The Aesthetics of Text-Based Virtual Realities," *Journal of Computer-Mediated Communication*, 1(2). Available online from <http://www.usc.edu/dept/annenberg/jcmc>.

McAfee, R.P., J. McMillan, and M.D. Whinston. 1989. "Multiproduct Monopoly, Commodity Bundling, and Correlation of Values," *Quarterly Journal of Economics*, 114:371-384.

McCall, William. 1996. "Man Who Gave Out Vehicle Records on the Net Forced off by Complaints," Associated Press, August 8.

McConnell, Sheila. 1996. "The Role of Computers in Reshaping the Work Force," *Monthly Labor Review*, 119(8):3-5.

McKinsey and Company. 1995. *Connecting K-12 Schools to the Information Superhighway*. U.S. Advisory Council on the National Information Infrastructure, Washington, DC.

McMillan, John. 1994. "Selling Spectrum Rights," *Journal of Economic Perspectives*, 8(3):145-162.

McNeil, Barbara J., and Karyn Nelson. 1990. "Meta-Analysis of Interactive Video Instruction: A 10-Year Review of Achievement Effects," Technical Report ED321761. Educational Research Information Center (ERIC), U.S. Department of Education, Washington, DC.

Melmed, Arthur (ed.). 1995. *The Costs and Effectiveness of Educational Technology: Proceedings of a Workshop*. RAND Corporation, Santa Monica, CA.

Memmott, Carol. 1997. "History Takes on Net Proportions," *USA Today*, June Bonus Issue.

Metcalfe, R. 1997. "Pollinate Lets You Rent the Software You Need for Just the Right Amount of Time," *Infoworld*, 19(23):111.

Milgrom, Paul. 1989. "Auctions and Bidding: A Primer," *Journal of Economic Perspectives*, 3(3):3-32.

Milgrom, Paul, and John Roberts. 1980. "The Economics of Modern Manufacturing: Technology, Strategy and Organization," *American Economic Review*, 80(3):511-528.

Moris, Francisco. 1996. "Semiconductors: The Building Blocks of the Information Revolution," *Monthly Labor Review,* 119(8):12-17.
Morrison, Catherine, and Ernst Berndt. 1990. "Assessing the Productivity of Information Technology Equipment in the US Manufacturing Industries," Technical Report 3582. National Bureau of Economic Research Working, Cambridge, MA.
Morrison, Ian, and Greg Schmid. 1994. *Future Tense: The Business Realities of the Next Ten Years.* William Morrow and Company, New York.
Mueller, Milton. 1996. *Universal Service: Interconnection, Competition, and Monopoly in the Making of the American Telephone System.* MIT Press, Cambridge, MA.
Mueller, Milton. 1997. "Universal Service and the Telecommunications Act: Myth Made Law," *Communications of the ACM,* 40(3):39-48.
Mueller, Milton, and Jorge Schement. 1996. "Universal Service from the Bottom Up: A Study of Telephone Penetration in Camden, New Jersey," *The Information Society.* Taylor & Francis, New York.
Murnane, Richard J., and Frank Levy. 1996. "Teaching the New Basic Skills: Principles for Educating Children to Thrive in a Changing Economy." *Publishers Weekly,* 243(26):38.
Murphy, Kevin M., and Finss Welch. 1993. "Lessons from Empirical Labor Economics: 1972-1992. Inequality in Relative Wages," *American Economic Review,* 83(2):104-109.
Narin, Francis, Kimberly S. Hamilton, and Dominic Olivastro. 1997. "Public and Private Research," technical report. CHI Research, Haddon Heights, NJ.
Narisetti, Raju. 1997. "IBM Planning to Research Internet Trade," *Wall Street Journal,* December 5, p. B10.
Nass, Clifford, and Byron Reeves. 1996. *The Media Equation: How People Treat Computers, Television and New Media Like Real People and Places.* Cambridge University Press, Cambridge, England.
Nass, Clifford, Jonathan Steur, and Ellen R. Tauber. 1994. "Computers Are Social Actors," *Proceedings of CHI 94.* ACM Press, New York.
National Center for Education Statistics. 1997. *Advanced Telecommunications in U.S. Public Elementary and Secondary Schools, Fall 1996,* Statistics in Brief, NCES 97-944. Office of Educational Research and Improvement, National Center for Education Statistics, Department of Education, Washington, DC.
National Information Infrastructure Advisory Council (NIIAC). 1995. "A Nation of Opportunity: A Final Report of the United States Advisory Council on the National Information Infrastructure," technical report. U.S. Government Printing Office, Washington, DC.
National Telecommunications and Information Administration (NTIA). 1995. "Falling Through the Net: A Survey of the 'Have Nots' in Rural and Urban America," technical report. NTIA, Department of Commerce, Washington, DC. Available online from <http://www.ntia.doc.gov/ntiahome/fallingthru.html>.
National Telecommunications and Information Administration (NTIA). 1997. "Privacy and Self-Regulation in the Information Age." NTIA, Department of Commerce, Washington, DC. Available online from <http://www.ntia.doc.gov/reports/privacy/privacy_rpt.htm>.
Netcraft. 1996. *The Netcraft Web Server Survey.* Netcraft Ltd., Bath, United Kingdom. Available online from <http://www.netcraft.com/survey>.
Netcraft. 1997. *The Netcraft Web Server Survey.* Netcraft Ltd., Bath, United Kingdom. Available online from <http://www.netcraft.com/survey>.
Network Wizards. 1998. *Internet Domain Survey, January 1998.* Network Wizards, Menlo Park, CA. Available online from <http://www.nw.com/>.
Nordhaus, William. 1969. *Invention, Growth, and Welfare.* MIT Press, Cambridge, MA.
Novak, T.P., and D.L. Hoffman. 1997. "New Metrics for New Media: Toward the Development of Web Measurement Standards," *World Wide Web Journal,* 2(1):213-246.

Noyelle, T. 1990. *Skills, Wages, and Productivity in the Service Sector.* Westview Press, Boulder, CO.
Nye, David E. 1997. "Shaping Communication Networks: Telegraph, Telephone, Computer," *Social Research,* 64(3):1067-1091
Office of Technology Assessment. 1987. *The Electronic Supervisor: New Technology, New Tensions,* OTA-CIT-333. U.S. Government Printing Office, Washington, DC.
Office of Technology Assessment. 1995. *Teachers and Technology: Making the Connection.* U.S. Government Printing Office, Washington, DC.
Oliner, Stephen D., and Daniel E. Sichel. 1994. "Computers and Output Growth Revisited: How Big Is the Puzzle?," *Brookings Papers on Economic Activity,* 2:273-334.
Oppenheimer, Todd. 1997. "The Computer Delusion," *Atlantic Monthly* 280(1):45-58.
Orlikowski, W.J. 1992. "Learning from Notes: Organizational Issues in Groupware Implementation," *Conference on Computer Supported Cooperative Work,* J. Turner and R. Kraut (eds.). Association for Computing Machinery, Toronto.
Orr, Julian E. 1990. "Talking About Machines: An Ethnography of a Modern Job," Ph.D. thesis, Cornell University, Ithaca, New York.
Park, R.E. 1916. "The City: Suggestions for the Investigation of Human Behavior in the Urban Environment," *American Journal of Sociology,* 20:577-612.
Park, R.E. 1955. *Society.* Free Press, Glencoe, IL.
Parks, Malcom R. 1996. "Making Friends in Cyberspace," Journal of Computer Mediated Communication, 1(4):80. Available online from <http://www.ascusc.org/jcmc/>.
Pelgrum, W.J., Janssen Reiner, and T.J. Plomp. 1993. *Schools, Teachers, Students, and Computers: A Cross-National Perspective.* International Association for the Evaluation of Educational Achievement, Amsterdam.
Perez, Carlota. 1983. "Structural Change and Assimilation of New Technologies in the Economic and Social System," *Futures,* 15(5):357-375.
Pool, Ithiel De Sola. 1984. *Communications Flows: A Census in the United States and Japan.* North-Holland, Amsterdam.
Porat, M.U. 1977. *Information Economy: Definition and Measurement.* OT Special Publication 77:12. U.S. Department of Commerce, Washington, DC.
Porter, Michael, and Victor Millar. 1985. "How Information Gives You Competitive Advantage," *Harvard Business Review.* Harvard University Press, Cambridge, MA.
President's Committee of Advisors on Science and Technology (PCAST). 1997. *Report to the President on the Use of Technology to Strengthen K-12 Education in the United States,* President's Committee of Advisors on Science and Technology, Panel on Educational Technology, Washington, DC. Available online from <http://www.whitehouse.gov/WH/EOP/OSTP/NSTC/PCAST/k-12ed.html>.
Press, Larry. 1997. "Tracking the Global Diffusion of the Internet," *Communications of the ACM,* 40(11):95-100.
Price Waterhouse. 1997. 1997 Price Waterhouse Consumer Technology Survey, Price Waterhouse's Entertainment, Media and Communications (ECM) Group, New York. (For information online about the ECM group, see <http://www.pw.com/us/2d96.htm>.)
Quarterman, John S. 1997. "1997 Users and Hosts of the Internet and the Matrix," *Matrix News,* 7(1).
Radner, R., 1992. "Hierarchy: The Economics of Managing," *Journal of Economic Literature,* 30:1382-1415.
Regan, Priscilla. 1995. *Legislating Privacy.* University of North Carolina Press, Chapel Hill, NC.
Resnick, Paul, and Hal R. Varian. 1997. "Introduction to Recommender Systems," *Communications of the ACM,* 40(3):56-58.
Resnick, Paul, and Jim Miller. 1996. "PICS: Internet Access Controls Without Censorship," *Communications of the ACM,* 39(10):87-93. Available online from <http://www.w3c.org/PICS>.
Rogers, Everett. 1995. *Diffusion of Innovation.* Free Press, New York.

Rohlfs, Jeffrey. 1974. "A Theory of Interdependent Demand for a Communications Service," *Bell Journal of Economics*, 5(1):16-37.
Romm, Celia T., and Nava Pliskin. 1997. "Toward a Virtual Politicking Model," *Communications of the ACM*, 40(11):95-100.
Rosenberg, Richard. 1997. *The Social Impact of Computers*, 2nd ed. Academic Press, San Diego, CA.
Rowe, Susan A. 1994. "Management Involvement: A Key Element in Preventing Musculoskeletal Injuries in Visual Display Unit Users in Australia," *Social Issues in Computing*, Chuck Huff and Thomas Finholt (eds.). McGraw-Hill, New York.
Rubin, Andee. 1996. "Educational Technology: Support for Inquiry-Based Learning," *Technology Infusion and School Change: Perspectives and Practices*, Model Schools Partnership Research Monograph. Transportation Emergency Rescue Committee, Cambridge, MA.
Ryan, Alice. 1991. "Metaanalysis of Achievement Effects of Microcomputer Applications in Elementary Schools," *Educational Administration Quarterly*, 27(2):161-184.
Sah, R.K., and J.E. Stiglitz. 1986. "The Architecture of Economic Systems: Hierarchies and Polyarchies," *American Economic Review*, 76(4):716-727.
Schement, J.R. 1990. "Porat, Bell, and the Information Society Reconsidered: The Growth of Information Work in the Early Twentieth Century," *Information Processing and Management*, 26(4):449-465.
Schmalensee, R.L. 1984. "Gaussian Demand and Commodity Bundling," *Journal of Business*, 57:S211-S230.
Scientific American. 1997. "The Internet: Bringing Order from Chaos," *Scientific American*, 276(3):50-82. Available online from <http://www.sciam.com/0397issue/0397intro.html>.
Scott, John T., and Albert N. Link. 1997. "Assessing the Infrastructural Needs of a Technology-Based Service Sector: A New Approach to Technology Policy Planning," *Best Practices in Technology and Innovation Policy*, Wolfgang Polt (ed.). Organisation for Economic Cooperation and Development, Paris.
Shapiro, Carl, and Hal Varian. 1997. "U.S. Government Information Policy," technical report. School of Information Management and Systems, University of California, Berkeley. Available online at <http://www.sims.berkeley.edu/~hal/Papers/policy/policy.html>.
Shapiro, Carl, and Hal Varian. 1998. *InfoTactics: Competitive Strategy for the Information Economy*. Harvard Business School Press, Cambridge, MA.
Shy, Oz. 1998. "The Economics of Software Protection and Other Media," *Economics of Digital Information and Intellectual Property*, Debora Hurley, Brian Kahin, and Hal Varian (eds.). MIT Press, Cambridge, MA.
Sichel, Andrew. 1997. *The Computer Revolution: An Economic Perspective*. Brookings Institution Press, Washington, DC.
Smart Valley. 1994. "Smart Valley Telecommuting Guide." Smart Valley, San Mateo, CA. Available online from <http://www.svi.org/>.
Smythe, D. 1977. "Communications: Blindspot of Western Marxism," *Canadian Journal of Social and Political Theory*, 1(3):1-27.
Smythe, D. 1981. *Dependency Road: Communication, Capitalism, Consciousness, and Canada*. Ablex, Norwood, NJ.
Solow, Robert. 1957. "Technological Change and the Aggregate Production Function," *Review of Economics and Statistics*, 39:312.
Solow, Robert M. 1987. "We'd Better Watch Out," *New York Times Book Review*, July 12, , p. 36.
Spence, Michael, and Bruce Owen. 1977. "Television Programming, Monopolistic Competition, and Welfare," *Quarterly Journal of Economics*, 91(1):103-126.
Sproull, Lee, and Sara B. Kiesler. 1992. *Corrections: New Ways of Working in the Networked Organization*. MIT Press, Cambridge, MA.

Sproull, Lee, and Samer Faraj. 1995. "Atheism, Sex, and Databases: The Net as a Social Technology," pp. 62-81 in *Public Access to the Internet*, Brian Kahin and James Keller (eds.). MIT Press, Cambridge, MA.

Sproull, Lee, Mani Subramani, Sara Kiesler, Janet H. Walker, and Keith Waters. 1996. "When the Interface Is a Face," *Human-Computer Interaction*, 11:97-124.

Stefik, Marc. 1995. "Letting Loose the Light," technical report. Xerox Palo Alto Research Center, Palo Alto, CA.

Stewart, Thomas. 1997. *Intellectual Capital*. Harvard Business School Press, Boston, MA.

Stipp, David. 1997. "The Idol of the Geeks, What They're Reading in the Computer Biz," *Fortune*, March 3, p. 40. Available online from <http://www.pathfinder.com/@@y1yRBQUAcc@UN2Gz/fortune/1997/970303/fir1.html>.

Stoll, Clifford. 1995. *Silicon Snake Oil. Second Thoughts on the Information Highway*. Doubleday, New York.

Sudweeks, Fay, Margaret McLaughlin, and Sheizaf Rafaeli (eds.). 1997. *Network and Netplay: Virtual Groups on the Internet*. AAAI/MIT Press, Cambridge, MA.

Tapscott, Don. 1996. *The Digital Economy: Promise and Peril in the Age of Networked Intelligence*. McGraw-Hill, New York.

Taylor, Lester. 1994. *Telecommunications Demand in Theory and Practice*. Kulwer Academic Publishers, Boston, MA.

Television Bureau of Advertising. 1991. *TV and Cable Factbook: The Authoritative Reference for the Television, Cable & Electronics Industries*. No. 60. Warren Publishing, Washington, DC.

Thurow, Lester. 1987. "Economic Paradigms and Slow American Productivity Growth," *Eastern Economic Journal*, 13:333-343.

Turkle, Sherry. 1984. *The Second Self: Computers and the Human Spirit*. Simon & Schuster, New York.

Turkle, Sherry. 1995a. "Computational Technologies and Images of the Self," *Life on the Screen: Identity in the Age of the Internet*. Simon & Schuster, New York.

Turkle, Sherry. 1995b. *Life on the Screen: Identity in the Age of the Internet*. Simon & Schuster, New York.

Tyack, David B., and Larry Cuban. 1995. *Tinkering Toward Utopia: A Century of Public School Reform*. Harvard University Press, Cambridge, MA.

U.S. Bureau of the Census. 1975. *Historical Statistics of the United States*, Bicentennial Edition, Series R190. U.S. Government Printing Office, Washington, DC.

U.S. Bureau of the Census. 1986, 1990, 1991, 1992. *Statistical Abstract*. U.S. Department of Commerce, Washington, DC.

U.S. Bureau of the Census. 1993. *Current Population Survey*. U.S. Department of Commerce, Washington, DC.

U.S. Department of Labor. 1991. *What Work Requires of Schools: A SCANS Report for America 2000*. U.S. Department of Labor, Washington DC.

U.S. Department of Labor. 1992. *Learning and Living: A Blueprint for High Performance*. U.S. Department of Labor, Washington DC.

U.S. Senate. 1995. "Cyberporn and Children: The Scope of the Problem, the State of the Technology, and the Need for Congressional Action," J104-36, 104th Congress, hearing before the Committee on the Judiciary, Washington, DC.

van Alstyne, Marshall. 1997. "The State of Network Organization: A Survey in Three Frameworks," *Journal of Organizational Computing*, 7(3).

van der Poel, Mart G.M. 1993. "Personal Support Networks," *Social Networks*, 15:49-70.

Varian, Hal R. 1995a. *Pricing Information Goods*. Harvard University Press, Cambridge, MA.

Varian, Hal R. 1995b. "The Information Economy, How Much Will Two Bits Be Worth in the Digital Marketplace?," *Scientific American*, 30(1)(September):200-201. Subsequently published in 1996 in *Educom Review*, (January/February):44-46.

Varian, Hal R. 1996a. "Differential Pricing and Efficiency," *First Monday*. Available online from <http://www.firstmonday.dk/issues/issue2/different/>.

Varian, Hal R. 1996b. "Economic Aspects of Personal Privacy," technical report. University of California, Berkeley. Available online from <http://www.sims.berkeley.edu/~hal/people/hal/papers.html>.

Varian, Hal R. 1996c. *Intermediate Microeconomics*. W.W. Norton, New York.

Varian, Hal R. 1997a. "Buying, Sharing and Renting Information Goods," technical report. School of Information Management and Systems, University of California, Berkeley. Available online from <http://www.sims.berkeley.edu/~hal>.

Varian, Hal R. 1997b. "Economic Issues Facing the Internet," *The Internet as Paradigm*, Charles Firestone (ed.). Aspen Institute, Washington, DC. Available online from <http://www.sims.berkeley.edu/~hal/people/hal/papers.html>.

Varian, Hal R., and Richard Roehl. 1996. "Circulating Libraries and Video Rental Stores," technical report. University of California, Berkeley. Available online from <http://www.sims berkeley.edu/~hal>.

Venkatesh, Alladi. 1996. "Computers and Other Interactive Technologies for the Home," *Communications of the ACM*, 39(12):47-54.

Vickrey, William. 1961. "Counterspeculation, Auctions and Competitive Sealed Tenders," *Journal of Finance*, 16(1):8-37.

Walsh, John P., and Todd Bayma. 1997. "Computer Networks and Scientific Work," pp. 385-406 in *The Culture of the Internet*, Sara Kiesler (ed.). Lawrence Erlbaum Associates, Rahway, NJ.

Warnke, Jacqueline. 1996. "Computer Manufacturing: Change and Competition," *Monthly Labor Review*, 119(8):18-30.

Webster, Frank. 1997. "What Information Society?," *The Information Age: An Anthology on Its Impact and Consequences*, David S. Alberts and Daniel S. Papp (eds.). National Defense University Press, Washington, DC.

Weill, Peter. 1992. "The Relationship Between Investment in Information Technology and Firm Performance: A Study of the Valve Manufacturing Sector," *Information Systems Research*, 3(4):307-333.

Weiss, Laura. 1996. *Buildings, Books, and Bytes: Libraries and Communities in the Digital Age: a Report on the Public's Opinion of Library Leaders' Visions for the Future*. Benton Foundation, Washington, DC. Available online from <http://www.benton.org/Library/Kellogg/buildings.html>.

Wellman, Barry. 1979. "The Community Question," *American Journal of Sociology*, 84:1201-1231.

Wellman, Barry. 1997. "An Electronic Group Is Virtually a Social Network," *The Culture of the Internet*, Sara Kiesler (ed.). Lawrence Erlbaum Associates, Hillsdale, NJ.

Wellman, Barry, and David B. Tindall. 1993. "How Telephone Networks Connect Social Networks," *Progress in Communication Sciences*, Volume XII, W.D. Richards, Jr., and George A. Barnett (eds.). Ablex, Norwood, NJ.

Wellman, Barry, and Milena Gulia. 1997. "Net Surfers Don't Ride Alone: Virtual Communities as Communities," *Communities in Cyberspace*, Peter Kollock and Marc Smith (eds.). University of California Press, Berkeley, CA.

Wellman, Barry, and Scot Worley. 1990. "Different Strokes from Different Folks: Community Ties and Social Support," *American Journal of Sociology*, 96(3):558-588.

Wellman, Barry, Janet Salaff, Dimitrina Dimitrova, Laura Garton, Milena Gulia, and Caroline Haythornthwaite. 1996. "Computer Networks as Social Networks," *Annual Review of Sociology*, 22:213-238.

Westin, Alan F., and Louis Harris & Associates. 1981. *The Dimensions of Privacy*. Garland, New York.

Wiley, Malcolm M., and Stuart A. Rice. 1933. *Communication Agencies and Social Life*. McGraw-Hill, New York.

Wilson, Diane D. 1995. "IT Investment and Its Productivity Effects: An Organizational Sociologist's Perspective on Directions for Future Research," *Economics of Innovation and New Technology*, 3:235-251.
Wolff, Edward N. 1996. "The Growth of Information Workers in the U.S. Economy, 1950-1990: The Role of Technological Change, Computerization, and Structural Change," Technical Report RR 96-41. Department of Economics, New York University, New York.
World Research, Inc. 1997. "Junk Email Survey." San Jose, CA. Available online from <http://www.survey.com/junkresults.html>.
World Wide Web Consortium. 1997. "Platform for Internet Content Selection." Available online from <http://www.w3.org/PICS>.

APPENDIXES

A

Workshop Agenda and Participants

AGENDA

Monday, June 30, 1997

8:00 a.m.   Registration and Breakfast

8:30   Welcome and Introductory Remarks
Hal Varian, Steering Committee Chair

9:30   Breakout Session 1

Session 1A: Information
Moderator: Clifford Lynch
Assigned Participants: Haim Mendelson, Peter Lyman, Kenneth Kraemer, Marvin Sirbu, Thomas Malone, Paul Resnick
Session 1B: Deployment Case Studies—Web and Collaboration Tools
Moderator: Scott Shenker
Assigned Participants: Jeffrey MacKie-Mason, John King, Mark Weiser, Lee Sproull, Amy Friedlander
Session 1C: Employment
Moderator: Erik Brynjolfsson
Assigned Participants: Frank Stafford, Alexander Field, N. Venkatraman, Richard Sutch, Timothy Bresnehan

12:30 p.m.   Lunch

2:00   Breakout Session 2

Session 2A: Commerce
Moderator: Marvin Sirbu
Assigned Participants: Richard Sutch, Timothy Bresnehan, Alexander Field, Haim Mendelson, Michael Froomkin, Erik Brynjolfsson
Session 2B: Communities—Existing and New
Moderator: Jorge Schement
Assigned Participants: Paul Attewell, Robert Kling, Claude Fischer, Mark Weiser, Paul Resnick, Frances Allen
Session 2C: Intellectual Property and Privacy
Moderator: Pamela Samuelson
Assigned Participants: Michael Froomkin, John King, Clifford Lynch, Carl Shapiro

5:00   Moderators from Monday sessions meet

6:00   Dinner

Tuesday, July 1

8:00 a.m.   Breakfast
Moderators for Tuesday sessions meet

9:00   Breakout Session 3

Session 3A: Human Capital, Training, and Education
Moderator: Richard Sutch
Assigned Participants: Frank Stafford, Alexander Field, Claude Fischer, John King
Session 3B: Content Regulation and Free Speech
Moderator: Paul Resnick
Assigned Participants: Michael Froomkin, Pamela Samuelson, Clifford Lynch, Peter Lyman
Session 3C: Organizations
Moderator: Erik Brynjolfsson
Assigned Participants: Thomas Malone, John King, Mark Weiser, Haim Mendelson, N. Venkatraman, Frances Allen

12:00 p.m.   Lunch

2:00   Synthesis—*Steering Committee*

4:00   Adjourn

PARTICIPANTS

Economics

Timothy Bresnehan, Stanford University
Joseph Farrell, University of California, Berkeley
Alexander Field, Santa Clara University
Jeffrey MacKie-Mason, University of Michigan
Carl Shapiro, University of California, Berkeley
Frank Stafford, University of Michigan

Sociology

Paul Attewell, City University of New York
Claude Fischer, University of California, Berkeley
Robert Kling, Indiana University
Robert Kraut, Carnegie Mellon University

History

Amy Friedlander, Corporation for National Research Initiatives

Information

Kenneth Kraemer, University of California, Irvine
Clifford Lynch, University of California, Berkeley
Peter Lyman, University of California, Berkeley
Haim Mendelson, Stanford University

Legal Aspects

Michael Froomkin, University of Miami
Pamela Samuelson, University of California, Berkeley

Organizations

John King, University of California, Irvine
Thomas Malone, Massachusetts Institute of Technology
N. Venkatraman, Boston University

Technology

Paul Resnick, University of Michigan
Marvin Sirbu, Carnegie Mellon University
Mark Weiser, XEROX Palo Alto Research Center

OBSERVERS

Jennifer Sue Bond, National Science Foundation
Eileen Collins, National Science Foundation
Edward J. Hackett, National Science Foundation
John E. Jankowski, National Science Foundation
Alan R. Tupek, National Science Foundation
Andrew W. Wyckoff, Organisation for Economic Cooperation and Development

B

Position Papers Submitted by Workshop Participants

RESEARCH ON INFORMATION TECHNOLOGY IMPACTS

Paul Attewell

*Graduate School and University Center,
City University of New York*

A few comments about past impact research are appropriate at the outset, because there are some important issues that ought to be considered before moving on to new topics and research priorities. We made some intellectual mistakes in the past that we can avoid repeating in the future. Since some of the workshop participants are new to this area of study, I think it would be helpful to lay out some of these issues.

Because technological change in information technology applications has been so rapid during the last 25 years, there has been a constant temptation to turn away from studies of current outcomes of existing information technologies and instead turn toward a kind of futurology or speculative stance about what might be the case in the future. Examples are found in the agenda for this workshop, where topics are articulated such as: "How will the nature of the employment contract change? . . .What will be the impact on K-12?" The future is important, and these kinds of questions are valid, but this stance has had some unfortunate implications for impact research in the past. Among these are the following:

• A tendency to support the development of theoretical models to predict what *will be* or *might be* the case, rather than pursue empirical studies of what actually *is* happening now. Since theorizing tends to be cheaper than data collection, this has tended to skew funding toward the former, and has often given this field a rather speculative feel. But speculation, even by very smart people, has often been far off the mark.

• A tendency to fund studies of "cutting-edge" applications, which tend to be located in large, dynamic (and resource-rich) firms, or superior schools, rather than looking at the kind of "ordinary" IT that is in place in average workplaces and ordinary schools—the point being that what one observes in the largest, most resource-rich, and most committed settings is *not* a good predictor of the typical effects of a technology in the larger world. (In the field of program evaluation there is a parallel phenomenon known as the *demonstration effect*: innovative programs are shown to work well initially in well-supported demonstration projects but then prove much less effective when widely implemented in more ordinary settings.) Studying cutting-edge applications in cutting-edge firms, schools, or universities is fascinating, but this is not the most rigorous approach to understanding how technological change is affecting the larger population of organizations and people. It tends to result in unrealistic scenarios.

• A tendency to direct money into prototyping new applications, and to rely on the authors of the prototype to do the impact assessment or performance evaluation themselves or not do an evaluation at all. This has occurred all over the "computer assisted cooperative work" field, as well as in the field of educational software. It is naive to expect that people who toil over developing new technology can provide an objective assessment of its performance, yet this approach dominates research. There is no equivalent in IT research of the "double blind" study, and replication is rare. Perhaps this is one arena in which engineers and social scientists could collaborate: if federal funders insisted that all prototype and development projects include an arm's-length performance assessment, this would be a major step forward.

• A tendency to discount findings that demonstrate negative or null impacts of IT as being intellectually uninteresting on the grounds that such impacts simply reflect early versions, or start-up problems, which will disappear when the next generation of machinery or software comes online. Studies indicate that there are large discontinuance/abandonment/non-use rates for important and much-hyped IT products. (Examples are Kemerer's recent studies of abandonment of fourth-generation software development tools and Detroit's ripping out advanced automated manufacturing from some plants.) Users of "what if" decision-tools have been found to use them mechanistically even when shown that they are producing inferior decisions. Computer searches of databases using current methods have been shown to generate large numbers of bad hits, and also to miss large numbers of relevant items.

If IT impact research were a normal social science discipline, such striking findings would be viewed as important scientific puzzles, unleashing a stream of follow-up research seeking insights into human-computer interactions implied by these failures. By and large this has not occurred, because of a widespread mentality that says that any problems with IT that impact studies unearth are simply minor implementation issues and will be overcome by the next generation of technology. This mentality reminds me of the anthropologist Evans-Pritchard's studies of Azande witchcraft. Whenever he contrived to show African believers in witchcraft that casting a spell/curse on someone did not work in a concrete case, the believers were unshaken, retorting that of course witchcraft worked, but that the spell had been performed poorly in this case. IT *does* work, but impact research should spend much more time looking at the many settings in which it works very differently than intended, and should mine these cases, as well as the successes, in order to understand the full picture.

APPENDIX B   135

- One of the most common findings in prior IT impact studies has been that outcomes are far from uniform across all kinds of settings and contexts. In earlier years we looked for *the* impact of IT on (say) organizational centralization, and scholars tended to hew to one end or the other of a bipolar spectrum: centralization versus decentralization; upskilling *or* deskilling; job destroying versus job creating. What scholars found, in almost every case, was that this was an unproductive way to conceptualize the issue. One almost always found evidence of both extremes of outcomes/impacts as well as many points in between (see Attewell and Rule, 1989). We finally realized that we were asking the wrong question. We should have asked, In what contexts does outcome A typically predominate, and in what contexts does outcome B tend to prevail, and when does one see A and B in equal measure? We found that a technology does not usually have *an* impact. The context or setting in which the same technology is used often produces strikingly different "impacts." This phenomenon has been discussed in terms of "Web Models" (Kling), or "structural contingency theory" (Attewell), or Robey's "Plus Ca Change" model. All imply that we fully appreciate the role of context in technology outcomes, and that we therefore expend sufficient research effort to measure the context, and to delineate its interactions with the technology. If we fail to do this, we return to the old "black box" paradigm, that is, attempting to measure only the input (say, a particular software program) and the outcome (say, kids' test scores) without bothering with the context (the classroom, the kids' family backgrounds) or the causal mechanisms. Black box research on impacts often discovered "inconsistent" outcomes across studies but proved unable to show why there was so much variation, because it neglected to measure the contextual variables that were moderating the effects of the input upon the output. For example, the old paradigm would phrase a research question so as to ask whether or not home PCs would improve kids' school performance. In contrast, research within the current contextual paradigm would ask under what conditions having PCs at home affects students' school outcomes. A piece of my own work has indicated, for example, that having a home PC currently has a minimal effect on the school performance scores of poor and minority kids but is associated with substantial positive effects on the school performance of kids with high socioeconomic status (SES), when other factors are controlled for (Attewell and Battle, 1997). Race and class/SES, in this example, prove to be very important contextual features moderating the impact of home PCs on school performance.

- Workshop organizers should be aware that because of the last three decades of research and the importance of context as discussed above, many distinguished scholars of technology avoid the term "technology impact." Using this term in framing the question would be viewed by some of them as indicating an ignorance of the body of scholarship in technology studies. For them, the term "impact" connotes a kind of technological determinism that is very dated and widely discredited. Personally, I am not so averse to the term "impact," but I do agree with their larger point about avoiding models based on simple technological determinism.

Distilling these arguments into positive recommendations: (1) future research should pursue empirical studies of existing technologies in real settings, as distinct from speculative or purely theoretical exercises; (2) care should be taken to include representative organizations/settings, not just cutting-edge or high-tech ones; (3) studies of unintended consequences of IT, such as failures and discontinuance, are important for what they tell us about these technologies and about the process of change more generally. Researchers should be interested in the full range of "impacts"—intended and unintended; (4) projects aimed at developing technology prototypes should routinely include a performance assessment or evaluation, and the latter should be conducted at arm's length from the former; (5) contextual variables should be studied rigorously, and their moderating effects on technology outcomes should be a major part of inquiry; (6) we should reconceptualize what we are doing as social and economic studies of computing and communications technologies rather than technology impact studies, and try to avoid technological determinism.

To move to the request about specific areas for research, here are some suggestions:

1. *The "productivity paradox,"* in my opinion, remains an important and unresolved issue. However, I suggest that we should move beyond dichotomous thinking (Does information technology have a payoff, or not?) and ask, In what areas/applications/settings do we see payoffs and in what areas don't we, and why? What mechanisms can be identified that attenuate potential payoffs, and how do we measure them? What interactions and contexts explain variation in productivity outcomes?

2. *Skills.* There is anecdotal evidence that the range in performance levels in computer-related work is greater than that found in noncomputerized tasks. In other words, the gap between skilled and mediocre users is larger in computer-related work. This suggests that skills in computer work are less well diffused, or are shared less than in other kinds of tasks. We need research on what constitutes skilled versus unskilled performance in computer work of various kinds, and a better understanding about why so many of us make mediocre use of these tools.

3. *Teenagers.* I suspect that personal computers are changing the lives of teenagers more than most other age cohorts, and that is both an opportunity and a concern. Computerized communication affords powerful opportunities for social affiliation (e.g., Sproull and Faraj, 1995) and for playing with identity, both preoccupations of adolescence. There have already been studies that suggest that teenagers are spending less time watching TV and more on the Web. There are a

host of policy issues surrounding their use. But our knowledge base of how young people are using the Web, and what they are getting out of it, is too sparse.

4. *Education.* As a researcher I find the literature on educational computing quite maddening. There are exciting claims of accelerated learning using computerized tools, but the research rarely gets replicated, and even the most lauded programs (e.g., the algebra tutor at Carnegie Mellon) never seem to cross into public use, in part because these prototypes are built on UNIX platforms in esoteric languages. As a result the field does not progress in a cumulative manner. There is clearly room for a serious review and analysis of the state of the art in educational software, and for research on the barriers to future progress of IT in education. Universal access to the Web is the only area I know that has received systematic treatment.

WHAT IF ALL INFORMATION WERE READILY AVAILABLE TO ALL?

Joseph Farrell

Department of Economics, University of California, Berkeley

Rapid improvements in information technology raise two grand issues. First, are we moving toward a world in which, to a reasonable approximation, all "information" (not, of course, the same as knowledge) is readily available to all, or are there major obstacles in the way that may prevent us from getting to that point? For instance, is there no such thing as "all information" relevant to a particular topic? Are standards problems, intellectual property rights problems, database search limitations, or other issues likely to bound us well away from that "all information available" state?

Second, if we do get to that state, what will it be like? Much of today's employment consists of clumsily dealing with information. Will the demands of more information be greater or less? If the problem gets "solved" rather than just increasingly addressed, what are the other main things that need to be done in an advanced society—in other words, what will today's information manipulators do instead?

CRITICAL ISSUES RELATING TO IMPACTS OF INFORMATION TECHNOLOGY: AREAS FOR FUTURE RESEARCH AND DISCUSSION

Alexander J. Field

Santa Clara University

There are several key issues that concern me as a scholar. First, as an economic historian and as someone who looks retrospectively as well as prospectively, I believe we face a major issue involving the archiving of data. There are two main issues. People say about magnetic media that it lasts 5 years or until it wears out, whichever comes first. That is probably a bit pessimistic. But even if the media persist, what about the input-output devices? It is getting more and more difficult to find a 5.25-inch drive, and woe to him or her who has data on 8-inch floppies! Tape backups are sometimes even worse. New backup software is sometimes not backwards compatible, so that one needs old copies of backup software as well as a compatible tape drive in order to restore data. We need mechanisms to ensure the retrievability of records that previously would have been stored as printed records. This issue is at least as important for individual records (both personal and professional) as for those pertaining to the corporation or organization as a separate legal entity. Whatever media are used, we need them to be at least as durable and stable as microfilm. Ideally these media should be relatively inexpensive, and equipment to read and/or write on them should be standardized and widely accessible. Will individual and private enterprise be sufficient to ensure retrievability? Is there an externality in terms of ensuring access that would warrant government subsidy or intervention in this area, perhaps as part of the activity of the National Institute of Standards and Technology?

A second issue: As a scholar I look forward to tremendous opportunities in terms of the archiving of old journal runs. This has an enormous potential capital savings impact (consider the linear feet of bookshelves in faculty offices that might be liberated). I look forward to being able to access 100-year runs of journals such as the *American Economic Review*, from CD-ROM or over a network through software such as Adobe Acrobat (thus text is searchable). I see this as less important for books and monographs (where being able to read through an entire volume, which presumably has some coherence) will still be desirable. Nevertheless, the ability to search the text of scholarly monographs would be useful. The cost of converting newly published material to this form will be small, since most of it now exists in machine readable form before it goes to be typeset. The real challenge will be older works. There is a potential for enormous efficiencies here in terms of research libraries and scholarly research. But who will pay? Is there a role for the Library of Congress? Can we get to the point that interlibrary loan involves the simple downloading of a large file? Will scholars assemble libraries of CD-ROMs attached to personal computers? Will they invest in juke boxes so that the disks are available and retrievable when needed? (CD-ROMs can be as inconvenient as the computers were prior to the advent of hard disks—one can never seem to find the disks when one needs them, and their smaller size renders them more vulnerable to misplacement than books.) Or will the material be available through servers in libraries or over commercial networks? Obviously, copyright issues are relevant for recently published works, but I am interested in materials for which copyright is no longer relevant. How will this affect the publishing business?

Finally, let me comment on ways in which new instructional technologies will affect the craft of teaching. I believe firmly that advances in information technology will play an important role in *complementing* rather than eliminating traditional classroom instruction. The advent of television and the video tape recorder were both heralded as sounding the death knell of traditional instruction. There is no evidence that this has occurred, nor that recent advances will have this effect either, any more than computers have eliminated the use of paper or videoconferencing facilities have spelled the demise of the 747. The effective instructor acts in a complex mixture of roles. In one role the instructor is a supplier of services to students (particularly when they are enrolled in course work beyond the age of compulsory schooling laws). In terms of this relationship students are in a real sense customers. But the effective instructor occupies another role as well—as, in a sense, a supervisor of students, and plays a role in motivating, encouraging, evaluating, and developing students that is totally foreign to the service provider-customer model. For any topic there will always be a small percentage of prospective students with the necessary background, motivation, and self-discipline to learn from self-paced workbooks or computer-assisted instruction. For the majority of students, however, the presence of a live instructor, will, in my view, continue to be far more effective than a computer-assisted counterpart in facilitating positive educational outcomes, just as for most work relationships, a live supervisor is going to be more effective than a computer replacement.

The most important impact of information technology will likely occur in increasing the productivity of the hours students spend outside of the classroom. Several years ago many universities, including my own, built computer classrooms with networked computers for every one or two students. While these have proved effective for training in the use of various kinds of software, in most cases they proved disastrous for standard classroom instruction. The computers created line-of-sight obstacles between the instructor and students, and students could sometimes not resist the temptation to play computer games during class time. In some instances such labs have been ripped out. Nor am I persuaded that the increasing use of presentation software on average improves the efficacy of classroom communication. The dimming of lights and the focusing of attention on an overhead screen distracts attention away from the facial expression and body language of an instructor, which gives away two of the most powerful benefits of live instruction. Expensive overhead cameras that convert documents to a video feed currently have lower resolution than standard overhead projectors.

The greatest potential for new information technology lies in improving the productivity of time spent outside the classroom. The norm of accrediting agencies is 2 hours' outside work for 1 hour in class. Making syllabi, solutions to problem sets, and, where copyright law will permit, assigned reading materials available on an inter- or intranet offers tremendous convenience. E-mail and more sophisticated groupware vastly simplify communication between students and faculty and among students who may be engaged in group projects and face enormous logistical challenges in setting up group meeting times.

COMPUTER-MEDIATED COMMUNICATIONS

Claude S. Fischer

Department of Sociology, University of California, Berkeley

Although not currently studying computing and communications, I nonetheless have several observations to make based, in some measure, on my past studies in the social history of technology. Most generally, I suggest caution. The major risk is to be carried away by the exaggerated claims about the consequences of computer-mediated communications (CMC). It is especially a risk for those of us who both heavily use and are fascinated by CMC. We should keep in mind that big devices can have small effects; that the effects of a technology can be contradictory and even self-canceling; that the extent of diffusion does not necessarily demonstrate social significance (cf. the VCR and the ATM, both nearly universal, with the cotton gin and the "pill"); and that the effects of a technology can be substantial but only in a specific section of society, such as the white-collar workplace.

Thinking about these issues requires focus and distinctions. One set of distinctions concerns the subject. "Information technology" is too large a field, including, among other items, television and photocopying. Clearly the interest is in the consequences of CMC, particularly e-mail and the Internet. Is that all? On the effects side, it would help to distinguish at least three contexts: (1) commerce and the workplace; (2) public institutions, such as government and schools; and (3) private life, including families and other social networks. (Some might suggest an additional realm: the psychological.) Not only are the dynamics likely to be different in each sphere, but so also are the quantity and nature of the available data. It is much easier to find out how marketing and job creation are affected by CMC than it is to find out how kin ties or neighborhood dynamics are affected. My own focus is on the third context.

What do we know about the social consequences—institutional or private— of CMC? My impression is: not much. We have some crude estimates of computer diffusion in U.S. households, by key demographic categories, but we know little about who uses CMC and for what, and probably know nothing about the implications of that CMC use. (Even our knowledge of who uses the household *telephone*, why, and with what end, is crude.) Perhaps some of that basic information is available in proprietary sources—and perhaps those sources could be opened to researchers. Much of the published research that I have seen tends to be small scale, focused on select groups, and often of marginal quality. In any case, we seem to have little that explains the who, what, when, where, why, and how of domestic CMC use. And even answers to these questions, as I cautioned above, may not tell us the answer to the key question—So what?

What do we need to know about (in the private sphere)? And how would we find out? We need to know more accurately and in greater detail who uses CMCs for nonwork purposes, how often, with whom or what, to what ends, and why; and conversely, who does not. Beyond those basics, several bigger questions have been raised, for example:

- Does use of CMC significantly affect use of other media? What is "displaced" by CMC? (Is, for instance, entertainment or social interaction displaced?) More generally, does CMC use significantly affect time budgets?
- Does CMC use significantly affect spatial activities? Does it, for instance, replace some number of trips? If so, which sorts of trips?
- Does CMC use significantly affect personal social networks? Are some social relationships developed? Some reinforced? Some ignored? Some dropped? (E.g., do CMC users shift some attention from, say, family, to distant friends?)

These types of questions might be answered with high-quality surveys and intensive ethnographies of *individuals*. Ideally, one might even design field experiments on some of these topics.

While important, the answers to these questions do not necessarily tell us what the aggregate, social effects of CMC are. Understanding these effects involves broader-scale and more difficult questions, such as the following:

- Does the diffusion of CMC significantly affect the spatial pattern of towns? (Are we ever going to get the dispersed world of telecommuting, first predicted in 1893?)
- Does the diffusion of CMC significantly affect subcultural segmentation? Does it contribute significantly to the formation and sustenance of specialized "social worlds," marked, for example, by "niche" magazines?
- Does the diffusion of CMC significantly affect political mobilization?

These types of questions cannot be easily answered by simply looking at individual use; these concern macro- or aggregate effects. Here, we need complex longitudinal and/or comparative studies of institutions or communities or even nations as CMC diffuses within them. (There are a couple of examples in the study of television.)

When journalists ask me, because I wrote a book on the early social history of the telephone, to comment on the effects of the Internet and such, I usually demur. Ask me after the dust settles, I often reply; it's too soon to tell now. But the policy challenge is to estimate where this CMC "football" is going to land even while it is still bouncing around on the field.

IMPACTS OF INFORMATION TECHNOLOGY: BEHAVIORS AND METRICS

Amy Friedlander

Corporation for National Research Initiatives

Barriers to the diffusion of information technologies and their commercial application are many: resolution of ambiguities in intellectual property and the relative importance of patent, copyright, and contract law; development of a viable financial model or models; and appropriate contexts for deploying technologies that provide security, afford adequate protection of personal privacy, and offer reasonable protection of free speech. Disputes and controversies that surround these issues make assumptions, usually silently, about who is doing what with information technologies. We appear to be in a phase of technology push more than demand pull. But whether we believe that technology is technologically, economically, or socially constructed, it is generally the business of the social and behavioral sciences to understand the context in which a technology or set of technologies is thrust.

The behavioral sciences, which span everything from history to social psychology, rely on observation of behavior whether embodied in dusty census records or recorded by telemarketers. The implications of this type of research in the networked information environment are potentially substantial. The mental model, which assumes that the audience can be characterized statistically and in some sense commodified, represents an (if perhaps dubious) achievement in radio, where ways to measure and characterize the audience were developed. These methodologies subsequently migrated into television. Conclusions drawn from this research are embedded in programming, commercial, and regulatory decisions.

These methods are hardly without controversy in broadcast communications, and their utility in the networked information environment is questionable. The simplest example is the problem of inferring the numbers of users. All too frequently, the interpretation of server logs conflates usage with users, i.e., it makes one file request the equivalent of one reader. But national caching as a way of improving network performance means that readership in Australia, for example, is greatly underreported in the server logs of the home directory. Proxy

---

NOTE: The opinions and views expressed herein are those of the author and do not reflect those of the Corporation for National Research Initiatives.

servers and bootleg mirror sites compound the problem, as do printing and hand-to-hand sharing of information whether in hard copy or on disks. There are a number of studies that are experimenting with ways around these issues (e.g., Carnegie Mellon University's HomeNet Project, which basically controls sample size and composition), but the issue of method seems to be one in which future research is warranted—that is, research projects in which method is the focus of the research and is not incidental to it. ("Cookies," code that resides on a user's computer, which is launched by the server when the user requests a file, have been proposed as a way around this problem. But the strategy is not without controversy.)

Accurate demographic characterizations are one dimension of use. Another is the cluster of issues typically subsumed into human-computing interactions, which is the subject of research at the University of Maryland's Human Computer Interaction Laboratory, the University of Michigan, and elsewhere. Many of these research efforts use the library context as an experimental setting and rely on two research traditions: (1) observation of users and (2) two information retrieval metrics—precision and recall. The former is typically limited to small samples and is vulnerable to oversimplification of the research design. The latter (precision and recall) were invented to assess the adequacy of indexing schemes and were subsequently adopted by researchers to evaluate searching behavior where the assumption was one of batch processing and the notion of iterative searching and query refinement did not exist. Neither metric considers user satisfaction but measures instead the relationship between what was found and what was available to be found.

In March of this year, Ron Larsen of DARPA called for developing new metrics to replace precision and recall, but more broadly, we have to ask how far the library paradigm can be pushed. That is, many information-seeking behaviors are captured in the way that people use libraries, both real and virtual. But the leap from the local reference desk to Yahoo or Excite deserves to be questioned, and the range of information-seeking behaviors requires attention. There is a clear bias in research projects toward research in academic settings, where so-called "experts" hold doctorates and "novices" are undergraduates. It is intuitively obvious that the way a physicist does a literature search is different from the way I might look for information on flight schedules. IBM has taken the approach that technologies appropriate for libraries will successfully migrate to other structured settings, notably corporations, where the economic pay-offs are potentially substantial. Nevertheless, in order for applications in the networked information environment to accommodate the variation in users and in uses (which is appreciated but not fully understood), much more research is required on information-seeking behaviors outside formal library and/or academic settings.

There is much in the future of advanced information technologies that will probably turn out to be familiar, including the need to understand the texture of use, whether we adopt a model of technology push or demand pull. However, the tools by which we will do that as well as the shape and form of products and services to be offered are likely to change. In the near term, this will closely resemble contemporary research that evaluates users' demand for and satisfaction with products and services. But the specifics will change as content and applications evolve in ways we have yet to imagine.

FIVE CRITICAL ISSUES RELATING TO IMPACTS OF INFORMATION TECHNOLOGY

Michael Froomkin

School of Law, University of Miami

The Argus State?

Decreases in the cost of video, audio, and other sensor technology, as well as cheaper data storage and information processing, make it likely that it will become practicable for both governments and private data-mining enterprises to collect enormously detailed dossiers on all citizens. This prospect raises a host of issues requiring research and debate. Among them:

- Who currently collects what data about individuals? How is it used? How is it shared? What are the trends?
- What are the existing default rules in different jurisdictions relating to the collection of information? Does the nature of default rules meaningfully alter outcomes? Do prohibitions on data collection (e.g., data protection laws), for example, affect outcomes? To what extent are existing rules vulnerable to foreign "data havens" and other regulatory arbitrage? To what extent do/will consumers choose alternatives to the default rules when such an option is available?
- What are the possible political, social, and economic consequences of extensive individual profiling? Is extensive profiling likely? Is the absence of a great deal of the privacy now taken for granted compatible with freedom? What difference does it make if the profiling is undertaken by (or available to) democratic governments? Non-democratic governments? Private industry? What would the economic and social consequences be of making profiling data available to some? To all? At a cost? At no cost? Would it be socially valuable to prohibit the creation of individualized dossiers? In an era of distributed databases, would it be technically practical to enforce such a prohibition?
- To what extent do different types of electronic cash and electronic commerce enable or disable profiling? To what extent do concerns about the control of electronic money laundering imply the power to restrict free speech or anonymous commerce? To what extent does the protection of free speech and a private social and economic space require the protection of anonymous speech and/or anonymous commerce? What are the current national policies regarding anonymous speech and commerce? In a networked world, what are the external and extraterritorial effects of one nation's policies regarding anonymous speech and commerce?

Legal Issues Affecting Digital Commerce

- *Non-repudiation?* How to find an accommodation between the stated requirement that (at least some) commerce based on certificate-verified digital signatures be non-repudiable (the X.509 tradition) and the traditional norms of consumer law in most countries which are designed to protect consumers from themselves as well as others (e.g., U.S. rules on credit card misuse).
- *Choice of law issues.* As it becomes clearer in at least some jurisdictions which domestic rules apply to certificates, digital signatures, and electronic commerce generally, the issue of selecting among, or meditating between, possibly conflicting rules in the various states and countries that could be associated with the transaction will become inescapable. A first step toward resolving these issues would be to undertake a considerable project of description, one that would look not only at the applicable substantive law, but also at the diverse choice-of-law rules that states might apply to transjurisdictional electronic commerce. With this in hand, it would be possible to identify more clearly the extent to which e-commerce actually contributes to "regulatory arbitrage" and the extent to which it merely replicates and expands existing practices.
- *Certification authority policies issues.*
  —It would be interesting to survey the content of existing certification authority (CA) policies (and background law) and especially to track them over time: Are they converging? Are they stratifying by quality of assurances offered to clients and relying parties—i.e., "race to the bottom" or "struggle to the top" or "product differentiation"? These data would inform any discussion of the regulation of CAs, as well as the debate over efforts to harmonize international standards.
  —One could also explore whether it is possible to design a standard semantics of CA policies—and perforce of applicable background national legislation—that could form the basis for users to set up rule-based decision making that could be built into e-commerce software. This software would allow the user to define properties that a certificate must have before it would be accepted. This would be an interesting case study of the potential for technological solutions to reduce (although they could not eliminate) the need for legal services, because currently users must make each decision manually for every certificate, either on advice of counsel or, if this is impractical for cost reasons, then based on the reputation of the CA.

The Economics of Trust and Reputation

It would be interesting and useful to know more about the psychology and economics of trust and reputation, between individuals and also between persons and institutions. Trust and reputation appear to be integral to the usefulness of networked communications between strangers. In an era of information overload and rapidly growing numbers of Web pages of indeterminate quality, does the future belong to editors and other reputation-enhancing quality certification organizations? This issue has obvious implications for news and other current information. But it also applies to many other things, such as education, in which one can imagine "Internet model" degree-granting institutions that certify the quality of various distance learning courses, and attest to the rigor of exams or administer exams directly.

Interesting questions for both empirical and theoretical study include, To what extent can "trust" meaningfully be transferred? Can transitive trust be modeled? If A trusts B, to what extent does B's assertion that C is trustworthy actually induce A to trust C? How much (and in what circumstances) *should* A trust C? What indicia other than a naked statement (or certificate) could/should B offer A regarding C? The answer presumably varies enormously with the context: different assurances are required regarding, e.g., scientific bona fides, general sincerity, and creditworthiness.

Distributional Effects of the Internet on Work and Economy

Although there has been speculation about the distributional effects of the Internet on the labor force and on institutional providers of services, there seems to have been little empirical work. It would be interesting to do sectoral studies, looking at provision of services such as travel services and banking, and the retailing of "commodity" products such as CDs and perhaps a "made to order" product also, in order to determine what effect the Internet has on industrial concentration, and on employment patterns.

Rule Formation in (Partial) "Anarchy"

Until very recently, the Internet has developed its technical standards and social practices without much government intervention. Of course, the Internet developed against an elaborate background of regulation of telecommunications, electricity, and many other things necessary to its operation. Nevertheless, in important ways both the Internet Engineering Task Force (IETF)-based standards process and the "Internet norms" of Usenet, e-mail, and mailing lists evolved in a meaningfully anarchic way. To what extent is the IETF decision-making model transferable to other realms? Can the fundamentally consensus-based model survive the growth and commercialization of the Internet? Is it possible to educate (socialize) large numbers of new users? Does the method produce "better" decisions (and according to what metric)? Is it fairer? Is self-selection a viable method for decisions that do not relate to technical standards, and which in most cases apply to issues that are neither life-threatening nor of widespread salience? What sort of social practices is the vigilante-style Internet method of enforcing social norms suited to? Where is it inappropriate?

CULTURAL INFLUENCES ON THE PROCESS AND IMPACTS OF COMPUTERIZATION

Rob Kling

Center for Social Informatics, Indiana University

Most of the popular, professional, and scholarly literature about computerization treats (1) computer-communication systems (CCS) as tools, (2) their adoption and use as parts of largely rational social processes, and (3) the impacts of CCS use as knowable by examining the social system of CCS users and the technical characteristics of CCS. This kind of conceptualization dates back (at least) to Leavitt and Whisler (1958) who argued that (upward reporting) organizational MIS would lead to a relative thinning out of middle managers and a resulting "hourglass shape" in the structure of organizations. Since the 1960s, the number of popular, professional, and scholarly books and articles about the social consequences of computerization have grown from a thin rivulet (1960s) to a stream (1970s) to a river (1980s) and now to a flood (1990s). The number of academic studies has grown at a modest pace and in the late 1980s and 1990s has been swamped by the volume of professional and popular writing.

In this seemingly vast literature, one can find a number of analytical strategies for understanding the social consequences of computerization. In popular and much of the professional writing it is easier to find elements of technological determinism. But in the academic studies, Leavitt and Whisler's technological determinism is relatively passé (although technological determinism reappears in various guises, such as the "cues filtered out" arguments in Sproull and Kiesler's CMC studies summarized in their book, *Connections: New Ways of Working in the Networked Organization* (1992).

In scholarly studies, the main alternatives to technological determinism have been various contingency analyses (with different stances about which social and technological factors are important contingency makers) and nondeterministic social process theories (such as Markus and Robey's (1988) "emergent process theories"). For example, deterministic analysis would hold that documentary networks such as Lotus Notes would encourage the sharing of information within organizations, whereas a contingency analysis would treat the organizational incentives for sharing information within specific groups as an important influence on the ways that Notes would be used in specific organizations.

In addition, some analysts have noted the ways that CCS of a given generic type can be implemented with important technical variations and social conventions for using them. For example, electronic forums differ in such respects as who has access to them, who controls their content, the nature of documentary archiving, the technological complexity faced by people who use them, and so on.

Most people who use CCS know about their possibilities through a combination of personal experience and accounts in the professional and popular media. When professionals were the primary users of CCS, the roles of computerization movements (Iacono and Kling, 1996) were specially important, although usually overlooked. Today, popular usage alters the social processes by which people come to learn about the possible social roles of new forms of CCS.

It is hard to estimate the role of the mass media in popularizing the Internet and the WWW in 1993-1994; but the enthusiasm of reporters and the sudden broad visibility of URLs in national media in 1994-1995 should not be ignored. However, ideas about the social shaping of CCS and social influences on their use have diffused rather slowly into professional and popular writing.

Many of the questions addressed in this workshop are answered, in part, by beliefs about how the public (including various professionals) will use CCS (and related services). I believe that we should take the popular cultural representations of CCS as serious influences on the ways that people will use these systems—and on their likely social impacts. These representations are not always homogeneous, and they will change over time (for example, from CCS as "giant brains" in the 1950s through "productivity machines" in the early 1980s through "communication media" in the 1990s). However, as vendors develop new technologies and services, the media play important roles in giving them meaning and popularizing them (e.g., how did Java become so popular so fast?).

QUESTIONS FOR RESEARCH

Jeffrey K. MacKie-Mason

Department of Economics, and School of Information, University of Michigan

What is currently known? What questions need to be addressed? Costs are falling exponentially for technologies built primarily with silicon and sand: computing cycles and bandwidth. The decline in data storage costs would also seem remarkable but for the comparison.

Almost, but not quite the same thing: technological progress in these areas is accelerating. (Possible research question: Is it? How is it measurable?) Ignoring cost, remarkable new things are possible each year. (A thousand IBM 360s connected with RS-232 cables would not a parallel-processing supercomputer have made.)

We have a long history of adapting to falling costs and technological progress. But we are not well adapted to such fast change. In the context of our history and institutions—social, political, cultural, at least—such rapid advancement is deviant. Deviancy threatens existing institutions.

Institutions (conventions; standard practices; social, business, and political norms) evolve to deal with problems that undermine the ideal of a competitive market equilibrium: positive externalities (standardization), public goods (government provision), and transaction costs (default rules, social conventions). But when relative costs and technological opportunities change rapidly, the problems that the institutions solved are no longer the same.

Problems are changing rapidly, but institutions change slowly and reluctantly. New problems, old institutions: things break, or progress is delayed. Examples:

- International spectrum allocation: need for global bandwidth reservations for low earth orbit satellites and other wireless networks.
- Governance of the Internet: need for assignment of domain names and Internet protocol numbers, routing policy, content control.
- International banking and currency control.
- International taxation, currently largely source-based: Where is cyber activity taking place? How easy will income shifting to find a low-tax-rate base become?

- Church, school, and other local community institutions being challenged as core communications channels for shared values, culture, and social norms. Rise of disembodied, asynchronous "community" (e-mail, Usenet, special interest groups). Paradox of improved communications channels increasing balkanization?

So, at least one set of fundamentally important questions for research involves looking beneath specific impacts to uncover the institutional structures, assumptions, and rigidities that are becoming dysfunctional, and then considering how to facilitate the transition to new institutions that are likely to accommodate the effects of exponential decreases in the costs of sand and silicon.

- What government core institutions underlie market interventions, subsidy and tax policies, and trade policies? What educational structures? What legal institutions?
- What do we take for granted about intellectual property (before we get to the question of protection)?
- What mechanisms for establishing trust, evaluating, authenticating, and providing assurance underlie conventional commerce, and how can a system of trust be evolved for electronic commerce?
- What law applies to artificial agents who participate in information exchange? What socially acceptable policies exist for dealing with deadly threats to the public health like outbreaks of Level IV computer viruses (Ebola-PC, Ebola-Mac)?
- What does universal service mean? When should government treat emergent network services with large potential positive network externalities as public goods that should be subsidized?
- Good advice: Assume CPU cycles and bandwidth are free. What then?

What will be useful methods to determine answers to such questions?

The cycle of change strains some traditional methods. It is hard to get data from "natural experiments" on which generalizable hypotheses can be tested. For example, Internet congestion seems to be a problem. Various approaches to allocating scarce, easily congested resources have been proposed, including different types of usage-sensitive pricing. Lots of concern: Will this increase information inequality? Squelch creative explosion of Internet applications? Slow adoption? Chase away independent, voluntary provision of content in exchange for industrialized creation and control of mass-market content? Some fundamental research questions: How much consumer surplus is lost due to congestion? (How much does waiting "hurt"? What applications are we not getting to use because they can't tolerate unpredictable congestion, and how much are those worth to us?) How would different classes of users respond to usage-sensitive pricing (if it constituted a small fraction of their consumption budget)? Thus, would the benefits (of less congestion in current services, and new services enabled with guaranteed quality of service) outweigh the adverse effects on adoption rate and social externalities of communication, reduced innovation, change in content, change (not necessarily increase!) in information inequality?

To answer these questions, we might normally run consumer demand studies to estimate user valuation of various service qualities at different prices, looking for natural experiments to assess the value of social externalities.

The problem: no data! And even as data start to become available, the data-generating process is nonstationary (stationarity is a prerequisite for classical statistical estimation and analysis): new services are introduced, users are on a learning curve, participation externalities are riding up the adoption curve. Example: How much do we learn about future Internet demand if we study pre-WWW demand? And if we wait to observe, strong network externalities and resulting standardization may lock us into policies and standardized solutions that are inefficient, inflexible, and limiting (e.g., Wintel architecture; the "mistakes" of QWERTY and VHS standards). The traditional pace of research and institutional adaptation is too slow.

Possible implication: Social science research may need to do more field and lab experimentation, rather than waiting around for the real world to toss up natural experiments.

There may also have to be some merger between traditional social science and engineering methodologies—some attempt to learn from results that are not fully general, developed, and rigorously tested following a modernist hypothesis testing method. Thus, look to find—and design—systems, policies, and institutions that "just work." Think about how to make them work better, without clinging too tightly to the "optimality" paradigm. Internet litmus test: "running code that works."

Likewise, traditional conceptual structures may need reworking.

Many observers—but not economists for the most part—have suggested that "traditional economics is dead," that there is a "new" economics of information. Yet the "special" features of information problems are familiar in economics: high fixed costs plus low variable costs, congestion externalities, positive network externalities, and tipping. What may be new is that several of these become simultaneously significant, and for a greater, more essential share of exchange. We are used to thinking of these and designing policies for them as special cases.

Nonetheless, we should not blithely discard hard-won principles. For example, some would have it that soon bandwidth will no longer be scarce: it will be infinite (effectively) and free. Not by the laws of physics, of course. Has anything ever become infinite and free? No, just relatively less scarce. It seems still very useful to study the relative scarcity of different resources—silicon, sand, labor, creativity, attention—and to focus on how relative scarcity is chang-

APPENDIX B   *155*

ing. Where the change in scarcity is occurring is where the opportunities and problems lie. The end of scarcity is a red herring.

A few areas on which to focus research:

- Information warfare: survivability of communications networks (civilian as much as military); institutions and policies for response to transnational terrorism and criminality (that uses or attacks information infrastructure);
- Artificial agent economies: how to harness the efficiency, stability and robustness of competitive economies for real-time management and control of complex systems (electric grids, telecommunications networks, smart highways, spread-spectrum bandwidth allocation); and
- Evaluation and social filtering: the economics of attention, trust, and reputation. Funding models for information and information services, and their effect on the creation and distribution of content.

ELECTRONIC INTERACTIONS

Paul Resnick

AT&T Laboratories

The Internet offers new opportunities both to support and to study interactions among people who do not know each other very well. I believe that recommendations, trust, reputations, and reciprocity will play important roles in such interactions and thus deserve attention from interdisciplinary research teams.

There are interesting topics in all stages of commercial interactions, from search processes to negotiation to consummation of transactions:

- Recommendations and referrals can help people to find interesting information and vendors. There is a need for continued research on techniques for gathering and processing recommendations (this is sometimes called collaborative filtering). Compilation of "grand challenge" data sets of recommendations would help this field advance.
- The structure of negotiation protocols and the availability of information about past behavior of participants will affect the kinds of outcome that are possible. Economists have theoretical results regarding many simplified negotiation scenarios, but there is a need for interdisciplinary research to apply and extend these results to practical problems of protocol design.
- Finally, in the transaction consummation phase, much effort has focused on secure payment systems. Some transactions, however, require a physical consummation (mailing of a product, for example) and hence must rely on trust in some form. Research can explore the role of reputations in creating trustworthy (though not completely secure) contract consummation. Such transactions may also have lower transaction costs than secure payment systems, even in the realm of purely electronic transactions.

Noncommercial electronic interactions also offer many interesting opportunities. Electronically mediated interactions are visible and available for analysis in a way that face-to-face interactions typically are not. For example, "softbots" could scour the Web to create various graphs of relations between people and information resources. Social network theorists have already devised a number of techniques for analyzing such graphs. One possible application would be to hypothesize about and then analyze the credibility of information sources in various parts of a social network. Another possible application of network analysis would be to analyze the flow of reciprocity (or gift exchange, as Esther Dyson put it) and perhaps devise ways to increase a social network's level of reciprocity.

In the last couple of years, I have become particularly interested in the concept of social capital, as articulated by James Coleman, Robert Putnam, and others. Social capital is a resource for action that inheres in the way a set of people interact with each other. I'm still struggling for various ways to connect this concept to specific research questions and projects. Some of the ideas above are born from those struggles, and I'd welcome any project ideas or new ways of thinking about these problems.

SOCIAL IMPACT OF INFORMATION TECHNOLOGY

Frank Stafford

University of Michigan

A great deal of attention has been given to new information technology as the main empirical force changing the wage structure and giving rise to wage inequality. Yet something on the order of skill-biased technical change is usually given no formal representation. The theory that could actually explain the changing wage structure is some type of unbalanced growth model. In fact the theory that could apply is not too hard to imagine. It is a closed economy "trade" model with "biased" technical change (Johnson and Stafford, 1998). Skilled and unskilled workers produce different goods. Suppose that there are three goods. Throughout, skilled workers produce Good A (professional services, most obviously), and less skilled workers produce Good C (including basic retailing). Initially, let us suppose that there is a large Good B sector, such as manufacturing and some other services, produced by less skilled workers. Then the new technology appears. It improves the ability of skilled workers to produce the Good B output, previously the domain of the less skilled workers.

What in general will happen to the equilibrium when this skill-biased technological progress occurs? The average real wage will rise, but the skilled workers will get more than 100 percent of the benefit, implying that the real wage of less skilled workers will fall. In contrast, if the new technology had allowed the skilled workers to be more productive at their traditional specialty (Good A), then the real wage of all workers would have risen.

A model of this simple sort would go a long way in organizing thought about some of the patterns reported in the literature on changing wage structure. Skilled workers have been substituted for less skilled workers in many Organisation for Economic Cooperation and Development manufacturing industries, for example. In that (Good B) industry there has been a rise in the ratio of nonproduction to production workers, and overall growth in manufacturing productivity has been strong. In contrast, high-skill service-sector (Good A) productivity growth has been generally slow. One need only think of higher education and legal services (and possibly medicine) as cases in point. The terms of trade within the domestic economy could be defined as the prices of goods produced by skilled workers and others. The price of the Good B sector has fallen because of biased technical change, and as additional less-skilled workers become available to produce more traditional Good C products such as retail services, they experience deteriorating terms of (internal) trade. For some countries with rather little trade, such as the United States, the closed-economy aspect of such a framework is most empirically relevant. For other countries, such as Japan, both trade and external as well as internal technological effects will be important to incorporate in an assessment of wage pressures.

Consider the price of tuition and the price of routine health care assistance provided by home health care aides. Data from the Bureau of Labor Statistics wage series show the latter to have been falling below the level of inflation since 1973. On a more optimistic note, if the new technology can be applied to improve the productivity of skilled workers in their traditional domains, both skilled and unskilled workers would be better off. The new information technology is so far helping the nonmarket productivity of skilled workers: use of the Internet will be providing a huge array of services via the household sector. Data available to study this aspect of technical change are close to nonexistent. The real standard of living may come to depend more on the nonmarket sector. We have developed a methodology for studying the value of nonmarket output though the use of time-use diary data, based on a grant from the National Science Foundation in the mid 1970s and early 1980s. We are currently studying the access of children under the age of 12 to information technology with time-use diaries both in the home and in schools. The data are being collected as a special supplement to the Panel Study of Income Dynamics, funded by the National Institute of Child Health and Human Development. Copies of our instruments are available at <http://www.umich.edu/~psid/>.

THE UNCALMING EFFECTS OF DIGITAL TECHNOLOGY

Mark Weiser

Xerox Palo Alto Research Center

The important waves of technological change are those that fundamentally alter the place of technology in our lives. What matters is not technology itself, but its relationship to us.

In the past 50 years of computation there have been two great trends in this relationship: the mainframe relationship and the PC relationship. Today the Internet is carrying us through an era of widespread distributed computing toward one of ubiquitous computing, characterized by deeply imbedding computation throughout the world. Ubiquitous computing will require a new approach to fitting technology to our lives, an approach we call "calm computing." Calm computing is not a natural result of increased use of technology—in fact unbridled digital technology naturally decreases calm.

Imagine the following experiment; or if you are brave, try it. Find two empty cardboard toilet paper tubes, and tape them over your eyes so that you are looking out through them. You now have no view up, down, left, or right, only a narrow cone of view straight in front. Now walk. What happens? You have lost the flow of information from the periphery into the center, and have only the center. Everything that you see is a surprise, because it just pops in without warning. Your head must constantly swivel or you will trip, run into things, miss people passing you, and generally bumble.

If you wear toilet paper tubes for a few hours you will feel exhausted and highly anxious. Your head will have been constantly swiveling to try to partially compensate for the lack of peripheral vision. You will feel overloaded with all the work you did to keep up with your world. You will be emotionally drained by all the surprises when things popped into view and when you had to compensate for the unexpected.

Wearing toilet paper tubes is like living in the digital age, where the feeling of exhaustion is called "information overload." Digital technology, like toilet paper tubes, tends to deliver information with a set of biases. These biases push us toward the center of our awareness and tend to leave out the essential periphery that helps us make sense of and anticipate the world around us. More and more of the economy and business and life are mediated through digital technology. If we lose the periphery, we may be smarter about whatever is right in front of us, but stupid to the point of ignorance about what is nearby but out of sight behind the toilet paper tube.

Proper action has always meant keeping the periphery and center in balance. The center is the domain of conscious, symbolic thought and action. The periphery is the domain of flow, of context, of intuition, and of understanding. The center is the domain of explicit knowledge of what to do, the periphery the domain of knowing how to do it. Take away either of these and near paralysis results.

There are 10 biases in today's digital technology that contribute to unbalancing center and periphery. These are saying, homogenizing, stripping, reframing, mono-sensing, deflowing, defamiliarizing, "uglying," reifying, and destabilizing.

1. Saying names the tendency of digital technology to make everything explicit.
2. Homogenizing is the delivery of digital information at an ASCII monotone that puts all information into the same pigeonhole.
3. Stripping is the loss of social context and frame that frequently comes with digital transmission.
4. Reframing results because there is always a social context and frame, and after stripping, a confusing or illegitimate context may result.
5. Mono-sensing is the emphasis on the eye over all other senses, reducing our inputs, our style, and our intelligence.
6. Deflowing is the loss of the context that lets us enter the "flow state" of greatest intelligence and creativity, and so reduces our anticipation and history.
7. Defamiliarizing is the loss of familiar social practices as we try to work and live on the net.
8. "Uglying" names, with an ugly word, the uncomfortable feeling with which the low state of design in digital technology leaves us.
9. Reifying results when implicit practices are cast in stone, removing the white space that lets anything work, as when a company puts all its processes online.
10. Destabilized is our emotional state after buffeting from all the above.

The above add up to a bias toward the center, and away from the periphery.

Understanding the power of balance between focus and periphery, and caring about both, can be a tremendous source of advantage in the digital age. Digital technology, through its homogeneous, ubiquitous, and voluminous provision of information, can enable an even richer periphery for action. The danger comes if we believe that only focus is effective. Trying to focus on the increasing volume of bits can overwhelm us, and we can badly misuse our full intelligence by ignoring attunement, community, and peripheral awareness. The opportunity for focus is greater than ever before, but only if we recognize that there is no focus without periphery, there is no center without a surround. If we can stay in balance, we can expect a world of greater satisfaction and effectiveness.

C

Commissioned Papers

INFRASTRUCTURE: THE UTILITY OF PAST AS PROLOGUE?

Amy Friedlander

Corporation for National Research Initiatives, Reston, Virginia

In 1890, advocates of direct current (DC) electric power systems employed alternating current (AC) to electrocute first a dog and then a condemned criminal at the Auburn (New York) state prison in a flamboyant attempt to demonstrate that AC was unsafe. The incident is perhaps the best-known episode in the so-called "War of the Systems," which came to an end with the invention of the rotary converter in 1892, which enabled existing DC distribution systems to be integrated into the more efficient AC systems, and completion of the Niagara Power Project in 1895, which showed that large generating plants and associated transmission lines capable of meeting regional needs could, indeed, be built.[1]

Electric power is one of four infrastructure history studies sponsored by the Corporation for National Research Initiatives (CNRI). The others address railroads, telephones and telegraphs, and banking; a fifth, radio, is in progress. These studies collectively examine attributes of infrastructure through literature reviews in American history, economics, political science, and sociology. Initially, three questions were posed:

- When and how did take-off occur?
- What were the public and private roles?
- And, how did an infrastructure—characterized by access, "shareability," and economic advantage—emerge?

These questions worked well for the first three studies: rail, telegraphy/telephony, and electricity. But the unspoken assumption behind these questions is technology—the application of engineering and science to accomplish a purpose. In the course of the fourth study, banking, which turned out to be about information, we began to look at the problem of infrastructure somewhat differently, examining properties of ubiquity, interdependence, and reciprocity, independent of a given technology or set of technologies. This focused attention on the

---

NOTE: The opinions and views expressed herein are those of the author and do not necessarily reflect those of the Corporation for National Research Initiatives (CNRI). © 1997 by the Corporation for National Research Initiatives. Reprinted by permission.

organizational and management structures, which had formed important elements of all of the preceding studies but had not occupied center stage.

Finally, all four of the infrastructures were subject to regulation during the New Deal. Indeed, much of the current deregulation is designed to dismantle the world that the New Deal put in place. From a policy perspective, then, the studies not only delineate more clearly what the relative and changing public and private roles were but also explain how the New Deal approaches to regulatory policy came to be, at least with respect to these four industries.

The Perils of Drawing Historical Analogies

The remainder of this paper discusses themes and observations common to all four of the subject infrastructures. But a word or two is necessary on the perils of drawing historical analogies. All four of these infrastructures obtained shape and form during a period of extraordinary growth. Between 1790 and 1850, the western boundary of the United States moved from the Mississippi River to the Pacific Ocean; population in the same period grew by an average of about 30 percent per decade. After 1860, population growth fell off to a mere 20 percent or so per decade until 1910.[2] Urbanization increased dramatically after 1870. In 1890, the U.S. Census Bureau announced that the frontier was closed, and three years later, historian Frederick Jackson Turner proposed his frontier thesis, which was at least partially a eulogy for this period in American history. By 1920, more than half of the nation's population lived in cities. This meant that through the second half of the nineteenth century and into the twentieth, there was a growing concentration of demand for networked technologies such as water, power, and communications as well as for inter- and intra-regional transportation and financial services. Moreover, the late nineteenth and early twentieth centuries saw prices fall so that construction of the physical infrastructure of electricity, for example—the generating plants, transmission lines, power stations, and substations—took place in an environment of declining real costs which could be passed off to consumers as lower rates while the companies still turned a profit.

The flip side was wages. Real wages increased in the 1920s, the period in which recognizably modern suburbia proliferated, creating an environment of new construction and consumer demand that made extension of power and phone lines attractive, easy, and relatively cheap. Indeed, the residential market for electricity, with its demand in the evening hours, now became more attractive as a means of continuing to balance peak load. The distribution system was largely in place, and the marginal cost of the "last mile"—that is, connections to individual residences—was relatively low compared with the total construction cost of the system, including the generating plant and long-distance transmission lines. Economies of scale based on improvements to generating and transmission technologies were increasing, and the cost as well as the price of electricity fell.[3]

This stands in marked contrast to current debates over strategies for funding construction of the "last mile" for the digital communications infrastructure.

The second cluster of differences concerns public/private roles. At the birth of the republic, most people thought of the government as local— parish or country—and perhaps as the state. The federal government was a dim presence, known to most of the people in the form of the postal system. Eligibility requirements, imposed by the states, meant that many men could not vote; universal suffrage for men was not the norm until the 1820s, and women were first granted the vote at the territorial level—in Wyoming in 1869. (Wyoming granted women the vote at the state level in 1890 when it entered the Union.) African Americans, enslaved or free, were denied the vote until passage of the 15th Amendment in 1870, and again, restrictive eligibility requirements excluded most blacks from the vote, particularly in the Deep South, until the twentieth century.

The vote is the most direct means of broad participation in civil life. Just as this participation was circumscribed on a number of grounds in the nineteenth century, so, too, was the government's perception of its intervention in the life of its citizens. The Civil War (1861 to 1865) represented a massive intervention in daily life, calling up "volunteers" in both North and South; levying direct taxation; and affecting the economy significantly through the sale of bonds, federal regulation of the currency, and procurement of goods and services, thus laying the foundation for a number of private fortunes. But these were the exception rather than the rule. Even the transcontinental land grants to the railroads— which amounted to an area greater than California and Nevada combined—were modest relative to the total cost. Carter Goodrich concluded that combined state and federal financial assistance to the transcontinental railroads amounted to about 13.5 percent of their total construction cost, and that this assistance was substantially *less* than that provided for canals.[4] Sustained intervention by the government in American daily lives, as measured by per capita increase in government revenues and expenditures, appears to have increased consistently after 1890 and to have begun with *local*—not federal—authority.[5]

Federal regulation, marked by the organization of the Interstate Commerce Commission (ICC) in 1887 to regulate the railroads, was initially a forum for resolving disputes and was embraced by some figures in the industry as a way of setting uniform national policy in an environment of competing state policies. However, by the New Deal, the regulatory agency was seen as a more active instrument, and the government, rather than acting as a mediator, was seen as having a positive obligation to ensure a minimal standard of security for its citizens. This is obvious in both social and economic programs, e.g., the Social Security Administration and the banking reform that expanded the scope of the Federal Reserve, established the Federal Deposit Insurance Corporation, and regulated the structure of the industry.[6]

Thus, for most of American history, government was a distant presence. Research labs, like Thomas Edison's in Menlo Park, New Jersey, arose with corporate support. His was dominated by the telegraph giant, Western Union, itself controlled by William Vanderbilt, who had financial interests in both rail and telegraphy. Not surprisingly, Western Union sponsored research into domains that resonated with its business goals. In 1873, Western Union announced its willingness to reward handsomely any inventor who could achieve multiplexing on its lines, thus increasing capacity without additional investment in the wired plant. This led directly to the simultaneous invention of the telephone by Elisha Gray and Alexander Graham Bell. Edison also came up with a receiver design at Western Union's behest. His lamp and associated DC generating and distribution system represented the most successful in a series of attempts to challenge the gas companies by producing superior interior illumination at a competitive price.[7] Thus, the great nineteenth-century infrastructures arose by processes of competition, compromise, and consensus in which the public presence was, at best, a facilitator and at times a mediator.

What Falls Out?

Economic growth, deflation, and different expectations of government are three important differences that shaped the development of the infrastructures studied. But six themes do fall out as common to all four of the studies:

- Period of experimentation,
- First-order substitutions and feedback effects,
- Evolution of new structures,
- Not always the "best" technology,
- Natural monopolies, and
- Physical plant and service.

Each of these observations is discussed in greater detail in the next sections.

Period of Experimentation: Winners and Losers

All of these examples witnessed a period of experimentation in which there were winners and losers and in which a new technology or technologies per se were necessary but not sufficient for take-off. Railroads are the obvious example. Most of the technologies required for self-propelled steam engines on rails (i.e., locomotives) were developed by the 1830s, but take-off, measured by a leap in miles of rail construction, did not occur until the 1850s. There were, moreover, numerous small railroad companies that were gradually incorporated into larger corporate systems. But this was a surprisingly slow and at times contentious process that required decades.

The standardization of the gauge is a case in point. By 1860, there were seven gauges for 30,626 miles of track. Of these seven, the standard, 4-foot, 8.5-

APPENDIX C

inch gauge represented the bare majority of mileage (53.3 percent). The second most common gauge was the 5-foot gauge, which was concentrated in the South, a region that was further isolated by insufficient intra-regional rail links, including a critical lack of bridges across major rivers. More generally, the effort by many southern cities to secure an urban hinterland resulted in highly localized lines emanating from the major cities but not connecting them.[8]

Three considerations drove conformity to the "standard" gauge, a precondition to interconnection: the big eastern railroad firms, eager to tap into the rapidly expanding markets in the West, particularly for western grain, which required transport across many states and many independent rail lines; the outbreak of the Civil War, which underlined the need for efficient east-west transportation and communications from both political and military perspectives; and finally, specification in 1862 of the 4-foot, 8.5-inch gauge for construction of the new transcontinental roads. Between 1870 and 1880, most of the companies outside the South adopted the uniform gauge; 3 percent merely built a third rail. Following a meeting among leading railroad interests in the South on February 2, 1886, the southern lines were brought into conformity with the 4-foot, 8.5-inch gauge.[9]

Standardization of gauge as well as increasing conformity in signaling, scheduling, and administrative procedures (e.g., cross-licensing access to track; through-ticketing and bills of lading; inventory control and management) enabled freight to flow across tracks and equipment controlled by competing interests. At the same time, mergers and acquisitions meant that many of the smaller companies built to service Portland, Maine, or Baton Rouge, Louisiana, were incorporated into larger entities, resulting in a pattern of many losers and a few big winners. Similar patterns characterized both telephony and electricity.

The Bell interests had enjoyed a 20-year patent monopoly in telephony, but with the expiration of key patents in 1893, the number of telephone companies serving local or regional markets exploded. Much to Bell's corporate dismay, the organization found itself confronted by a potential welter of services, technical standards, and lively competition. Indeed, in 1903, more than half of the nation's 1,051 incorporated towns and cities hosted more than one telephone company. In 1915, at least 40 percent of the telephone exchanges in cities with a population of 5,000 or more competed with another local exchange, and dual service continued to exist in parts of the Midwest and Plains until 1924. By the end of that year, however, AT&T, then under the jurisdiction of the Interstate Commerce Commission (ICC), had bought 223 of the 234 independent telephone companies subject to the agency's jurisdiction.[10]

Electricity tells a similar story. Until the widespread adoption of AC technology, service areas, limited by the short, one-mile range of DC distribution, tended to be relatively compact. It was fairly easy for a small electric utility to identify a market. Thus, between 1887 and 1892, 28 separate firms offering electric service were formed in Chicago alone—not including users who purchased independent, self-contained plants. In their analysis of the structure of the electric utility industry in 1897-1898, Hausman and Neufeld conclude that most firms were only marginally profitable. Weaker firms found it difficult to raise capital, which is one reason put forth for the founding of municipally owned electric plants.[11]

The integration of DC into AC systems meant that economies of scale and scope were technologically possible as well as desirable since high-voltage AC transmission over distance was more efficient but meant higher threshold costs. Hausman and Neufeld found that strong power companies offering a higher rate of return tended to be older and larger, to have bigger generators, to rely on hydro rather than steam, to have a strong commitment to AC generation, and to have a better load factor (i.e., the ratio of average to peak demand). These firms had the potential to enjoy substantial cost savings—conditions, the authors observe, "which would be expected to presage a major period of consolidation," and which did, indeed, occur. Power generation and transmission companies evolved notions of holding companies as a way to leverage capital and manage broad distribution. Led by Samuel Insull of Commonwealth Edison, industry executives cultivated state regulatory agencies that mandated standardized service and interconnection. By 1924, 7 holding companies controlled 40 percent of the nation's generating capacity, and 16 holding companies generated three-fourths of the nation's electrical power. Thus, even the publicly owned municipal utilities, which provided service to end-users, were dependent on private power providers and transmission line companies for access to bulk power.[12]

First-Order Substitutions

So far, we have discussed the overall shape and form of these industries. In each case, there was an initial period of expansion and proliferation followed by consolidation into a few—or one, in the case of telephony—corporate giants. This was in some cases pushed by the requirements of the technology, e.g., electricity. But this was not necessary; telephony, for example, could have existed as a series of interconnecting yet independent companies—corporate consolidation and management were not necessary.

In each of these cases, there was a product that let end-users or consumers do something or have something better. The substitution effect is most obvious in electricity. There already existed a market in interior illumination provided by candles, kerosene, and gas. Edison intentionally set out to provide a superior product that was cost-competitive with the equivalent gas service, and the pricing of electricity was established in terms of competition with gas.[13]

Telephony was also an improvement on existing local communications technologies. In 1873, Western Union enjoyed a monopoly over telegraphic service, which was primarily between cities. About 10 years earlier, the telegraph giant had begun to experiment with combined telegraphic and delivery services as a way to provide local communications connections. Western Union also began to explore switching technologies that allowed financial information to flow from several banks to a single clearinghouse and then from the clearing house back out to the banks. The initial market for telephony was believed to be local, thus filling the gap in service. Telephony was initially constrained by signal attenuation to a range of about 20 to 30 miles in urban environments where cable was laid below grade, although transmissions across distances of 800 miles could be achieved with open-air lines. By 1890, Bell interests were already pursuing interurban transmission in head-to-head competition with the telegraph monopoly.

Rail transport was also conceived of as a substitution, in this case, for transport via canal or overland. Although canals had achieved the first major cost savings, rail held the advantage in perishables and high-value goods, where the desire for speed outweighed higher costs.[14] The differential between rail and water has been a matter of some debate. In general, though, competition between rail and water tended to lower all freight charges. Similar inter-product competition also tended to keep electric utility rates relatively low and encouraged utility executives to cooperate with regulatory agencies, thus distancing themselves from the contentious and adversarial positions taken by the gas companies.

**Evolution of New Structures:
Niches, Organization, and Efficiency**

Eventually, niches for different services formed and new structures and services evolved. For example, early nineteenth-century turnpike companies, never as profitable as hoped, quickly gave way in the long-distance market to both canals and railroads. On the other hand, expanding numbers of middle- and long-distance routes via either rail or water increased the need for short-distance overland services of 15 miles or less. This increased demand more than offset the loss of long-distance business. Plank roads, constructed on the same principle as wooden sidewalks, were introduced after the mid-1830s, and wagons dominated the short haul, that is, distances less than 15 to 20 miles long, where the rate was cheaper than either rail or canals and time was not a constraint. This was seen as an advantage to some entrepreneurs. John Murray Forbes of Boston, who controlled the Michigan Central, avoided construction of branch lines and encouraged local construction of plank roads affording access to the railroad without his having to expend capital to reach markets. Water transport via coastal, lake, or river steamer or by canal barge had the advantage in medium to long hauls, averaging 650 miles, especially where the commodities shipped were high bulk and low value. Innovations during the nineteenth century tended to reduce costs mainly over medium to long distances. Waterways were good albeit not perfect substitutes for rail and generally had the advantage in shipping high-bulk/low-value goods over long distances. Rail possessed the advantage in shipping high value items over medium and long distances and in shipping high-bulk/low-value commodities over medium distances.

Similar differentiation characterized power. Competition with electric companies spurred gas producers to cut prices and improve the product. "Water" gas, introduced in 1880s, was considered greatly superior to the earlier coal gas; it was cleaner and provided better light. The manufacturing process required a larger scale of operation, which increased the costs of entry but also resulted in economies of scale. In a newly competitive environment, Consumers Gas of Chicago was able to offer still lower prices, thus forcing the price of gas to fall from $3.00 to $1.75 per 1,000 cubic feet. The new gas technology resulted in similar price competition in Houston and a 40 percent decrease in local rates. With electricity beginning to encroach upon the lighting market in upper- and upper-middle-class households and commercial establishments, gas seemed poised to capture the market of middle and working class homes where kerosene light was still the norm.

Discovery of natural gas fields and realization of the thermal applications of gas led to further service and product differentiation. Between 1900 and 1940, higher-income urban households adopted electricity first and tended to prefer electricity for lighting and natural gas for hot water and perhaps cooking, with an oil burner for heat. Middle- and lower-income residents converted to new energies more slowly. They selected electricity for light first, then shifted from a coal to a gas stove, and finally added a gas hot-water heater.[15] Thus, consumers chose among multiple energy technologies, and the urban energy landscape as late as the 1920s was characterized by a mix of coal, oil, gas, and electricity.

Applications of electricity in the heavy industries took place after World War I as a result of continued advances in technology as well as soaring prices for both coal and labor. But the implications of electrification were more profound than substitution of one power source for another. Applications of central station-generated electricity in manufacturing and industry had begun in the 1890s among small users who realized the advantages of the small AC electric motor in providing fractionalized power in highly segmented, labor-intensive processes where needs were historically too small to justify a large investment in a steam engine: the apparel industries, chemicals, printing, and several equipment manufacturers (electrical, non-electrical, and transportation), and metal fabrication. This cluster of industries remained at the forefront of electrification through 1954. Large-scale enterprises, characterized by substantial sunk costs in existing technology and by power- and heat-intensive processes (lumber, paper, petroleum, stone/clay/glass, and primary metals), consistently lagged in adopting electric power. Given the scale of their facilities and the importance of the heat by-product (e.g., steam) to their industrial processes, managers of these industries tended to install self-contained electric generating plants when they did decide to go electric after 1919.[16]

Electricity thus offered small-scale enterprises access to power that formerly they did not have. In both the heavy and light industries and manufacturing plants, electrification revolutionized the organization of work. Prior to the introduction of electricity, industry relied on centralized, belt-and-shaft systems linked to a single prime mover (either water or steam-powered). The advent of electricity and the electric motor enabled a restructuring of industrial processes to a more efficient, decentralized unit drive system where energy was made available at the point of use. Unit drive systems possess numerous advantages. Elimination of the centralized line shaft system reduced fuel inputs and increased energy efficiency by reducing friction losses implicit in belt-and-shaft distribution. Factory structures no longer needed to support heavy mechanical systems, permitting lighter, single-story factory layouts, which in turn permitted better materials handling and flexible work flows. Finally, components of the process became independent, and having to fix a problem in one did not shut the entire system down. Walter Devine, who has conducted the seminal work on electrification and organization of industrial processes, argues that reduced energy requirements resulting from efficient application of electricity in unit-drive systems resulted in higher productivity of capital and labor. And economist Harry Oshima finds that in textiles, six labor-intensive mechanized processes in the era of steam were reengineered to 25 processes without a concurrent increase in labor inputs.[17] Thus, electrification enabled efficiencies in industrial and manufacturing processes.

Not Always the "Best" Technology

The efficiency *cum* labor substitution argument set forth by Oshima is part of a larger literature that addresses the relationship between technology and growth in the American economy in the late nineteenth and the twentieth centuries. Two themes in this literature resonate with contemporary concerns: one is the relationship between technology and labor, and the second is the so-called "productivity paradox." The productivity paradox consists in the fact that although electricity was adopted as early as 1889, measurable gains in *aggregate national productivity* began to appear only in the 1920s, after large industrial plants—metals, petroleum, transportation—shifted to electric power. Why the lag?

For one thing, early adopters were small, labor-intensive manufacturing plants where good light and access to fractionalized power were important. But their impact on the total industrial sector was small relative to the heavy industries, which did not electrify until after 1919. According to economist Arthur Woolf, this transition occurred in the context of rapidly falling prices for electricity, escalating prices for coal, and increased costs of labor. Woolf concludes that firms took advantage of cheaper energy costs to offset higher labor costs by restructuring their operations.[18]

His analysis has been criticized as overly reductionist and too reliant on the costs of electricity and labor as the principal determinants without taking into account the engineering flexibility and efficiencies that electric power enabled or the process of incremental adoption that began with smaller enterprises.[19] Finally, the expectation that a new technology will be quickly recognized and adopted underestimates the significance of the process of experimentation, which characterized all of the infrastructure technology we have studied, as well as the implied costs of converting an installed base and investment in the status quo to something new. Indeed, the existing investment in DC systems and technologies is one reason for the emotional intensity that characterized the "War of the Systems" in the 1890s.

The pace of adoption of electricity—or any technology—is one dimension of understanding technological diffusion. A second is the "goodness" of that technology. Here, a certain tautology tends to enter the discussion, which goes as follows: technology x enters the common use and is considered the "best" solution because it has become the successful solution, and success is equated with value.[20] There is substantial evidence to the contrary. The adoption of the standard gauge, for example, was the consequence of tradition, the founder effect, and the advantages of a network. The standard 110 volts in power distribution is a function of the economic analysis that one of Edison's researchers undertook to determine the costs of a system that would be price competitive with gas, where the principal cost was the price of copper. Finally, William Paul Barnett's dissertation on the diffusion of telephony challenges this tautology and elucidates the interaction between technology diffusion and demand.

The explosion in demand and proliferation of companies after 1894 had created a manufacturing bottleneck. Western Electric, a wholly owned Bell subsidiary, could not keep pace with the demand for equipment. As a result, lesser but still satisfactory devices were developed and used by the independent companies. During the first decade of the twentieth century, there were basically two competing technologies: the common battery system, which presumed a common power source and a physically centralized system; and the more primitive "magneto" instrument, which relied on local, individualized battery power contained in each device.[21]

Barnett is interested in the relationship between technology and competition. He found that independent telephone companies offering combinations of local and long-distance services both cooperated and competed with each other. Successful companies enjoyed cooperative relationships within a technological standard, even though that standard was not necessarily the most sophisticated technology available. Thus, relatively primitive, single-exchange common-battery companies, offering local service, thrived in complementary relationships with multiexchange companies, providing regional long-distance service, so long as local and regional servers shared a standard technology and interconnection was possible. Technological sophistication only appears to have mattered when two companies competed for the same market niche, as in the competition for regional long-distance service. There, companies with a more advanced technology enjoyed an advantage. Thus, Barnett describes a gradual process of successful local and long-distance market/service differentiation within the context of a standardized and interoperable—but not necessarily the most sophisticated—technology.

What is the "best" technology then? Barnett's research suggests that it is the technology that satisfies end-users, which may or may not be the most sophisticated available. These results were confirmed by Kenneth Lipartito's research on telephony in the South. Lipartito found that Southerners did not necessarily want the sophisticated—and expensive—service offered by AT&T. When telephone service was introduced to Huntsville, Alabama, a local newspaper editor observed that residents wanted connections to nearby towns—not to New York City or Washington, D.C.[22]

Whither "Natural Monopoly"?

We come now to the vexing theoretical question of natural monopoly. Explanations of natural monopoly begin with a model of the market based on supply and demand, and focus their analyses on factors affecting supply (or production). Thus, one definition of a natural monopoly looks at the production plant and finds that natural monopolies are characterized by high fixed costs of the physical plant. Another definition of natural monopoly argues that a natural monopoly exists if multiple producers will result in excess capacity and waste.

The railroad companies quickly learned that excessive competition could result in overbuilding and waste. Frustrated by the Pennsylvania Railroad's dominance of the Pittsburgh market, for example, Andrew Carnegie financed William Vanderbilt's efforts to build a parallel line into Pittsburgh. Vanderbilt had his own quarrel with the Pennsylvania Railroad: the company had bought an interest in the New York, West Shore, and Hudson, which, in 1881, proposed to build a line into New York City on the west side of the Hudson River—thus duplicating the exclusive rail route into Manhattan owned by Vanderbilt's New York Central. By this time, however, J.P. Morgan had developed a substantial interest in the rail companies as an underwriter as well as a financier. Concerned by the overbuilding and ruinous rate wars between the Pennsylvania Railroad and the New York Central, he assembled the principals of both firms on his yacht, the *Corsair*, and a deal was struck.[23]

In the case of networked systems, the issue of competition is complicated by the question of network externalities—that the value of the system increases as more members join it. Thus, with respect to telephony, the natural monopoly thesis argues that the inherent value of a single, integrated network to consumers, together with the wastefulness of multiple systems, meant that large systems tended to devour small ones, and that efficiencies increase when the system encompasses the maximum number of users. The theory—frequently articulated by AT&T representatives in the twentieth century—seems to confirm the traditional view of telephony as a natural monopoly, which provided cost-effective, high-quality service to its subscribers.[24]

There are, however, a few problems. For one, interconnected and networked systems do not necessarily achieve economies of scale, a lesson railroaders learned quite painfully and the telephone companies relearned when they tried to design switchboards that could accommodate large numbers of users.[25] For another, the model presumes that demand is constant and homogeneous, a contention that historical data do not support.

Barnett demonstrated differentiated demand in Iowa and Pennsylvania, and Liparito also showed that Southern users were uninterested in superior technology and long-distance connections; they prudently bought the cheapest service. It is a rational decision from an economic point of view, but it is not consistent with the theory. Southern consumers clearly did not seek to maximize their network access, and the nature of Southern demand was obviously different from the interests clamoring for broader access. Even within the South, different strategies were required in North Carolina from those that had worked in Georgia.[26]

Finally, Claude Fischer's analysis of the spread of telephony between 1900 and 1940 finds that early subscribers wanted residential telephone service for a combination of reasons. Some, notably physicians, saw its commercial and professional value. Indeed, one of the entrepreneurs in Antioch, California, was a doctor who, it is said, envisioned substituting telephone service for homing pigeons to maintain communication with his dispersed, rural patients. A second group of subscribers saw its social value; this group contained a disproportionate number of women and rural residents, precisely the group left out of the AT&T business plan, which, based on the example of Western Union, emphasized national service for businesses. But Fischer found that telephone service tended to be adopted first among professional and socially elite households and then to percolate more slowly through the local socioeconomic structure.[27]

Fischer's underlying interest concerns the diffusion of technology, and he sees in the example of the telephone evidence that consumer behavior and demand affect technological development and expansion of service. Thus, cheaper alternatives such as direct dialing and party lines, initially resisted by corporate AT&T because they might diminish AT&T's high quality of service, were implemented to capture the consumer market in some cases already served by independent competitors. Fischer also found that corporate advertising first focused on business and commercial applications. When the marketing message was adjusted again in the 1920s to stress the sociability of telephony, the change in content came in response to patterns of consumer behavior, rather than in anticipation of them.[28]

These studies all challenge the association of natural monopoly and telephony by demonstrating the importance of consumer demand (rather than production efficiencies) to the process of diffusion of technologies and related services. In Chapter 3 of his dissertation, Mueller constructs a series of purely theoretical models in which he considers outcomes based on either a single service, dual service, or concentration of demand. He argues that dual service can exist in situations in which demand is concentrated but not uniform. Conversely, interdependent demand and widely distributed communication patterns tend to result in convergence. This finding resonates both with the patterns that Lipartito found in North Carolina and Virginia as well as with the success of the local independent company in Fort Wayne, Indiana, where communications demand was primarily local and regional and could clearly be met by the local independent company.[29]

Finally, despite AT&T's undisputed technological advantage in long-distance service, Mueller points out that demand for long-distance service was small and concentrated in a limited stratum of business users.[30] Theoretically, at least, this type of demand can sustain dual service, with different entities offering service in complementary niches—just as they, in fact, did in Barnett's analysis. Under the latter scenario, AT&T's superior long-distance capability could have enjoyed complementary relationships with regional companies. Since dual service, which would have afforded integrated local/long-distance service through cooperating organizations, is theoretically possible (hence monopoly is neither natural nor inevitable), he looks elsewhere for an explanation, turning his attention to strategy.

The key decision, he argues, was interconnection. Bell initially refused to interconnect with the independent telephone companies, fighting competition with lawsuits over alleged patent infringement and rate wars. Independent companies in Wisconsin and Ohio also initiated lawsuits, attempting to compel Bell to provide them interconnections because the telephone was a common carrier and therefore obligated to provide service impartially. These suits were generally either unsuccessful or were withdrawn, when independent companies realized that providing access for Bell to their subscribers ceded a valuable asset. By 1897, both AT&T and the independents subscribed to a theory of competition, which posited subscriber access territories (that is, the geographical areas in which subscribers were physically located) as a fixed resource. Thus, telephone service offered by one company necessarily diminished the potential market of a second company. Neither AT&T nor the independent companies recognized that the distinct communication needs of urban businessmen and those of small-town and rural residents might in principle have been served by overlapping telephone service areas.[31]

Physical Plant and Service

Bell's business model was consciously patterned on Western Union: high-end, national service to business clients under a single corporation that controlled both the wired plant and the service delivery. This was quite similar to the railroads, which owned the roadbed and the rolling stock and provided transportation services. In their day, this was a departure from existing practices: early nineteenth-century turnpike companies constructed roads and charged a toll for access and use. They failed.

Despite the innovation in management represented by the railroads, over time the profitable and competitive enterprises were frequently those in which the service was separated from the physical plant and in which the physical system was segmented. American Express is a case in point. American Express was begun as a fast freight service; shippers promised their clients rapid delivery, used the railroads as a common carrier, and were able to charge a selection of affluent clients what the market would bear. This meant that American Express targeted the lucrative end of the market, where the profit margins were high, and did not bear the cost of maintaining the plant itself. Rather, American Express could take advantage of what competitive pricing did exist from the transport companies while charging end-users for a special service.

A similar differentiation in service occurred in the electrical power industry. The industry evolved into a tripartite organization of large power-generating plants, transmission line companies, and local utilities that provided service to end-users. The most profitable part of this system was in long-distance transmission. Transmission line companies did not have to bear the extremely high cost of constructing power generating plants but controlled access to bulk power by the local utilities. In this case, the profitability was in segmenting the service and controlling the intermediary function. This was—and is—also the competitive part of the industry, suggesting that monopoly control is not necessary for profitability even though excessive competition can result in overbuilding and ruinous competition, as the railroads discovered and the *Corsair* incident illustrates.

A Word on Banking

All of the above examples have been drawn from the infrastructures that developed around science and technology. Banking feels like the odd man out. Banking is fundamentally a service industry based on information; it is the sum of a series of informational transactions, based on shared concepts, procedures, and relationships that enabled commodities and funds to flow within and among regions. Banking is, therefore, an infrastructure of and about information—information in the form of discounts, interest, and prices, and information (or misinformation) that allowed consumers (including other bankers and investors) to make decisions about spending and saving.

Eighteenth- and early nineteenth-century merchants considered banking an auxiliary of trade. After about 1840, the volume and complexity of financial transactions, which resulted from expanding population, public works, and economic development, precipitated specialization among the emerging financial services. Finance became separate from commerce, and banking segmented into commercial and investment houses. The range of financial intermediaries, which

APPENDIX C

included savings and loans, brokerages, and insurance companies, enabled the nation's savings to be invested in countless projects ranging from home mortgages to railroads. Of these, commercial banks were probably the most important,[32] and much of the shape and form of banking varied within increasingly restrictive thresholds and boundaries established by state and federal laws, mediated by local demands for credit and opportunities for investment.

Antebellum banks provided a source of credit and a circulating medium of exchange by issuing redeemable bank notes. An antebellum bank made money if it invested wisely, and if its notes stayed in circulation. Most of the bank's investment capital came from its investors. If a bank failed, not only did the investors lose whatever they had put into it, but the various noteholders—who ranged from small merchants and households to other banks—also suffered because the bank notes were now unredeemable and hence worthless. Thus, early banking is largely about managing currency, but in the process, a series of cooperative structures emerged.

The Suffolk system (1819 to 1858) in Massachusetts was one response to the problem of shaky bank notes and represented an attempt to stabilize the system by increasing confidence, or trust, in bank notes. The Suffolk Bank intended to reverse Gresham's Law by driving out bad money with good; to a large extent the bank succeeded, partially by threatening to redeem large numbers of notes issued by irresponsible banks, and partially by compelling other banks to participate in the system and to maintain reserves with the Suffolk bank as security for their notes.[33] Free banking (1837 to 1863) was another strategy; states established minimum entry requirements and stipulated purchase of public securities that were held as security against bank note issues. Finally, discount rates, which emerged in the context of domestic money markets, were a key indicator of the relative risk associated with a given bank's notes, and the market itself discriminated between good money and bad, while facilitating flows of capital within and among regions.[34]

Two antebellum tools, reserve requirements and discount rates, remain features of the modern banking infrastructure and have become instruments of regulatory policy. Vestiges of three other antebellum innovations also survive in modern practice: cooperative bank insurance, correspondent relationships, and the clearinghouse. Of these, the clearinghouse may be the most significant as an example of emergent cooperative behavior in a competitive system.

New York City emerged as the nation's financial center in the 1850s, and not surprisingly, many innovations originated there or in Albany. The New York Clearinghouse was organized in 1853. Like Suffolk, it relied on cooperation among interdependent institutions to achieve greater operational efficiency and institutional stability among the members and hence to instill greater public confidence in the banking system. Clearinghouses required reserves, instituted disclosure requirements, and came to act as a lender of last resort by issuing loan certificates, which member banks used during periods of financial stress. Interdependence among banks was furthered by correspondent relationships among banks and bankers' balances (reserves deposited by one bank in another as security for checks and notes), which were codified by New York state law. The New York state hierarchical model of country and city banks took on national proportions, and by the Panic of 1857, actions by New York City bankers had wide impacts.[35] Not surprisingly, the Civil War legislation, which mapped out a pyramid of relationships among banks patterned on New York's law and practice, also set New York City at the apex. Elements of the clearinghouse system were even perpetuated in the Federal Reserve system (1913), including check clearing, hierarchical organization based on the size of the bank and the population it served, and voluntary membership. The irony—and the conundrum—is that structural interdependence, which strengthened the position of any one member, also enabled weakness in one part of the system to travel throughout it,[36] as evidenced in crises in 1857, 1907, and 1929-1930.

More Questions

This paper carries a question in its title. If the utility of history is to provide solutions, then the answer is "proceed with caution," because the solutions that were right in 1890 are unlikely to work in 1990, and it would be folly to map rate structures from 1900 to 2000. Indeed, the Bell system's initial decision to pattern its business strategy on Western Union's successful national monopoly fundamentally misunderstood the implications of telephony as a social phenomenon, and the error brought Bell intense competition in many local and regional markets. But if the point is to provide a common framework and baseline of experience, then history has something to offer.

Whether by abstracting service delivery from the physical plant or by segmenting the system, differentiation of services as a means of providing competition and introducing a profit incentive carries a few questions. How will the physical plant be built and who will maintain and upgrade it? And what can be done about cream-skimming, that is, offering services that skim off the lucrative end of the market so that serving the entire market becomes unprofitable? Historically, both the telephone company and the electrical power companies have used cross-subsidization among market segments as a pricing strategy. In the 1920s, residential electric rates subsidized industrial rates, and from the end of World War II until 1974, long-distance telephone rates subsidized local rates.

Federal intervention has been one means of ensuring fairness, either through regulation or by creating incentives through tax-advantaged or below-market loans in the case of rural electrification. Indeed, the Rural Electrification Administration (REA) is considered a success story. In 1930, about 10 percent of the farms in the United States had access to electricity; by 1946, half of the nation's farms were electrified and the program was solvent. Nearly every dollar that had been loaned out had been repaid. The REA did result in the organization of more than 1,000 decentralized, small-scale cooperatives serving 5 million families. In the postwar period, it also led to competition with local utility companies that effectively increased their range of service. In some instances, the power companies skimmed off the most lucrative customers by building their lines through the most profitable areas, thus depriving local cooperatives of an important segment of their customer base. Moreover, in the late 1940s, efforts by the Truman administration to continue to expand public power were frustrated by Congress' refusal to fund construction of transmission lines. In 1952, transmission line construction was included in the appropriation to Southwest Power. Through a combination of REA funding and federal flood control policies, which resulted in hydroelectric dam construction, national electrification was accomplished in the 1950s.[37]

Federal intervention clearly resulted in expansion of electricity to underserved rural populations. However, it is less clear whether public intervention has historically best served the interests of the consumer or those of the producer. Consider the example of banking. Key concepts and relationships of the banking infrastructure, which were invented to improve its stability and shore up public confidence, migrated from the private to the public sector, where legislation and regulation broadened the scope of their impact. These include the discount rate, reserves, checks and check clearing, and interdependence through cooperative structural relationships. Many historical and contemporary observers argue that banking remains sound and profitable so long as public confidence in it remains strong; panics occur when the public loses confidence. But when voluntary private cooperative solutions seemed to fail, public reform efforts have stepped in, and public requirements, whether in the form of free banking thresholds or New Deal mandates, have become a means of building public confidence in what is ultimately a private system.

On the other hand, the contents of the New Deal reforms do not appear to have addressed the underlying economic causes of the Great Depression,[38] and the separation of investment from commercial banking—the core New Deal reform—in fact met the needs of bankers themselves. During the expansionist 1920s, the distinctions between investment and commercial banking had blurred. Real wages were rising, and large numbers of small accounts became attractive, since they could accumulate into significant pools of capital. In this new market, the commercial banks enjoyed several advantages. They had access to a new source of funds through depositors' accounts; both investment banks and trust companies had traditionally relied on the resources of a select clientele. It was very successful. Between 1927 and 1930, the percentage of bond issues that originated with banks and their affiliates doubled, while the influence of private investment banking shrank accordingly. But when the crash came, more people experienced the collapse directly, and their bankers became their targets. Faced with hostile hearings on Capitol Hill, private investment bankers, who had seen commercial banks encroach upon their securities business in the 1920s, lined up behind the separation of investment and commercial banking, thus reducing competition in a declining market. Commercial bankers themselves came on board in part to forestall more severe regulation and in part because the new legislation promised to exclude investment banks from demand deposit business, relieving commercial banks from the need to pay interest on demand deposits and securing them a part of the market.[39]

Proponents of the capture theory of regulation—wherein the industry subject to regulatory authority "captures" or subverts the commission or agency to its own ends—can easily see in the structure of early regulatory agencies how stabilization of the industry met corporate needs by limiting competition. Indeed, Gregg Jarrell argues that utility and power companies that were subject to regulation after 1912 actually saw relatively higher profits, higher rates, and lower output after regulation than before. Thus, he believes that state regulation at the turn of the century was a "proproducer policy."[40] William Emmons in his dissertation in business economics comes to somewhat similar conclusions with respect to regulation in the 1930s. Namely, state regulation appears to have had little or no effect upon prices, but prices tended to fall when competition was present. Thus, competition—not regulation—resulted in lower prices to consumers.[41]

Whether the private sector would have expanded into otherwise unprofitable or marginal markets in electrical power or telephony without federal involvement through mandates, preferential loans, and hydropower construction projects is a separable and as-yet unanswered question. Moreover, as the history of banking illustrates, with liquidity crises and panics occurring with depressing 20-year regularity between 1800 and 1930, the price of competition may be a level of instability that is considered unacceptable.

For the near term, we are likely to live out the curse of interesting times. But based on these historical examples, I would venture a few predictions:

1. There will be several, not one, "killer apps" in the information technologies and they will possess the following characteristic. They will be *services* that clearly meet users' immediate needs—product substitution—and enable consumers to begin to do things differently, just as small consumers of central power sources took advantage of fractionalized delivery of power to obtain interior illumination and to begin to mechanize their labor-intensive processes. We have already seen this in the introduction of word processing and spreadsheet programs as well as the deployment of intranet and e-mail technologies. Recall, too, that the demand is differentiated, and not all "users" are conventional end-users. For example, there will be a market for intermediate services just as there exists a machine tool industry to support manufacturing. The information technologies will thus ripple through our institutions, so becoming ubiquitous, sometimes noticeable, like the lamp on the wall, and sometime invisible, like the wiring behind it.

2. These "killer apps," like Edison's lamp, will not be ends in themselves but will unlock an underlying technology and science that are sufficiently robust to support other kinds of activities, just as the significance of the lamp was not interior illumination but the system of power generation and delivery that eventually enabled the creation of a power infrastructure. Many of today's information applications themselves will thus migrate into the information infrastructure wherein the defining characteristic is the ability to support more advanced applications and services.

3. There will be winners and losers. We have already seen this exemplified in former household names that are now barely memories. This is not an aberration of the high-technology world but rather characterizes all of the infrastructures we have studied from railroads to banking. How stability and fairness will be achieved—whether through government regulation and/or incentives, or through market mechanisms, such as pricing strategies, or through a combination of public and private strategies—remains to be seen. History is replete with examples and experiments, some of which succeeded and some of which failed. What they show conclusively is that we humans are inventive and time will tell.

NOTES

1. Thomas P. Hughes, *Networks of Powers: Electrification in Western Society, 1880-1930* (Baltimore and London: The Johns Hopkins University Press, 1983), 108; Thomas P. Hughes, "The Electrification of America: The System Builders," *Technology and Culture* 20 (January 1979): 143.
2. Population data are based on the U.S. census and are tabulated in the appendices to Bernard Bailyn et al., *The Great Republic* (Lexington, Massachusetts: D.C. Health and Company, 1977), xviii.
3. David E. Nye, *Electrifying America: Social Meanings of a New Technology* (Cambridge, Massachusetts: MIT Press, 1990), 260–61.
4. Carter Goodrich, *Government Promotion of Canals and Railroads, 1800-1890* (New York: Columbia University Press, 1960), 271. On the size of the grants, see Lloyd J. Mercer, *Railroads and Land Grant Policy: A Study in Government Intervention* (New York: Academic Press, 1982), 7.
5. See J.B. Legler, R. Sylla, and J.J. Wallis, "United States City Finances and the Growth of Government, 1850-1902," *Journal of Economic History* 48 (1988): 347-56.
6. The expansion of federal authority into social welfare issues during the New Deal is discussed in Robert L. Rabin, "Federal Regulation in Historical Perspective," *Stanford Law Review* 38 (1986): 1192, 1243-1261.
7. On corporate support for Edison's research, see Hughes, "The Electrification of America," 130-32; on Western Union's competition and the invention of the telephone, see David A. Hounshell, "Bell and Gray: Contrasts in Style, Politics, and Etiquette," *Proceedings of the IEEE* 64 (September 1976), 1306; on the significance of Edison's systems approach, see Hughes, *Networks of Power*, 21; on prior experiments in electric lamp design, see Robert Friedel and Paul Israel, *Edison's Electric Light: Biography of an Invention* (New Brunswick, N.J.: Rutgers University Press, 1986), 115; on the competition with gas, see ibid., 123, 206-207.
8. George Rogers Taylor and Irene D. Neu, *The American Railroad Network, 1861-1890* (Cambridge, Massachusetts: Harvard University Press, 1956), 14, 42-45, 48.

9. Taylor and Neu, *The American Railroad Network,* 52-58; Goodrich, *Government Promotion of American Canals and Railroads,* 179-81; Thomas E. Root, *Railroad Land Grants from Canals to Transcontinentals* (Tulsa, Oklahoma: Natural Resources Law Section Monograph Series, No. 4. Section of Natural Resources Law, American Bar Association and the National Energy Law and Policy Institute, University of Tulsa, 1987), 19-20.
10. William Paul Barnett, "The Organizational Ecology of the Early American Telephone Industry: A Study of the Technological Cases of Competition and Mutualism" (Ph.D. dissertation, University of California, Berkeley, 1988), 12; Milton Mueller, "The Telephone War: Interconnection, Competition and Monopoly in the Making of Universal Telephone Service, 1894-1920" (Ph.D. dissertation, University of Pennsylvania, 1989), 3; Peter Temin and Louis Galambos, *The Fall of the Bell System: A Study in Prices and Politics* (Cambridge: Cambridge University Press, 1987), 11.
11. William J. Hausman and John L. Neufeld, "The Structure and Profitability of the U.S. Electric Utility Industry at the Turn of the Century," *Business History* 32 (April 1990): 232-33.
12. Hausman and Neufeld, "The US Electric Utility Industry," 238-39, 241; Hughes, "The System Builders," 157-59. American Power and Light was, for example, instrumental in organizing Utah Power and Light; see John S. McCormick, "The Beginning of Modern Electric Power Service in Utah, 1912-1922," *Utah Historical Quarterly* 56 (winter 1988): 4-22. On the extent of electrical power controlled by the holding companies, see Jacobson, "Water Works, Electric Utilities, and Cable Television," 83. On the dependence of municipal utilities on private companies for bulk power, see Richard Rudolph and Scott Ridley, *Power Struggle: The Hundred Year War Over Electricity* (New York: Harper & Row, 1986), 38-41.
13. Friedel and Israel, *Edison's Electric Light,* 123, 206-207.
14. Prior to the opening of the Erie Canal in 1825, the costs of shipping one ton of wheat or flour from Buffalo to New York City show that the price fell from $100 by road to $10-$12 by the Erie Canal. Moreover, a single canal barge could haul a load ten times the size of that drawn by a four-horse Conestoga wagon on the best toll roads. Robert William Fogel, "Notes on the Social Saving Question," *Journal of Economic History* 39 (1979): 30, 49-50; Patrick O'Brien, *The New Economic History of the Railways* (New York: St. Martin's Press, 1977), 83; on the primacy of the transfer from road to water, see Albert Fishlow, *American Railroads and the Transportation of the Antebellum Economy* (Harvard Economic Studies CXXVII. Cambridge, Mass.: Harvard University Press, 1965), 44, 55, 77; John B. Rae, *The Road and Car in American Life* (Cambridge, Mass., and London: MIT Press, 1971), 20; John F. Stover, *Iron Road to the West: American Railroads in the 1850s* (New York: Columbia University Press, 1978), 160-64. There has been extensive discussion with respect to calculating the rates via water and rail reflecting the variations by commodity, distance, and destination as well as widespread rebating. For a review of the technical literature on this issue, see David L. Lightner, "Railroads and the American Economy: The Fogel Thesis in Retrospect," *Journal of Transport History* 4 (1983): 21-26.
15. Harold L. Platt, *The Electric City: Energy and the Growth of the Chicago Area, 1880-1930* (Chicago: University of Chicago Press, 1991), 46-47; "Houston's First Battle Over Utility Rates," *The Houston Review: History and Culture of the Gulf Coast* 9 (1987): 59-68. The principal output of petroleum refineries from 1859 to 1900 was kerosene, which was used as an alternative to gas and electricity for interior illumination. Gas required connections to a central source. Although electricity might be obtained from a self-contained plant, the threshold cost was relatively high, and there remained the problem of exhausting the heat generated by the plant. Kerosene, however, was easily transported, provided acceptable, steady light, and did not require hook-ups to a centralized system. Still, by 1900, petroleum refiners could see that electric lighting would soon displace kerosene and focused their attention on developing stoves and furnaces, which had been available but were not widely used. Oil burning furnaces went on the market in the 1920s but did not begin to displace coal-burning furnaces until the price of

APPENDIX C

coal soared after World War II; see Ruth Schwartz Cowan, *More Work for Mother: The Ironies of Household Technology from the Open Hearth to the Microwave* (New York: Basic Books, 1983), 94-95; Mark H. Rose, "Urban Environments and Technological Innovation: Energy Choices in Denver and Kansas City, 1900-1940," *Technology and Culture* 25 (July 1984), 532-34.

16. Richard B. Du Boff, *Electric Power in American Manufacturing, 1889-1958* (New York: Arno Press, 1979), 64, 71-74, 98-100, 134-35.
17. In a group-drive system, one energy source supplies power to several machines; in a unit-drive system, there is one energy source per machine. Walter J. Devine, "From Shafts to Wires: Historical Perspective on Electrification," *Journal of Economic History* 43 (June 1983): 347-68, 371; Harry T. Oshima, "The Growth of U.S. Factory Productivity: The Significance of New Technologies in the Early Decades of the Twentieth Century," *Journal of Economic History* 44 (March 1984): 164. This summary of the advantages of unit-drive systems, which is based on Devine's important essay, is found in Paul A. David, "The Dynamo and the Computer: An Historic Perspective on the Modern Productivity Paradox," *American Economic Review* 80 (May 1990): 358.
18. Arthur G. Woolf, "Electricity, Productivity, and Labor Saving: American Manufacturing, 1900-1929," *Explorations in Economic History* 21 (April 1984): 178, 189. The average price of electricity fell by 50 percent between 1910 and 1929; coal prices tripled in the same period, and wages doubled.
19. David E. Nye, *Electrifying America: Social Meanings of a New Technology* (Cambridge, Massachusetts: The MIT Press, 1990), 186-87. Nye somewhat oversimplifies Woolf's thesis, since Woolf himself acknowledges (based on Devine's research) "the tremendous amount of freedom in plant design" (p. 177) afforded by electric power, although he predicates willingness to use electric power on its falling prices. Moreover, Woolf goes on to conclude that "the process of electrification allowed for substantial management and factory design changes that greatly enhanced productivity"; see Woolf, "Electricity and Productivity," 189.
20. This tautology is particularly acute in the history of the internal combustion engine and the automobile, although it also riddles the history of telephony. For a discussion, see David A. Kirsh, "The Electric Car and the Burden of History: Studies in Automotive Systems Rivalry in America, 1890-1996" (Ph.D. dissertation, Stanford University, 1996), 5, 22-31.
21. Barnett, "Organizational Ecology of the Early American Telephone Industry," 13, 16-17.
22. Kenneth Lipartito, *The Bell System and Regional Business: The Telephone in the South, 1877-1920* (Baltimore: The Johns Hopkins University Press, 1989), 93.
23. Stover, *Iron Road to the West: American Railroads in the 1850s*, 117.
24. Kenneth Lipartito, "System Building at the Margin: The Problem of Public Choice in the Telephone Industry," *Journal of Economic History* 49 (June 1989): 323; *The Bell System and Regional Business: The Telephone in the South, 1877-1920* (Baltimore: The Johns Hopkins University Press, 1989), Chapter 1.
25. Milton Mueller, "The Switchboard Problem: Scale, Signaling, and Organization in Manual Telephone Switching, 1877-1897," *Technology and Culture* 30 (July 1989): 534-60, *passim*.
26. Lipartito, "System Building at the Margin," 332.
27. Claude S. Fischer, *America Calling: A Social History of the Telephone to 1940* (Berkeley: University of California Press, 1992), 136, Chapters 4, 5, and 7 for detailed discussion of conclusions stated on pp. 261-63.
28. Fischer, *America Calling*, 47-48, 81-83; see also "'Touch Someone': The Telephone Industry Discovers Sociability," *Technology and Culture* 29 (January 1988): 32-61.
29. Milton Mueller, "The Telephone War: Interconnection, Competition and Monopoly in the Making of Universal Telephone Service, 1894-1920" (Ph.D. dissertation, University of Pennsylvania, 1989), 132-33; Lipartito, *The Bell System and Regional Business*, 167.

Mueller bases his argument on interdependent demand theory, particularly as articulated in 1989 by W. Brian Arthur, at that time a professor of economics at Stanford University. Arthur postulated a theory of "increasing returns," by which he meant that the utility of a given technology increases as more people select that technology. However, Arthur also stresses that the initial selection may be a matter of historical accident, rather than the result of economic efficiencies or technological superiority. Over time, as increasing returns tend to create positive feedback that magnifies otherwise random variation, the process of adopting technology will tend to converge on a standard. Arthur describes the process of technological adoption as "a random walk with absorbing barriers," wherein the absorbing barrier is the point at which a given technology has a large enough market advantage to compel most users to conform to it, a phenomenon he calls "lock-in." The firm that controls the critical technology will, therefore, have obtained a monopoly position. The synopsis of Arthur's thesis is based on Mueller's discussion; see Mueller, "The Telephone War," 44-46. The original paper is W. Brian Arthur, "Competing Technologies and Lock-in by Historical Events," *The Economic Journal* 99 (March 1989): 116-31. The most obvious, current example of the phenomenon Arthur describes is Beta versus VHS. Arthur is not the only architect of the theory of increasing returns, but he has given it a rigorous, econometric expression that nonetheless provides for fuzzy vagaries of historical circumstances.

30. Mueller, "The Telephone War," 47-48.
31. Mueller, "The Telephone War," 183-97.
32. On the importance of commercial banks relative to other financial services entities, see Larry Schweikart, "U.S. Commercial Banking: A Historiographical Survey," *Business History Review* 65 (1991): 606-607. Schweikart's essay is an excellent review of the literature as of about 1990 as well as an introduction to the fundamental issues in the field.
33. On the Suffolk system, see Donald J. Mullineaux, "Competitive Monies and the Suffolk Bank System: A Contractual Perspective," *Southern Economic Journal* 53 (1987): 884-98.
34. There is a substantial literature on free banking. In addition to Schweikart's essay, the following offer some perspectives on this period: James A. Kahn, "Another Look at Free Banking in the United States," *American Economic Review* 75 (1985): 881-85; Hugh Rockoff, "Institutional Requirements for Stable Free Banking," *Cato Journal* 6 (1986): 617-34; "The Free Banking Era: A Reexamination," *Journal of Money, Credit, and Banking* 6 (1974): 141-68; Arthur J. Rolnick and Warren E. Weber, "Inherent Instability in Banking: The Free Banking Experience," *Cato Journal* 5 (1986): 877-90; "New Evidence on the Free Banking Era," *American Economic Review* 73 (1983): 1080-91; George A. Selgin and Lawrence H. White, "The Evolution of a Free Banking System," *Economic Inquiry* 25 (1987): 439-57.
35. Charles W. Calomiris and Larry Schweikart, "The Panic of 1857: Origins, Transmission, and Containment," *Journal of Economic History* 51 (1991): 807-34 provides an overview of the literature as well as a context-dependent explanation of the panic itself based on the structure of the financial markets and contemporary events. See also: Richard H. Timberlake, "The Central Banking Role of Clearinghouse Associations," *Journal of Money, Credit, and Banking* 16 (1984): 1-15; Gary Gorton, "Clearinghouses and the Origin of Central Banking in the United States," *Journal of Economic History* 45 (1985): 277-83; Gary Gorton and Donald J. Mullineaux, "The Joint Production of Confidence: Endogenous Regulation and Nineteenth Century Commerical-Bank Clearinghouses," *Journal of Money, Credit, and Banking* 19 (1987): 457-68.
36. See, for example, Bruce D. Smith, "Bank Panics, Suspensions, and Geography: Some Notes on the 'Contagion of Fear' in Banking," *Economics Inquiry* 29 (1991): 230-48.
37. On federal flood control policy, see D. Clayton Brown, *Electricity for Rural America: The Fight for the REA* (Contributions in Economics and Economic History, No. 29; Westport, Connecticut: Greenwood Press, 1980), 109-13; Jeanette Ford, "Electricity for a Region: The Southwest Power Administration," *Chronicles of Oklahoma* 60 (Winter 1982-1983): 455; Charles Coate, "The New School of Thought: Reclamation and the Fair Deal, 1945-1953," *Journal of the West* 22 (April 1983): 58-59. On competition between rural cooperatives and

local power companies, see David Mitchell, "The Origins of the Robertson Electric Cooperative," *East Texas Historical Journal* 25 (2, 1987): 71-79.
38. Explaining the Great Depression, which is notable primarily for its duration, has taken on a contentious life of its own. Current explanations emphasize its complexity and combination of macroeconomic, internal, and monetary dimensions. What is clear, however, is that it was not caused by commercial bankers invading the precincts of investment bankers. For overviews, see Barry Eichengreen, "The Origins and Nature of the Great Slump Revisited," *Economic History Review* 45 (1992): 213-39; Schweikart, "U.S. Commercial Banking," 633-35; Eugene Nelson White, "Before the Glass-Steagall Act: An Analysis of the Investment Banking Activities of National Banks," *Explorations in Economic History* 23 (1986): 52.
39. George J. Benston, *The Separation of Commercial and Investment Banking: The Glass-Steagall Act Revisited and Reconsidered* (New York: Oxford University Press, 1990), 136-38; White, "Before the Glass-Steagall Act," 34-37; "The Political Economy of Banking Regulation, 1864-1933," *Journal of Economic History* 42 (1982): 39; Robert Eli Litan, "An Economic Inquiry into the Expansion of Bank Powers" (Ph.D. dissertation, Yale University, 1987), 45-47; Vincent P. Carosso, *Investment Banking in America* (Harvard Studies in Business History 25; Cambridge, Mass., Harvard University Press, 1970), 249-51; George David Smith and Richard Sylla, "The Transformation of Financial Capitalism: An Essay on the History of American Capital Markets," *Financial Markets, Institutions & Instruments* 2 (no. 2, 1993), 27.
40. Gregg A. Jarrell, "The Demand for State Regulation of the Electric Utility Industry," *Journal of Law and Economics* 21 (October 1978): 292-93.
41. William Monroe Emmons III, "Private and Public Responses to Market Failure in the U.S. Electric Power Industry, 1888-1942" (Ph.D. dissertation, Harvard University, 1989), 172-73.

COMPUTER AND COMMUNICATION TECHNOLOGIES: IMPACTS ON THE ORGANIZATION OF ENTERPRISE AND THE ESTABLISHMENT AND MAINTENANCE OF CIVIL SOCIETY

John Leslie King and Kenneth L. Kraemer

University of California, Irvine

Introduction

This paper is the first step toward a comprehensive review of critical issues in the social and economic impacts of computers and communications technologies. It is broad in its coverage, corresponding to the charge we were given.[1] The paper considers social and economic impacts of at several levels: groups, organizations, trans-organization, and society. It also discusses the policy-relevant implications of the research and issues for future research. It is grounded in empirical research as well as established and emerging theory. However, it proceeds from the assumption that the changes being wrought by computers and communications technology are of such magnitude that fundamental theoretical aspects of social understanding might be challenged. Thus, we are not bound by the isomorphic constraints of existing disciplinary tradition in our analysis. The ultimate purpose of the paper is to challenge the community of scholars engaged in research on the profound socio-economic and socio-technical changes under way.

The audience for the paper includes scholars in the social sciences, broadly defined, including economics, sociology, political science, psychology, communications, and management. It concerns, as well, scholars from the science and engineering disciplines who are concerned with the effects of their creations and with a desire to learn more about how the processes of technological design, development, implementation, and maintenance can be improved in the general interests of human welfare. Finally, it includes scholars from the humanities and

---

[1]The charge for this paper was given by Hal Varian in a message of May 5, 1997: "I suggest that you try to broaden your overview to include a survey of the potentially policy-relevant economic and social science contributions to computers and communications issues. Relevant issues include the role of government, privacy, free speech, intellectual property issues, employment, training/education, commerce, communities, and organizations. I realize that you cannot address all of these issues in depth, but it would be useful to look at as many as possible."

the arts who are interested in the changes, actual and potential, that computers and communications technology imply for human experience and self-reflection.

The paper is preliminary, as any paper of this breadth must be. It is a collage, assembled by the authors based on their own research and that of others. Despite the limitations of this preliminary paper, it supports several strong conclusions with implications for future research. The paper hopefully provides a background for, and a stimulus to, discussion at the workshop.

Organization of This Paper

This paper discusses three areas:

- The organization of enterprise,
- Establishment and maintenance of civil society, and
- Recommendations for research.

The rationale for this organization is dependent on several underlying assumptions that must be understood if the discussion is to make sense. The first assumption is that all social phenomena must ultimately be understood in ways that account for individual action. Although our analysis takes place above the individual level, beginning at the lowest point with characteristics of goal-oriented work groups, we recognize that the foundations of our discussion must be traced to explanations of individual intention and action, no matter how extensively mediated or channeled by higher-level social forces or conditions of the natural world. Moreover, we assume that the closer our analysis is to the individual level, the greater will be the power of individualistic explanations in accounting for what we observe. At the higher end of our analysis, at the broad levels of culture and society, the power of individualistic explanations is expected to weaken considerably.

These assumptions justify our selection of the categories of enterprise and civil society as the two levels of discussion for our purposes. We acknowledge that other conceptual schema can work to organize this discussion. However, we feel that this scheme has the advantages of capturing all the major social science perspectives needed for the task, while remaining parsimonious and indicative of the distinction between "micro" and "macro" approaches to social phenomena common throughout the social sciences.

Enterprise in our use refers to those human activities that are undertaken for the direct production of goods and services, whether under a market-based governance structure or a policy-based regime. Enterprise includes everything from local businesses to multinational firms in the private sector, and everything from special districts for services such as flood control to multinational military forces in the public sector. The defining features of enterprise include the pursuit of production objectives within specific production constraints, an inherent logic of production (however poorly understood by the participants in the enterprise), and tangible measures of performance in the accomplishment of the objectives. We adopt a perspective that is influenced primarily by microeconomics, social psychology, and organizational politics, each of which has close ties to individualist views of social behavior. The operating assumption is that the people involved in enterprise will, to the extent that they are able, act in ways that conform to economic rationality, are socially tractable at the group level, and are politically stable and salient. The successful pursuit of these goals will produce equilibrium conditions that are not easily disturbed. This implies that existing equilibria, produced largely before the advent of recent computers and communications technologies, will not be easily disturbed. The onus, from this perspective, is on showing that impacts from those technologies are real, significant, and lasting.

Civil society refers to the larger social order that makes economic rationality, social tractability, and political stability possible at the local level of groups, organizations, and production sectors. This position proceeds from the premise that democratic government is a satisfactory, though not necessarily optimal, form of social governance for achieving those ends, while other forms of social governance, such as autocracy, oligarchy, and plutocracy, are not. Our focus is mainly on social institutions that shape the organization of enterprise, and is predicated on the assumption that civil society enables particular organization of enterprise, and not the other way around. Our assessment of computers and communications technologies in the realm of civil society draws on intellectual perspectives from political theory, the sociology of institutions, and cultural anthropology, and to a lesser degree, institutional economics.

We have attempted to anchor our discussion in empirical research findings whenever possible, although in this draft we have not specifically cited the research we have used. However, a hallmark of research on the social impacts of computers and communications is that coverage of this vast field has been sporadic and episodic. In addition, the high probability that use of these technologies is changing fundamental aspects of enterprise and civil society makes it exceedingly difficult to anchor some of our conclusions and recommendations in established empirical evidence. As we suggest in the conclusion to this paper, a major challenge for the research community is to define, design, and implement research into the social impacts of computing and communications that serve as sound guidance for technology design and development, organization of enterprise, and the establishment and maintenance of civil society in the information age.

Clarification of Some Terms

Computers, in this review, refer to substantially more than the basic machines associated with computing. Computer technology is a "package" that encompasses a complex, interdependent system comprising people (computer specialists, users, managers), hardware (computer mainframes, peripherals, telecommunications gear), software (operating systems, utilities, and application programs), techniques (management science models, procedures, organizational arrangements), and data. Computing and communications technologies are increasingly intertwined in the everyday functioning of socio-technical systems at all levels of organizations and society. Other information technologies, especially mass communication technologies such as film, audio recordings, radio, television, and print, have implications for organizations and society, but we do not include them in this analysis. We focus on computers and those key information technologies that tend to be closely linked with computers, mainly data communications.

The Organization of Enterprise

We begin with the assumption that the underlying drivers that shape individual actions leading to the organization of enterprise are individual desires for economic rationality, social tractability, and political stability. These objectives are meaningless unless understood within a context of civil society that embodies abiding social values, and thus must be seen as derivative of rather than generative of those values. It might therefore seem that the organization of enterprise is determined by civil society, but this is not the case. Certain forms of social order make particular kinds of enterprise difficult or even impossible, but within the space of what is possible under a given social order, the organization of enterprise can be seen as a matter of choices made by individuals and groups. It is further assumed that the individuals and groups making such choices are at least to some degree blind to the outcomes that particular choices entail, and thus, the discovery of satisfactory organization schemes will be at least to some degree discovered through trial and error as opposed to created entirely by design.

This section deals with the organization of enterprise by dividing the subject into key issues that relate to computers and communications technologies. These are the concept of organization, the organization of production and distribution, organizational structure, enterprise boundaries, mediation patterns, organizational politics and process, and work life.

The Concept of "Organization"

Perhaps the most important potential impact of computers and communications on organizations is a shift in the very concept of "organization" as an economic and social entity. Once considered to be semipermanent and routinized by definition, ideal organizations increasingly have come to be seen as flexible, change-oriented, and able to shift their boundaries, alliances, and partnerships rapidly to meet changing conditions. Computers and communication technologies increasingly permit anytime, anywhere communication, synchronous and asynchronous collaboration, and tight linkages in operational processes within and between organizations (e.g., manufacturers and their suppliers and distributors, and manufacturers and the direct buying public). The concept of the "adhocracy"—a fluid organization in which members come and go as interests change—has emerged as competition for the concept of bureaucracy. After many decades of increasing vertical integration of production and growth as a totem of success, many organizations have divested themselves of every function that was not a core competence, and that could possibly be "outsourced" or bought on the market. Small really did become beautiful, at least in principle. Young entrepreneurs who started little companies in their garages built novel ideas into huge companies and fortunes, capturing the imagination of the world. And the mighty such as AT&T, IBM, and GM appeared shaken as the world they had built started to collapse around them.

Yet, as recent history has shown, organizations such as AT&T, IBM, and GM have by no means been pushed aside by the changes of the information age. They have adopted and adapted the technologies and harnessed them in ways that have allowed radical "downsizing" of work forces while retaining and in some cases enhancing top management control over firms' performance and profitability. And the start-up companies created in garages have found it necessary to adopt time-honored aspects of organizational hierarchy in order to function effectively. This lesson from recent history reveals an important but frequently overlooked aspect of the information revolution: that its revolutionary character is being channeled through pathways established by powerful social and institutional forces that are not necessarily swept aside by the effects of technology, no matter how powerful those effects are.

Much of the rhetoric about profound change in organizations has been speculative and undisciplined, based more on idealized views of what organizations ought to be rather than on the practical realities that shape organizational form and function. One can construct scenarios of organizational demassing and decentralization, but one also can just as easily construct sound arguments that computer and communication technologies give new life to the traditional bureaucracy. Functions normally carried out by middle managers—information gathering, decision making within directives, communications with lower-level staff, and monitoring and upward-reporting of activities carried on below—can be replaced to some extent with technology. The resulting "flattening" of the organization through the elimination of middle managers has been said to bring greater "empowerment" of remaining employees. But technological change can just as easily allow significant increases in organizational centralization, tighter monitoring of employee activity, more effective enforcement of compliance with the desires of top management, and the redesign of tasks in ways that make it difficult for employees to act outside of prescribed patterns.

There are reasons to be confident about profound changes under way in the character and concept of organizations as a result of new computer and communications technologies. At the same time, it is important not to let ideological enthusiasm substitute for careful reasoning and empirical research. The remainder of this section on the organization of enterprise explores the ways in which impacts might arise, and forms the base for discussion of needed research.

The Organization of Production and Distribution

Economic activity has long been divided into production of goods and services and their distribution to the final consumers. Neither production nor distribution makes sense without the other, and the concept of the value chain has emerged to unite them in an end-to-end scheme. Of particular importance is the concept of coordination. Coordination is both necessary and costly, and in the past several decades much attention has been focused on transaction costs— easily observable costs of coordination—to explain how and why production and distribution are organized the way they are. In particular, the focus has been on the choice between organizing by hierarchy, meaning the imposition of a policy regime to ensure coordination of various components of production and distribution, vs. organization through markets, meaning interaction among parties governed by the balancing of supply and demand through the marketplace.

It is misleading to place hierarchy in opposition to market mechanisms, because this implies that the two are in some consistent way substitutable for one another. In practice, they tend to be complementary. At the most rudimentary level, markets can be seen as an organic innovation to facilitate economic exchange between individuals with minimum social overhead and no social direction other than to permit participants to pursue their own welfare. In this characterization, hierarchies evolve mainly for coping with imperfections in markets such as occur in the case of public goods that, for various reasons, are socially desirable but unlikely to be provided by individual investors in a market setting (e.g., national defense). Although not directly substitutable for each other, here is an important sense in which societies choose to organize production and distribution predominantly around either hierarchies or markets.

An extreme comparison is the command economies vs. market economies, characterized by the two sides of the Cold War. A more useful example for this discussion is that between vertical integration of production and distribution of products and services, conceivably under a single company throughout the value chain, versus a disaggregated value chain in which products and services are passed along from one organization to another through sale in markets, being "assembled" as they go, before reaching the final consumer. Where workable, markets are usually considered to be more efficient than hierarchies, and in a condition of open choice among options, hierarchies emerge mainly as a consequence of market failures. The political position that derives from this is that the market should govern as much of production and distribution as possible, while hierarchies serve as a kind of back-up in the event of market failure. Given that we have already segregated civil society from this discussion, it is not necessary to argue this point in detail at the level of organization of enterprise.

It has been argued that computers and communications technologies can precipitate a shift from hierarchical organization of production and distribution to more market-like forms. The logic of this argument is that an infrastructure of computing and communication technology providing 24-hour access at low cost to almost any kind of price and product information desired by buyers would reduce the informational barriers to efficient market operation, and presumably facilitate a shift from hierarchy to market organization. If this infrastructure also provided the means for effecting real-time transactions such as sales based on such information, whole classes of intermediaries such as sales clerks, stock brokers, travel agents, and so on, whose function is to provide an essential information link between buyers and sellers, might be eliminated. Removal of intermediaries would not only prune the existing hierarchies that now govern buying and selling, but would also reduce the costs in the production and distribution value chain, further encouraging the shift toward markets.

Organization Structure

Organization structure refers to the social organization of authority and responsibility assignments within groups with production objectives, predicated on needs of specialization and division of labor. A long-standing concern in organizational structure is over the centralization versus decentralization of decision authority within organizations. Research indicates that use of computers and communications technologies per se has neither a centralizing nor a decentralizing influence. The prevailing organizational context in which the technologies are used is a much stronger influence on whether organizations centralize or decentralize than is the technology, which can support either type of arrangement. In general, use of these technologies tends to reinforce existing organizational tendencies, and in some cases can be a powerful tool in facilitating organizational changes. An organization that wishes to decentralize can implement information systems that provide to lower level managers the information necessary for decentralized decision making. Organizations wishing to centralize can use the technologies to facilitate surveillance by top management over lower-level managers. Computers and communications technologies have been used to downsize middle management when there is congruence between the centralization of authority in the organization and centralization of control over use of computing resources. In organizations where both are decentralized, middle managers use the technology to enhance their value to senior management and to maintain their relative influence and size.

Enterprise Boundaries

Computers and communications technologies have enabled the emergence of the trans-organizational enterprise. As producing organizations downsize and outsource in order to focus on their core competencies and shed organizational weight and overhead, they become less capable of providing full-range products and services for the markets they supply. This is particularly true in the case of highly complicated, limited production products (e.g., large information systems and commercial aircraft) but also extends to more traditional manufacturing sectors. The "manufacturer" in many cases is not deeply involved in the actual fabrication of parts, or even in assembly. These arrangements are quite different from those represented by the large, integrated manufacturers who bought large numbers of supplies and parts from small suppliers. These arrangements often entail interlocking minority ownership arrangements, long-term supply/buy commitments, sharing of product and market information, cooperative design and manufacturing, and risk sharing. They depend on rapid and effective communication and information links among partners, supplied through information technology.

The trans-organizational enterprise can alter alliances and allegiances and create community at various social levels. For example, Detroit was the center of the global automobile industry while the U.S. automobile industry dominated the world. As Japanese competition emerged, the result was not a shift in centers (e.g., Detroit to Yokohama), but rather, industry realignment around a global market for "world cars," with manufacturing and assembly taking place in many countries. This shift has had many ramifications, including imbalances in merchandise trade, use of transborder transfer pricing to manipulate national taxation systems, and the shifting patterns of employment as jobs are sent "offshore." While not directly causative of these changes, computers and communications technologies have made them possible. The technologies also have brought about a blurring of the traditional links between employment and place. Large U.S. firms have set up major information processing centers in India and the Philippines, where skilled programming talent can be found at low prices. These foreign workers "commute" to work as "virtual" guest workers over the satellite and fiber-optic links that tie them to their employers. In a sense, the technologies have eliminated national borders, and in the process have made many national labor policies moot.

Mediation Patterns

Many aspects of enterprise rely on mediation to function correctly within the larger production system. For example, many supply and distribution chains use the mediation of brokers, expediters, agents, and so on. Mediators often survive through successful exploitation of information asymmetries, such as the knowledge necessary to match a cargo carrier's excess capacity to the needs of a one-time shipper. In principle, computers and communications technologies can facilitate disintermediation by linking the parties along the value chain and reducing information asymmetries. For example, these technologies have facilitated the evolution of enhanced "mail order" retailing, in which goods can be ordered quickly by using telephones or computer networks and then dispatched by suppliers through integrated transport companies that rely extensively on computers and communications technologies to control their operations. Nonphysical goods, such as software, can be shipped electronically, eliminating the entire transport channel. Payments and reconciliation can be done in new ways. The result is disintermediation throughout the distribution channel, with cost reduction, lower end-consumer prices, and higher profit margins.

Another, more subtle example can be seen in heavily computerized "warehouse" department stores that have taken market share from traditional department stores by capitalizing on the cost-saving advantages of advanced supply chain management. In the simplest form of this model, the end retailer and the manufacturer disintermediate the distributors that once sat between them, driving associated costs from the system. In the more extensive model the retailer disintermediates itself from the traditional job of retailing—buying wholesale and reselling—by never taking possession of the merchandise. In this model, the manufacturer receives point-of-sale (POS) information on sales of its products at a given location directly from the retailer, updates its planning for manufacturing and distribution, sends a restocking order to distribution, dispatches the goods to the retailer location, and stocks the shelves. The manufacturer still owns the merchandise, which the end-consumer then picks up and carries through the point-of-sale terminal, beginning the cycle again. The retailer is no longer a retailer in the traditional sense of the term, but rather an "access provider" through which end customers are delivered to the manufacturer's point of presence, and who charges the manufacturer an "access fee." The traditional distributors and their costs are disintermediated in this model, and transaction costs associated with the retailer's purchase of goods from the manufacturer are eliminated.

Mediation, Hierarchy, and Markets

These changes raise interesting questions about the possible shifts from hierarchies to markets in production and distribution. The examples above appear to reduce the operation of markets and result in vertical integration or at least vertical channel partnerships, wherein suppliers and retailers develop close and perhaps collusive relationships. Market dominance could only reemerge if exclusive vertical partnerships proved to be unsustainable. The crux of the arguments favoring markets over hierarchies revolves around the powerful attractor of reduced transaction costs and the possibility of greater innovation in transactions than is possible under the constraints of hierarchy. It has been argued that economic organizations predicated on ongoing auction, negotiation, and coalition-building behaviors, without the overhead and conservatism of hierarchy, could unleash an unprecedented wave of economic growth and innovation.

Still, the question of whether hierarchy can or should be replaced by markets is open. Many interorganizational information networks have been used to forge stable and long-lasting relationships among selected economic partners—quite the opposite of the impersonal "spot market"—and the ecology of these networks can be quite complicated. For example, travel agents theoretically are able to move freely among various computerized airline reservation systems, and airlines can easily disintermediate agents by building direct connections to passengers. In fact, agents tend to lock into one system as their primary reservation aid, and build their business around that system. The companies that own the reservation systems were originally owned by the airlines, and they kept tight hold on travel agents through incentives and constraints, such as forgiving costs of terminal rentals and discouraging agents from using more than one system. This behavior was so common that federal regulation was enacted to make reservation systems "neutral" in order to reduce anticompetitive practices. In this case, the hierarchy of the government stepped in to ensure the vitality of the market, which was threatened by the use of computers and communications technologies.

There are important questions about who benefits from movement toward markets in place of hierarchies. Those who occupy key positions in existing hierarchies are likely to fight loss of power, and the elimination of old hierarchies will probably give way to new hierarchies as the new market structures become understood and exploitable for the long-term advantage of particular parties. Already the consumer credit network industry that has made possible "profile" advertising has come under severe criticism from privacy advocates and consumer groups for invasion of privacy and appropriation of consumers' "information property." It is not clear that the powerfully seductive vision of the move from hierarchies to networks in economic organization is comprehensive in its consideration of what must change.

Organizational Politics and Process

The fundamental question of organizational politics is who gains and who loses from change. Some have predicted that computers and communications technologies will shift power to technocrats; others have suggested that use of these technologies will strengthen pluralistic features of organizations by providing different interest groups with the tools to respond to their opposition. Most research suggests that such power shifts are rare, and that organizational elites typically use their control over resources to shape the acquisition and application of computers and communications technologies in ways that perpetuate their power. However, there are exceptions. The availability of data in electronic form can empower new participants in decision-making processes, while the spread of networked PCs, e-mail, and other technologies provides opportunities for new actors to gain influence. The unresolved issue is whether, and to what degree, these technologies alter systematically the balance of political power within organizations.

Decision Making

The use of computers and communications technologies enhances the ability to organize, maintain, and retrieve information needed for decision making and allows modeling in which large amounts of information can be mined to provide insights that help decision makers evaluate different scenarios. Applied to group decision making, these technologies seem to enable efficient handling of complicated decision problems that are not easily managed without technological support. More broadly, the use of these technologies in decision making appears to have the effect of enforcing a stronger discipline on the process of deliberation, with more careful attention to underlying assumptions and sensitivities.

Work Life

Computers and communications technologies allow individuals to communicate with one another in ways complementary to traditional face-to-face, telephonic, and written modes. They enable collaborative work involving distributed communities of actors who seldom, if ever, meet physically. They permit individuals, groups, and organizations ready access to rich arrays of information, often in machine-readable form, that permits data exchange for local or remote processing without costly conversion. These technologies utilize communication infrastructures that are both global and always "up," thus enabling 24-hour activity and asynchronous as well as synchronous interactions among individuals, groups, and organizations.

Computers and communications technologies can change the nature of work by altering the quality of the work environment, the nature of job skills, and the quality of social interaction within the organization. One effect involves the levels of job stress and work pressure experienced by information workers. Some studies have found that automated systems decrease time pressure, while others suggest that the technologies have speeded up work and increased the level of stress and time pressure on workers. Other studies have found the technologies have had a positive effect on workers' job satisfaction, sense of accomplishment, and interest in their work, a greater sense of control over their work, and a sense of enhanced status among coworkers and clients. With few exceptions, the technologies have not resulted in "*deskilling*" of work, but instead have expanded the number of different tasks that are expected of workers and the array of skills needed to perform those tasks. The exceptions appear in certain types of factory floor and clerical work, in which the use of the technologies has resulted in some deskilling if not elimination of such jobs.

Social interaction in organizations has been affected by the use of computers and communications technologies. Peer-to-peer relations across department lines have been enhanced through sharing of information and coordination of activities. Interaction between superiors and subordinates has been made more tense because of social control issues raised by the use of computerized monitoring systems, but on the other hand, the use of e-mail has lowered barriers to communications across different status levels, resulting in more uninhibited communications between supervisor and subordinates.

The impacts of computing on work life have been basically positive with respect to individuals' job satisfaction, sense of accomplishment, interest in their work, control over their work, and social interaction with peers and superiors. However, computers and communications have also speeded up work, increased job pressure and time pressure, deskilled low end clerical-type jobs, and eliminated certain clerical and factory-floor jobs.

Employment and Unemployment

There has long been concern over the impacts of computers and communications on employment. The ability of computers and communications to perform routine tasks such as bookkeeping more rapidly than humans led to concern that people would be replaced by computers and communications. The response to this argument has been that even if computers and communications led to the elimination of some workers, other jobs would be created, particularly for computer professionals, and that growth in output would increase overall employment.

The net effect of computers and communications on employment is still a matter of considerable debate. Employment in particular jobs, such as telephone operators and bank tellers, has undoubtedly decreased with the increased use of computerized switching systems and automatic teller machines. Such clear-cut cases are uncommon, however. The statistical measures used to determine employment conditions are not precise enough to isolate the effects of one factor such as the use of computers and communications. After decades of computerization of all sectors of the economy, the United States has generally achieved full employment periods of economic expansion, while experiencing cyclical unemployment during periods of recession. The ratio of public-sector to private-sector employment has not changed much either. It is more likely that computers and communications have led to changes in the types of workers needed and in wage rates for different occupations rather than to changes in total employment. For example, research shows that computer users receive higher pay than noncomputer users in the same jobs. It does appear that use of computers and communications has resulted in a shift of jobs from the United States to other countries, particularly to Asia but also to generally lower wage locations.

Establishment and Maintenance of Civil Society

Civil society is the social order in which the "rules of the game" are articulated and enforced for individuals, groups, organizations, and sectors. Our primary focus in this discussion is on the institutions involved in the construction of democratic government, and on the relationships between the people and government. We also address the process by which individuals are elected and appointed to serve in institutionally defined positions of influence and authority in the democratic governance structure.

Democratic Governance

Computers and communications technologies have taken on a highly visible role as tools of government and as symbols in the ongoing debate about how government ought to function. There has been considerable speculation over whether use of these technologies can and will alter the functioning of democratic government. There are a variety of forms of democratic government. We choose to focus our discussion on the constitutional form of democratic government found in the federated structure of the United States. The United States is the oldest and greatest user of computers and communications technologies among large democratic countries; effects on its democratic institutions should by now be apparent.

Our discussion covers three areas: effects on the fundamental structure of democratic institutions predicated on separation of powers and the concept of federalism; effects on the relationship between government and the people; effects on the processes of deliberation and constitutional operation. It also touches on risks inherent in high levels of dependence on technology.

Effects on Democratic Institutions

The U.S. form of democratic government is predicated on two key assumptions. The first is the separation of power horizontally across the key functions of government—the legislative, executive, and judicial—in order to ensure that each branch holds the others in check. In principle, differential use of computers and communications technologies by one of the branches could undermine the checks, thereby providing substantive, procedural, functional, or symbolic advantage compared to the other branches. The second assumption is that power should be separated vertically in order to keep as much of the authority of government as close to the citizen as possible. In principle, the construction of national information systems for criminal justice, taxation, welfare, and so on might enhance the power of the central government in comparison to the regional and local governments.

The introduction of computers and communications technologies in the U.S. federal government was accompanied from the start by speculation that power would accrue to the branch with the most technology. Given the preponderance of technology in the executive branch, one would expect it to gain advantage over the legislative and judicial branches. In fact, no such power shift has occurred.

APPENDIX C

The separation of powers doctrine ensures that each branch has separate functions, that each is constitutionally and politically independent of the other, and that each has inviolate recourse through which to check the others. Computers and communications technologies do not and cannot fundamentally change these constitutional relationships. Three examples serve to illustrate:

- *Example 1.* Assume that, as a result of its greater computing, information, and analytic capabilities, the executive branch gains power over the smaller, less experienced, and diffuse bureaucracies supporting the legislative branch. The legislative branch can limit and control executive branch computerization by stopping the purchase of new computer systems through legislation, by strangling the procurement process through audits and inquiries, and by raising politically damaging questions of faulty procurement, cost overruns, mismanagement, and other evils resulting from executive computerization. The legislative branch can also request data from executive agencies, which are usually willing to comply in exchange for favorable treatment of their appropriations. Finally, the legislative branch can buy its own computers, develop its own information systems, and operate its own analytic models with its own staff. Through these mechanisms, the legislative branch can readily establish parity with and independence from the executive branch.
- *Example 2.* Assume that the executive branch tries to influence judicial review or overload the judicial branch with data from its vast stores of computer databases. The judiciary is the least computerized of the three branches of government and so is considered most vulnerable to the information that the executive branch can amass in support of its legal and policy preferences. The judiciary, in response, can use its tremendous power over legal proceedings to hold the executive branch to answer for its actions. The judiciary can grant or deny standing of parties, can determine the materiality of information, and can in effect declare all or part of the executive branch's information to be "non-information" and therefore inadmissible in any of its proceedings. The judiciary, alone among the branches, has the power to decide what information "is" within its own house.

The judiciary can also force the executive branch to provide the information it wants, when it wants it, and in the form it wants it, regardless of whether the information yet exists or what it costs the executive to get it. Finally, where violations of federal law may be involved the judiciary can override executive branch attempts to withhold information under claims of "executive privilege." In summary, the judiciary's powers overwhelm any advantage the executive branch may gain from computers and communications technologies.

- *Example 3.* Assume that the legislative branch seeks to gain advantage over the executive through the use of computers for oversight. Even if an "ideal" computerized system for legislative oversight were in place, the executive could stall in the provision of information, could provide misinformation and disinformation, and could refuse outright to provide information requested by the legislative branch. In such a confrontation, only the judiciary would have the power to mediate the disagreement. The most powerful response of the executive branch is the ability of the executive to take his or her viewpoint directly to the citizens, thereby marshaling popular support and potentially nullifying the effects of oversight by the legislature. The use of computers and communications technologies is unlikely to produce power shifts from the executive to the legislative branch in this area either.

The branches are able to check one another in virtually any case where computers and communications technologies play a role, simply because the powers of democratic institutions transcend whatever advantage the technologies can confer.

Another possibility is that acquisition of vast computer databases could give one level of government exceptional power over other levels. The most common speculation has been that the central government gains power at the expense of the regional and local governments. There is no evidence that this has happened, and moreover, it is unlikely that such a shift could happen. For one thing, the central government does not need computers and communications technologies to gain a power advantage because it already has the supremacy of federal law on its side. The states have wide powers of autonomous action (i.e., the residue of powers not conferred by the Constitution upon the federal government) but not independence. Also, intergovernmental relationships seldom involve the federal government "ordering" state and local governments about. Instead, most federal actions affecting states involve the federal government paying for national programs, such as unemployment and social welfare, that are implemented by state or local governments, or holding out carrots and sticks to induce state and local governments to adopt particular policies or programs.

It is conceivable that the careful use of computers could permit the federal government to be more heavy-handed in its superior role by enabling federal agencies to better monitor state compliance with federal expectations. However, the current political trend is in the opposite direction. The dominant trend of federalism is toward devolution of funding, administration, and oversight responsibility to the state and local level. As in the case of separation of powers across the branches of government, the distribution of power across the levels of the federated government system is itself a central part of democratic governance and the institutions that ensure such governance. Use of computers and communications technologies is highly unlikely to affect this as time goes on.

Effects on Relationships Between Government and the People

In the foregoing discussion we address the impacts of computers and communications technologies on democratic institutions. At a more fundamental level, there is concern that these technologies can affect the relationship between government at all levels and the citizens of the country. A central principle of the U.S. form of democratic government is the desire to protect citizens from government tyranny. At issue is whether the use of computers and communications technologies could give government the power to overwhelm constitutional safeguards against abuse of individuals or groups. Creating a well-balanced distribution of power between individual citizens and the government created by and for those citizens is a central problem in the maintenance of civil society. The issue is not whether individuals are imperiled by a faceless government armed with computers, but rather whether duly elected representatives, working through appropriate constitutional mechanisms, will engender computer-dependent abuse of individual rights.

Most of the concern over this issue is expressed in the debate about computers, databanks, and personal privacy. There has been considerable speculation and discussion of scenarios about the potential problems for privacy due to the computerization of government record-keeping activities, but there has been little empirical evaluation of the privacy-related consequences of the use of computers and communications technologies. The debate has at times been largely ideological. With enough data and the right computer systems, authorities will be able to monitor the behavior of large numbers of individuals in a systematic and ongoing fashion. The issue is no longer what authorities can do, but what they choose to do in surveillance of the population.

Privacy is a politically sensitive topic, but as a concept in society and law it is surprisingly not well developed. Existing uses of computerized databanks have not yet abridged personal privacy sufficiently to require constitutional action or even substantial Supreme Court action on the matter. Nevertheless, the privacy issue is being played out in the realms of rhetoric, legislation, and executive action. The controversy is likely to persist due to the creation and interconnection of large systems containing personal information and the relatively weak enforcement of existing privacy legislation.

Effects on the Political Process

Computers and communications technologies do not appear to be serious agents of change in democratic government, at least as seen thus far. However, there is a chance that these technologies will have a very substantial influence on the political processes that lead to the election of representatives and the mobilization of national political movements. Much has been written about the effects of communications media, particularly the mass media of radio and television, on the processes by which public opinion is formed and guided, and on the political contests that determine who will govern. The addition of advanced forms of public opinion sensing and computerized direct-mail systems has created a package of tools that are transforming the nature of the political process. There is concern that the extensive manipulation of public moods through the use of technology will decrease the electorate's overall awareness of the issues, and increase the tendency toward the election of individuals on the grounds of media image and single-issue direct-mail advertising. The ultimate concern is the deliverance of the role of political opinion making, and thereby the mobilization of political bias, into the hands of technicians who stand between actual political leaders and the electorate. This can result in reduced influence of the electorate over political leaders, and potentially, the means for wholesale distortion of the issues by political leaders with skilled "image-making" technocrats.

The impact of computers and communications on political fund raising and campaigning could prove to have significant effects on the political process, not because of any particular weakness of the Constitution itself or as a result of changes in the structure or function of the governmental system, but because changes would be part of larger effects of automation on the mobilization of bias among interest groups in the population. The concept of constitutional democracy depends on an informed electorate, capable of discriminating among candidates based on their overall strengths. Critics contend that extensive use of television in campaigns has decreased the quality of debate and reduced attention to the issues. Highly targeted, single-issue fund raising and campaigning conducted through computer-assisted direct mail or targeted telephone solicitation could contribute to such a trend. The Constitution itself addresses only the major offices and issues of enfranchisement, and not the protocols of party behavior or campaigning. It is possible that computing-based changes in the conduct of political contests will eventually have an effect on the ways the Constitution is interpreted and implemented.

An orthogonal view of technology and its impact on social life implies more subtle and possibly more important concerns for democratic government. This view engages concern over the application of computers and communications technologies to mass surveillance, national information systems, and political campaigning—in particular, to the question of what is really important in the determination of who should govern. This concern is manifest in Aldous Huxley's *Brave New World*, in which technological advancements were deliberately, and to a large measure democratically, applied toward elimination of need and stabilization of the social order. The new world was the epitome of successful technocracy, to the point that circumstances that gave rise to jealousy were preempted through ubiquitous use of technology. Technology was used not to give expression to malicious and destructive tendencies, but rather to support well-intentioned efforts to eliminate the causes of strife. In the process, the removal of strife eliminated existential choice, and thereby, freedom. Technology maximized efficiency in exchange for unavoidable limitations on individual privacy, choice, and freedom.

This story is useful for considering the ultimate impacts of computers and communications technologies on democratic government. The world depicted by Huxley evolved over a protracted period of time, and each step along the way posed a choice: to live with the contradictions of the present, or to remove them with technical solutions. To the extent that democratic government is threatened by the application of information technology, the threat does not come from weaknesses in the Constitution or the government it shapes. Rather, the threat comes when the governed fail to protect and defend their rights to personal privacy. Whether the growing use of information technologies in mass social surveillance or in partisan political contests is leading to this end remains to be seen. However, this analysis gives sufficient evidence to warrant renewed concern and to prompt increased monitoring of computing activities conducted by government or used in political processes.

Technology, Dependency, and Risk

A civil engineer working on the large California Water Project, which brings water from the Sacramento/San Joaquin river delta to Southern California, once remarked, "If we don't build this canal, we won't need it." The creation of vital infrastructure ensures dependence on that infrastructure. As surely as the world is now dependent on its transport, telephone, and other infrastructures, it will be dependent on the emerging information infrastructure. In a sense, this is an inevitable price of technological progress—dependency occurs only when the thing depended on is very valuable to the dependent. At issue here is the character of dependence that is likely to evolve, and the institutional responses to that dependency.

Dependency on technology can bring risks. Failures in the technological infrastructure can cause the collapse of economic and social functionality. Regional blackouts of electricity service in the Northeast during the 1970s and 1980s resulted in significant economic losses. Blackouts of national long-distance telephone service, credit data systems, electronic funds transfer systems, and other such vital communications and information processing services would undoubtedly cause widespread economic disruption. Dependency can also result in unanticipated, downstream consequences in the form of negative externalities such as pollution. Reliance on nuclear weapons as a key component of strategy during the Cold War resulted in an at-any-cost development and production program that left large areas of the United States terribly polluted, perhaps so badly that they must eventually be entombed and sacrificed as a cost of the war. Although it is difficult to imagine dependence on information technology producing an equivalent environmental catastrophe, toxic materials used in the manufacture of semiconductors and other hardware components have polluted manufacturing sites throughout the country that must now be cleaned up.

Perhaps most important, high levels of technological dependency create more than the risk of economic difficulty from failure. When technologies are instrumental in the construction and maintenance of institutions, and workable substitutes are not available in the event of failure, institutional collapse is possible. A useful example of this is the uni-modal transportation infrastructure of the Los Angeles region. The entire region is dependent on a single transportation infrastructure: vehicles on roadways. The failure of any major component of that infrastructure—fuel availability, roadways, traffic controls—for any lengthy period of time would bring the entire region of 12 million people to a halt. The Los Angeles region is at risk not only because the existing infrastructure constitutes a single point of failure capable of threatening the region, but also because commuting long distances to work using that infrastructure is a widespread and accepted cultural norm. The failure of transportation would strike at the heart of a nondiscretionary social institution. The collapse of two bridges on the Santa Monica Freeway during the 1993 Northridge earthquake was minor given the hundreds of miles of freeway in the region, yet the cost to the city's economy was at least a $1 million per day during the reconstruction, even after every available alternative transport mode and scheme was implemented.

In summary, technological dependency is not necessarily something to be avoided; in fact, it is probably impossible to avoid altogether. What must be considered is the exposure brought from dependency on technologies with a recognizable probability of failure, no workable substitutes at hand, and high institutional and social costs as a result of failure.

Conclusions and Implications

Research Issues

Computerization Is a Complex Social Phenomenon. The process of automation involves more than the acquisition and implementation of discrete components of technology. Automation is a social phenomenon involving a "package." The adoption and diffusion of information technology are influenced by both demand-pull and supply-push factors. Demand forces dominate the evolution of large, complex, custom applications, while supply forces appear to exert a major influence on the evolution of smaller packaged applications.

The Impacts of Computers Are Seldom as Predicted. Common predictions about the effects of using information technology frequently fail to materialize as expected. The failure of a prediction is not a signal that the outcome is negative. Rather, it is a sign that the impacts are richer and more complex than anticipated. Computerization has not resulted in widespread job displacement of middle managers because it has actually increased their job scope and roles in many cases. And, while management information system skill bureaucracies do not fit the ideal-type service bureaucracy, they frequently produce leading-edge applications of the technology. The important lesson from the research, then, is that failures of expectation and prediction are commonplace in the world of automation. The technology and its applications are best characterized as evolutionary in impact rather than revolutionary. Indeed, many organizational managers desire stability and work against surprises. Therefore, new information technology is generally introduced slowly so that it can be adapted to meet the organization's needs, and so that the staff can adapt to the technology's introduction.

Technology Is Political. Rational perspectives on change seldom acknowledge the explicitly political character of technology. They emphasize organizational efficiency, concentrate on the positive potential of technology, and assume organization-wide agreement on the purposes of computing use. In contrast, political perspectives see efficiency as a relative concept, embrace the notion that technology can have differential effects on various groups, and reflect the belief that organizational life is rife with social conflict rather than consensus. From a political perspective, organizations are seen as adopting computing for a variety of reasons, including the desire to enhance their status or credibility, or simply in response to the actions of other organizations. Moreover, applications of the technology can cause intra-organizational conflicts. Decisions about technology are inherently political, and the politics behind them may be technocratic, pluralistic, or reinforcing, with different consequences for different groups in each case.

Political perspectives are essential for understanding technology's role in organizations. Technocratic politics helps explain the relationships between the technologists and end-users; pluralistic politics helps explain the relationships among various user interests vying for access to computing resources; and reinforcement politics helps understand the effects of computing on power and authority in organizations. Reinforcement politics has proven to be important in explaining decisions about computerization in organizations, wherein the technology is used primarily to serve the interests of the dominant organizational elites. Reinforcement occurs sometimes through the direct influence of the elites, but more often it occurs through the actions of lower-level managerial and technical staff in anticipation of the interests and preferences of the elites. The political mechanisms used to determine the course of organizational automation will vary, depending on the broader political structure of the organizations themselves, and these mechanisms tend to remain stable over time.

Management Matters in Complex Ways. Prescriptive literature is full of admonitions about the importance of management in effective use of information technology. However, empirical research into the role of management and the efficacy of management policies is lacking. Research of the Irvine School has demonstrated the crucial role of management action in determining the course of automation, even in cases where major environmental changes were present. Moreover, there are distinct patterns of management action that yield different outcomes. Effective management of computers and communications technologies is much more difficult than suggested, however. Specific policies are contingent in their effects on the state of computing management as well as the characteristics of the organization. Policies recommended in the practitioner literature have proven to be associated with serious problems in the computing environment, and it is unclear whether the policies are not working, whether they have not yet had time to work, or whether they work only under special conditions.

Methodology

Research Requires the Use of Multiple Perspectives. Review of the research shows that systematic research into social impacts requires understanding and use of multiple disciplines for viewing the interaction of technology, organizations, and society. The work reviewed has used perspectives from the social sciences (political science, economics, sociology, psychology, communications, and management) and from the social analysis of computing in the information and computer sciences. Perhaps more important than the multidisciplinary character of this research, however, is the value of drawing on multiple intellectual perspectives when exploring fundamental causes of social change.

All meaningful explanations of the social aspects of the use of information technology proceed from an ideological base. All scholars have interests and values that influence the theories and explanations they construct. These interests are important not only in prescriptive work; they also figure markedly in the descriptive and explanatory work in the field. By recognizing the fact that explanations are at least in part ideological, and that ideology is an essential and required component of social analytic work, we are able to "triangulate" on a set of facts from several explanatory positions. This approach permits explaining social phenomena more comprehensively and precisely by gathering insight from various points of view, and using contrasting elements from various perspectives to test the intellectual coherence of alternative perspectives. The multiple-perspectives approach leads to increased self-consciousness during observation and explanation, and increased precision, because explicit perspectives can be examined in light of the facts and other perspectives for explaining the facts.

The dominant analytical perspectives in the computer and communications field have traditionally been tied to the supply-push world of technical development, coupled with a rational-economic interpretation of managerial behavior. These explanatory perspectives have considerable power and have yielded useful results. However, they have distinct limits. Technological determinism and narrow managerial rationalism do not explain the variance observed in the patterns and processes of adoption and routinization of information technology in various tasks, and they fall far short of explaining the considerable differences in successful use of the technology across organizations. Indeed, such perspectives are at a loss to explain the fact that "success" in the use of information technology is singularly elusive. As economist Eliot Soloway has stated so succinctly, the effects of the information revolution have shown up everywhere but in the profit figures.

There certainly are technical and economic-rational elements to be considered in understanding use of information technology in organizations. Missing, however, are the more finely grained explanations of volition in shaping the behaviors of those that adopt and use the technology, or that react to the effects of its use. While it is clear that information technology has brought major opportunities for change to organizations, it is the individuals and features of the organizations within which they work that determine whether given technologies are adopted and how they will be absorbed into the complex of factors operating in modern organizations. Organizations are political, social, and managerial constructions that involve interactions among competing and cooperating groups, each of which seeks to pursue some mix of its own and common interests, within the framework of broader organizational and social constructions of what is appropriate and expected. Since the true consequences of using information technology are unforeseeable, the actions of individuals in organizations are always based to some extent on faith, social pressure, perceived political advantage, and other factors, in addition to "cost-benefit" calculi covering applications to given activities.

Research Requires a Critical Perspective. Research indicates that there is often a gulf between expectations and subsequent experience with the use of information technology. It is important, therefore, that research proceed from a critical stance. It should be concerned with challenging existing ideas, examining expectations about technology and organizations, and counteracting unsubstantiated biases in both. It should focus particularly on the important role played by ideology and expectations in the use of information technology. The expectations of managers and others in organizations influence the choices they make in adopting and using technology. Managers who believe in technological solutions are likely to introduce information technology on faith, while discounting other considerations. And experiences with technology shape future expectations about the efficacy of technology in meeting organizational needs. The ongoing relationship between expectations and outcomes is a crucial part of understanding the dynamics of use of information technology in organizations.

In taking a critical stance, it is useful to start from common expectations and accepted explanations, and then attempt to corroborate them with empirical evidence. When the corroboration is incomplete, explanations can be modified, expanded, or displaced in order to develop a more accurate fit of theory with the facts. The combination of the critical stance and the multiple-perspectives approach reveals biases inherent in popular claims and provides leverage to think critically about alternative explanations.

Social Analysis Requires Innovation in Research Design. The Irvine School has produced methodological as well as substantive contributions. Most are innovations in research design that are especially suited to social analysis. The basic research strategy of the group is that the scale of research has to match the scope of the problem one seeks to address. Large, complex, and multifaceted problems require similar approaches. Given customary constraints (shortage of knowledge, resources, and talented people), one is challenged to focus both energy and effort.

Five recommendations can guide research. The first is to focus on leading adopters of the technology when studying the effectiveness of policies for managing computing. This focus enables determination of what works and what does not in the process of innovating, and can lead to advice that will bring others up to the level of the leading performers. The second, when studying policies, is to sample sites at the extremes of policy application (e.g., high and low centralization, insignificant and extensive user training). This approach maximizes the variance on the policies and provides a better indication of the basic direction in the relationships. The third is to use census surveys to investigate the extent of a technology's diffusion, the extent of its use, and the nature of its organizational impact. In addition to elimination of sampling bias, a census provides a good indication of the distribution of patterns of diffusion throughout a population of organizations. The fourth is to concentrate on long-term study of organizational and social impacts. Such impacts cannot be studied over the short term because changes occur slowly, the effects of the use of technology are indirect more often than direct, and the organization and the technology are interactive. The fifth is to use a mix of methods—quantitative and qualitative secondary data analysis, survey research, longitudinal research, international comparative research—and a mix of measures in the research in an effort to achieve better measurement and to triangulate the results of various studies.